Tolkien and
the Modernists

Tolkien and the Modernists

Literary Responses to the Dark New Days of the 20th Century

Theresa Freda Nicolay

McFarland & Company, Inc., Publishers
Jefferson, North Carolina

Quotations from Tolkien's letters are reprinted by permission of Harper-Collins Publishers Ltd. *The Letters of J.R.R. Tolkien* © The J.R.R. Tolkien Copyright Trust, 1981.

LIBRARY OF CONGRESS CATALOGUING-IN-PUBLICATION DATA

Nicolay, Theresa Freda, 1962–
    Tolkien and the modernists : literary responses to the dark new days of the 20th century / Theresa Freda Nicolay.
        p.   cm.
    Includes bibliographical references and index.

    ISBN 978-0-7864-7898-9 (softcover : acid free paper) ∞
    ISBN 978-1-4766-1720-6 (ebook)

    1. Tolkien, J. R. R. (John Ronald Reuel), 1892–1973— Criticism and interpretation.   2. Tolkien, J. R. R. (John Ronald Reuel), 1892–1973. Lord of the rings.   3. Modernism (Literature)   I. Title.
    PR6039.O32Z6977 2014
    823'.912—dc23   2014016136

BRITISH LIBRARY CATALOGUING DATA ARE AVAILABLE

© 2014 Theresa Freda Nicolay. All rights reserved

No part of this book may be reproduced or transmitted in any form or by any means, electronic or mechanical, including photocopying or recording, or by any information storage and retrieval system, without permission in writing from the publisher.

On the cover: Gollum from *The Lord of the Rings: The Return of the King*, 2003 (Photofest)

Printed in the United States of America

McFarland & Company, Inc., Publishers
   Box 611, Jefferson, North Carolina 28640
   www.mcfarlandpub.com

to Joseph and Elle
sine qua non

Table of Contents

Introduction	1
ONE. Rekindling an Old Light	9
TWO. Industrialism, Instrumentality and "antiquity so appealing"	25
THREE. *The Lord of the Rings*: "Insubstantial dream of an escapist"	55
FOUR. Modernist Disaffection and Tolkienian Faith	77
FIVE. The World as Wasteland: The Landscapes of Loss	101
SIX. The Wasteland Within: Alienation in Tolkien and the Modernists	135
SEVEN. Postmodern Monsters and Providential Plans	162
Bibliography	187
Index	191

Introduction

For as long as there have been storytellers, humanity has looked to stories as a way to preserve the past, guide the present, and shape the future. The stories that we invent and pass down through generations not only describe our experiences, but the lessons and insights that literature offers teach and inspire us to live more mindfully and humanely in the present so that we may create a more hopeful future. Many storytellers, themselves immersed in the narratives that preceded them, reflect on the past and carry forward the values and wisdom that they find there, whether that place in time is near to them or as remote as ancient times. And while some writers hope to break free of old forms and create new ones, even they cannot help but to be influenced in some way by the very traditions they seek to reject. In its inevitable engagement with the past, literature invites us to consider our shared humanity with those who came before us, to hear their voices, however rich and strange or ordinary and familiar they may be. This is one way among many to regard literature: as a self-reflective, multi-voiced, and ongoing narrative of human history, of humanity's part in what J.R.R. Tolkien called "the Whole Story."

During periods of great cultural change, literature can play an especially profound role in shaping the experience of the individual as well as society. This is especially true of the mid-nineteenth and early twentieth centuries, when the Industrial Revolution gained full momentum and irrevocably changed the familiar patterns of human existence. The turn of the century in particular encompasses a liminal period during which writers looked back at the effects of industrialism, then took stock of their world, and in many cases were repelled by what they saw. Tolkien's sensibility grows out of this nineteenth-century

Introduction

landscape of change: the rise of industrialism and capitalism; new theories in science, the social sciences, and the arts; changing attitudes toward religion and politics; and an apparent diminution of the quality of human experience in terms of both the individual and the community.

The effects of such rapid change along with a growing alarm about the damage to the natural world reveal themselves in the work of many nineteenth-century writers, including, among others, Charles Dickens and William Blake. Such writers described the ugliness of the landscape and the loss of the humane brought about by so-called modern improvements. In many cases, labor-saving machinery that was meant to improve life often brought with it instead new forms of suffering, both physical and emotional. Herman Melville's mid–nineteenth-century short story "Bartleby the Scrivener: A Story of Wall Street" dramatizes the potential of capitalism to break down community, to destabilize identity, and to transform human beings into robotic creatures. Melville implicitly asks the reader to contemplate Cain's question to God: "Am I my brother's keeper?" Throughout his relationship with his clerk, the narrator of "Bartleby" struggles with this question; however, he ultimately fails to make any kind of meaningful connection with the story's title character, an everyman who ends his life in unmitigated isolation and loneliness.

One of the twentieth-century's first novelists to consider the damage done to humane fellowship by the forces of industrialism is E. M. Forster. In his 1910 novel, *Howard's End*, Forster presents a number of dichotomies that reflect the preoccupations of the day. Among these oppositions are wealth and poverty, machinery and nature, and a capitalist in contrast to an aesthetic sensibility. These dichotomies are embodied by the characters Henry Wilcox and Leonard Bast, two men at opposite ends of the social and economic spectrum of Edwardian England. Mediating between these opposing forces are the Schlegel sisters, Margaret and Helen, whose lives repeatedly intersect with those of the Wilcoxes and the Basts. The young bank clerk, Leonard Bast, has an aesthetic and intellectual sensibility that is unique among his working class peers. Early in the novel we find him attending a Beethoven concert where he first comes into contact with Margaret and Helen Schlegel. This meeting sets off a chain of events that will end catastrophically

Introduction

when consummate Victorian optimism and self-assuredness collide with the grim reality of Edwardian England's economic determinism. If Melville's "Bartleby, the Scrivener" asks the question, "Am I my brother's keeper?" Forster's *Howard's End* answers, one might say, "Yes, whether you realize it or not."

There are two prevalent literary responses to the increasing feelings of alienation, fragmentation, and dislocation brought about by industrialism, secularism, and the Great War. On the one hand, some nineteenth- and twentieth-century writers strived through their own imaginative constructs to demonstrate the possibilities of human connection and community that could be achieved through the values of sympathy, compassion, selflessness, and a sense of stewardship regarding other people as well as the natural world. On the other hand, many writers chose to focus on the damage done to Western civilization and its inhabitants. Modernist writers in particular tended to underscore the failure of communication and community in the post-war world-as-wasteland, or to create characters whose focus has turned so completely inward as to cut them off not only from community but from their own psyches. In this regard, J.R.R. Tolkien diverged from his contemporaries: while he portrays characters that inevitably go mad from the kind of self-absorption depicted by the modernists, he presents a much stronger case for the life-sustaining and community-building powers of kindness, compassion, selflessness, and spiritual faith.

Tolkien's life and his life's work reflect a set of enduring values that was grounded in a belief in the fundamental goodness and decency of human beings, along with a profound faith in God. He appears to have maintained throughout his life a firm belief in a providential order overseen by a being greater than ourselves, whose love for humanity offered ultimate hope. Tolkien's letters, collected by Humphrey Carpenter, demonstrate very clearly that his Christian faith played a daily role in his life, whether that meant praying, attending mass, interpreting the events of his lifetime as they unfolded, or acting as "God's instrument" by keeping the light of Truth alive in a world that was growing increasingly dark.

Tolkien's letters also show very specifically his belief that these values could reside in narratives that would offer meaning and worth to current and future generations, just as so many ancient legends contain the wisdom of the past that can inform our actions in the present. For example, many of the values that Tolkien embodied in his characters and their stories are those that the eleventh-century Anglo-Saxon poet put forward in his portrayal of the pagan warrior, Beowulf. Tolkien meant to bring those qualities into vivid life by creating characters that he set against the most potent evil imaginable, just as the *Beowulf* poet set his hero against a monster that represents the darkness that encircled the mead hall, itself a metaphor for human existence and fellowship. In his imaginative construction of a world in which individuals rise above their various differences as well as their own weaknesses in order to confront and cast down the incarnation of evil in their world, Tolkien shows his readers the dignity and nobility of the human spirit, which transcends time and thus speaks to us even today.

The whole idea of connection, of the ability to move beyond the self to form life-sustaining relationships and communities, is of central importance in *The Lord of the Rings*. For Tolkien, the ability to feel pity, compassion, and forgiveness toward others, especially those who are unlike ourselves or those who have somehow injured us, is among the highest of virtues. This ability is so important because it emulates the love that God demonstrates toward human beings. Tolkien's friend, C.S. Lewis, in his book *The Four Loves*, explains that the fourth love, "charity," calls upon us to love one another in the same way that God loves humanity, not out of want or even need, but for the sake of "Love" itself (128). Lewis describes "charity" as "Divine Gift-love" which comes from the grace of God and gives a person the ability "to love what is not naturally lovable; lepers, criminals, enemies, morons, the sulky, the superior and the sneering" (*The Four Loves* 128). In *The Lord of the Rings*, Tolkien brings these qualities to life most vividly in Frodo. Through a divine grace, the hobbit exhibits *caritas* for Sméagol/Gollum, a creature who for many reasons occupies a liminal space in the cultural worlds of Middle-earth. In this and other respects, Sam, the most provincial of the four hobbits, is the foil to Frodo: the humble gardener demonstrates what Lewis would call "natural love" (*Four Loves* 128), since it would be easy for anyone to love such a good and kind friend as Frodo is to Sam. But who could love such a creature as Gollum, whose long ownership of the One Ring has made him monstrous? Sam is unable to rise to the

Introduction

level of pity and caring that Frodo achieves; rather, he feels only mistrust and repulsion toward Gollum.

That Frodo is capable of this highest form of love is also evident in his relationship to the Fellowship itself. In her essay, "*The Lord of the Rings*: Tolkien's Epic," Jane Chance explains that Frodo exhibits *caritas* in his attempt to set out on his own from Amon Hen in order to save his companions. Frodo, Chance writes, "acts as that savior of the Fellowship earlier witnessed in the figures of Tom Bombadil and Strider in the first book and Gandalf and Galadriel in the second" ("Tolkien's Epic" 213). By removing himself and, in consequence, the corrupting power of the One Ring from the Fellowship, Frodo hopes to ensure the safety of its members. In this regard, he clearly puts the needs of others ahead of his own, in spite of his fear of the terrifying path that lays before him. The importance of Frodo's feelings of charity cannot be overestimated, for it is the hobbit's compassion and devotion to others that quite literally save the world.

The strength of Tolkien's Frodo rests largely in his selflessness and his ability to cast his thoughts outward, far beyond his own welfare. The characters of the modernists, in contrast, often find themselves imprisoned in the world of their own consciousness, their own minds; thus their thoughts are always turned inward on themselves, and they struggle, most often in vain, to achieve genuine reciprocity with others. Any one of these characters might, as C.S. Lewis says of A.E. Housman, "storm and rage and shake his fist at the universe" (*The Four Loves* 140), but such outcries have little or no impact on the world. Over and over again, twentieth-century literature demonstrates the disastrous outcomes of this paralyzing preoccupation with the self: loneliness, grief, despair, alienation, even death. Rather than forging community through the imaginative act of connection, identity becomes unstable, even breaks down, under the pressure of self-absorption.

* * *

During the nineteenth and early twentieth centuries, industrialism and war profoundly damaged the human community as well as much of the world itself. In the aftermath, many British and American writers looked to the past to restore the present. The work of the literary modernists concerns itself rather specifically with the individual's efforts to create order out of fragmented and chaotic experience. Tolkien's work, on the other hand, addresses the role of the individual in promoting and sustaining both the human community and the natural world in the face of those forces that would make a wasteland of it. Like the modernists, Tolkien looks to the past, but his models and guiding principles derive from his Christian faith as well as the ideals and themes of Romantic (as opposed to "realistic") literature, from epic poetry such as *Beowulf* to the fairytales of George MacDonald and the romances of William Morris.

Tolkien was greatly influenced by the work of William Morris, himself a person who was disaffected with Victorian notions of progress, which encompassed rapid growth in technology and mass production. These advances brought great wealth to some, but at the same time they brought great poverty as well as poor living and working conditions to many. In Morris' invented worlds, such as in *The Well at the World's End*, we find virtuous and kindly knights who succeed in their quests and share their good fortune with kingdoms near and far. We find also brave warriors who place the good of the community above their own welfare, bringing together many "houses," or tribes, against a common foe in order to preserve their way of life in the wilderness, as in *The House of the Wolfings*. Such themes are very familiar to readers of *The Lord of the Rings*. William Morris looked to the medieval past and even farther back, as did the *Beowulf* poet before him, to a pagan past which he ennobled by highlighting its virtues of courage, bravery, loyalty, and fellowship across diverse groups. In many ways, Tolkien was striving to do the same thing, as his fiction, letters, and essays demonstrate.

In responding to the changing landscapes of the Western world, writers engaged with the past for various purposes: to bring forward values that they felt had been lost to the present time; to help them construct order and meaning where they perceived chaos and randomness; to use remnants of the past to create wholeness where they perceived fragmentation; and, finally, to help them regain that sense of human sympathy which is necessary to build a community capable of affirming and sustaining life, thereby providing assurance that the existence of each and every individual has meaning. There is no denying that Tolkien and the modernists shared many of the same concerns for the world in

Introduction

their time. However, they diverged most profoundly in the possibility of hope that their imaginative constructions offer for posterity. Tolkien's work, particularly *The Lord of the Rings*, concerns itself with the reality of the human condition and offers the foundation stones upon which humane community rests.

ONE

Rekindling an Old Light

In 1919 John Ronald Reuel Tolkien was living in Oxford, England, and working on the "W" section of the new *Oxford English Dictionary*. At twenty-seven, his days were finally settling into a routine of marital life and work as both a lexicographer at the OED and a tutor for several Oxford students. How quiet and ordered this life must have seemed after the muddy trenches, the artillery barrages, and the immediacy of death that was the Battle of the Somme. And though Tolkien's family was growing, his world was at the same time diminished by the loss of two of his three closest friends. Together the four, who had met during their years at King Edward's School in Birmingham, made up a group who called themselves the "TCBS," which, as Humphrey Carpenter explains, stood for "Tea Club and Barrovian Society," signifying their clandestine meetings both at school and in a nearby store (*Letters* 8–9).

The young men shared more than tea, of course. Much of their time was taken up with discussions of theological and literary questions, often focusing on their own writing, which they shared with and reviewed for each other. All four hoped to live lives of meaning and value. To this end, they believed that the TCBS was greater than the sum of its parts. The death of even one member gave Tolkien the feeling that world had become an irrevocably changed place, as though, he wrote, "something has gone crack" (*Letters* 10). Such was the death of TCBS member Rob Gilson, who lost his life in the Battle of the Somme during the earliest part of the Allied offensive. On August 12, 1916, Tolkien wrote to another TCBS friend, Geoffrey Smith, who would also be killed in the war, of his conviction that the four friends were meant, with the grace of God, to achieve greatness in a troubled world (*Letters* 10). Tolkien believed that through the grace of God the TCBS had been gifted with the ability to have a real impact on the world of their time, either individually or as a group. These young men, he wrote, were bound to "rekindle an old light in the world"; in other words, they would, by their lives or deaths, Tolkien wrote, "testify for God and Truth" (Tolkien, *Letters* 10). For Tolkien, this meant incorporating the Truth of the Gospels into his life's work: the history of Middle-earth and its peoples, including and especially, *The Lord of the Rings*. Tolkien's literature would be just such a testament to his catholic faith.

In the "Foreword to the Second Edition" of *The Lord of the Rings*, published in 1966, Tolkien reminds his readers that World War I had profound effects on the lives of all those who were forced to endure it. He writes that only firsthand experience with war can help one to truly understand its many deprivations, but fifty years later even memories of the Great War seemed to him to be fading from the collective consciousness of the Western world. He tells his readers that to live through the First was just as traumatic as to live through the Second World War. For him this trauma had much to do with the losses of his dear friends, Rob Gilson and Geoffrey Smith (Tolkien, *The Fellowship of the Ring* xix). War, death, marriage, fatherhood: these were the touchstones of J. R. R. Tolkien's coming-of-age, rites of passage that took place at a pivotal moment in the history of Western civilization, for World War I, as John Garth notes in his book, *Tolkien and the Great War*, "inaugurated the modern age" (39).

* * *

During the second half of the nineteenth and the beginning of the twentieth century, the rapidity of technological and social change caused people to experience a profound anxiety about the world, as Western culture became increasingly urbanized and industrialized. For the first time in history, large numbers of people could travel great distances relatively quickly and easily, and this meant that people from different cultures, classes, and ethnicities were much more likely to come into contact with one another than ever before. On a personal level, identity itself became unstable as identity became less anchored in a traditional social order. The anxiety was due also to changes in intellectual thought, along with ever increasing secularization and the demystification of nature throughout the nineteenth century. Over the course of that century in particular, a confluence of theories from a variety of disciplines changed the intellectual atmosphere of the Western world. Literary modernism itself is one of the end results of "modernity," a phenomenon which Patrick Curry, in his book, *Defending Middle-earth*, describes as

> a "world view" that began in late seventeenth-century Europe, became self-conscious in the eighteenth-century Enlightenment, and was exported all over the world, with supreme self-confidence, in the nineteenth. It culminated in the massive attempts at material and social engineering of our own day. Modernity is thus characterized by the combination of modern science, a global capitalist economy, and the political power of the nation-state [12].

The rise of secularism and the concomitant growth of large cities brought with them the virtual demise of social structures based around agrarian and village lifestyles that followed familiar patterns based on the cycles of nature as well as on religious rituals. At the same time, a new working class emerged to meet the demands of industrialization. The living and working conditions of these "masses" in the new industrialized society became a central subject of writers and intellectuals from Karl Marx to John Ruskin to D.H. Lawrence, to name a varied few. The horrifying culmination of the rapid growth in technology was the wide scale violence and devastation of World War I, which for the modernists represented an abrupt break in the ostensibly smooth progression of Western history.

The first half of the twentieth century, especially the period beginning with the First and ending with the close of the Second World War, encompasses that period of British and American literature known as Modernism, a literary movement that is associated with writers such as T.S. Eliot, Virginia Woolf, and D.H. Lawrence in England and Robert Frost, Wallace Stevens, and F. Scott Fitzgerald in America. Much of the literature of this period depicts the world as a wasteland and its inhabitants as marked by a sense of existential despair as well as feelings of alienation, dislocation, and loss. What had been lost, at least for many people, were the old beliefs that helped to give order and meaning to the world, including the individual's particular place within it. Religious faith, and with it the belief in a divine purpose or providential order within the world, the Victorian optimism in science and progress that fueled industrialism, the stability of the social order as well as cultural norms of gender and class: these were some of the old convictions with which the modernists took issue. After the First World War, many people cast aside the traditions, values, and beliefs of the past that had once anchored them within the vastness of a universe that they had once believed was created and watched over by a benevolent and loving God. When these anchors were swept away what remained in their place was a profound emptiness, one that left many individuals feeling as though they had been set adrift in a universe that was at best indifferent and at worst hostile to humanity, a universe in which events happened at random.

Without faith in a benevolent power that orders and gives meaning to life and circumstances within both the temporal and the eternal worlds, many people found it difficult to cope with the events of the early twentieth century, especially the First World War. In his essay, "Nihilism in the Twentieth Century: A View from Here," Clyde Manschreck explores the roots of nihilism in Western culture. He asserts that while it can be traced as far back as the Old Testament, by the twentieth century expressions of nihilism had come to permeate all aspects of society (Manschreck 85). Manschreck links twentieth-century nihilism to "a mood of despair," and his description of this state of mind might well be a list of the central themes of modernist literature, including "a sense of emptiness and meaninglessness, a loss of transcendence, a feeling that life finally ends in the nothingness of death, that moral norms cannot be validated, that relativism and subjectivism render all statements about truth suspect and untenable" (86). All of these feelings and beliefs can be linked to the abandonment of the conviction that a Supreme Being is at work within and beyond the world. Belief in such a power invests human existence with meaning and worth, provides a set of moral absolutes to guide the actions of individuals, and carries with it the promise of eternal life and an end to human suffering. Indeed, belief in such a power can help to make sense of adversity and pain, thereby helping individuals as they struggle to understand and accept the more dire circumstances of life, such as the precipitous loss of a loved one.

According to Manschreck, twentieth-century secularization, the rise of science and nationalism, and an increasing sense of the primacy of the individual eclipsed the notion of a providential and God-centered universe (86). "By the latter half of the nineteenth century," he writes,

> relativism and subjectivism had so eroded traditional values, and science had made so much progress in explaining the mysteries and miracles of this world (especially with Darwin's *Origin of the Species*, 1859) that Fredrich Nietzsche boldly celebrated the death of God and "exposed" the old values of love, kindness, and humility as no more than power substitutes evolutionized by weak people herded together to gain strength [Manschreck 87].

Nietzsche's book, *Also sprach Zarathustra* (*Thus Spake Zarathustra*), published between 1883 and 1892, the year of Tolkien's birth, contributed greatly to the anti-religious sentiment that had been growing throughout the nineteenth century. As Joseph Pearce writes, "Convinced that Christianity was bankrupt [Nietzsche] proclaimed Schopenhauer's 'will to power' and emphasized that only the strong ought to survive" (*Literary Converts* 2). By "the strong" Pearce is referring to Nietzsche's "ubermensch," or "Superman," whose centrality replaced for the philosopher that of God. Like Schopenhauer, Nietzsche placed the greatest emphasis on the individual rather than society or an aspect of it, such as religion.

This concept of the strong enduring and the weak subsiding calls to mind Darwin's notion of the "survival of the fittest." As Manschreck notes, Nietzsche believed that Christian virtues such as "love, kindness, and humility" were merely evolutionary adaptations by which powerless people attempted to ensure their survival. In the period between Schopenhauer's *The World as Will*, published in 1819, and Nietzsche's *Zarathustra*, Charles Darwin published two revolutionary scientific works. *On the Origin of Species*, published in 1859, and *The Descent of Man*, published in 1871, put forth Darwin's theories about evolution and natural selection, ideas that deeply challenged the belief that God created and gave meaning to life as part of His divine plan. Rather, according to Darwin, life originates and progresses through the exigencies of nature. Despite their implications for Christianity, Darwin's theories moved beyond the academic world and into the wider culture.

Along with these movements in philosophy and science, the nineteenth century also brought with it new theories of politics, economics, and psychology. Among the most significant of these is Karl Marx and Friedrich Engels' *The Communist Manifesto*, originally published in 1848, which points to the eventuality whereby the working class would overthrow the ruling class to ultimately bring about a classless society. Marx's *Das Kapital*, the first volume of which was published in 1867, explores his theory of political economy and argues that in a capitalist system, a small number of owners of the means of mass production retain the benefits of industrialism while a vastly greater number of laborers suffer economic hardship. The socioeconomics of industrialism would culminate in the rise of larger-than-life captains of industry such as the American Henry Ford, who by 1914 would so refine the methods of mass production that the term "Fordism" came into the language, and the notion that "machines can do it" would come to be associated with his name. In the world of psychology, new concepts about identity and the mind itself were emerging, led by Sigmund Freud, whose major contribution to the intellectual atmosphere of pre-war Western civilization is his 1899 book, *The Interpretations of Dreams*. In this work, Freud develops the concept of the mind as working on two levels: the conscious and the subconscious. What was so groundbreaking at the time of the book's publication was the notion that we are guided not only by our reason and intellect, but by an area of our minds that is beyond our control, that is, our subconscious. This claim had profound implications for the primacy of rationality, since rationality itself might be the result of irrational drives.

Taken together, theories such as these, with their drive toward secularization and their emphasis on the individual as well as various forms of determinism, prepared the ground for the anti–Christian, anti-rational, anti-moral response, astonishingly comprehensive in scope, which would spring up seemingly full-blown in the early decades of the twentieth century. Manschreck asserts that this phenomenon constituted a "psychic, epistemological condition gnawing like a cancer inside Western culture" which was subsequently "compounded by an overwhelming consciousness of death and the dehumanizing effects of megatechnocracy" (88). When the First World War hit, the intellectual atmosphere of the nineteenth and early twentieth centuries became operationalized, and its effects were ubiquitous as new movements in art, architecture, music, and literature came to the fore.

The literary modernists took part in this split with traditional beliefs by attempting to capture in their prose and poetry the feelings of alienation and loss that coincided with their sense that there was no central and stabilizing agency that made sense of both the world and human experience within it. In his book, *Tolkien: A Cultural Phenomenon*, Brian Rosebury situates Tolkien in relation to his contemporaries. Rosebury discusses the twentieth-century shift from a religious to a secular perspective, arguing that modern writers were working with "a background cultural assumption of unbelief" (153). "The existence of a transcendent order giving value to the world," Rosebury asserts, could "no longer credibly be propounded as datum, but must be glimpsed, as a possibility, or a hope, through a persuasive evocation of human experience" (153). Examples of such glimpses can be found in modernist texts such as Virginia Woolf's *To the Lighthouse*, where a sublime vision is bestowed on humanity in general only to disappear as suddenly as it had appeared.

In the absence of faith in a divine intelligence that orders the universe and invests human existence with meaning, the modernists perceived of the world as a wasteland, both literally and figuratively. They often use the image of the wasteland as an "objective correlative" to express their sense of the barrenness of the Western world after World War I. The term gained currency when T.S. Eliot adapted it to describe a way of using what is external to the self in an effort to signify an internal state or feeling. In "Hamlet and his Problems," which appears in *The Sacred Wood*, a collection of essays composed between 1917 and 1920, Eliot explains: "The only way of expressing emotion in the form of art is by finding an 'objective correlative'; in other words, a set of objects, a situation, a chain of events which shall be the formula of that particular emotion; such that when the external facts, which must terminate in sensory experience, are given, the emotion is immediately evoked" (100).

Eliot's concept of the objective correlative can be illustrated by considering Robert Frost's 1914 poem, "Home Burial," in which a husband and wife engage in fruitless argument over their responses to the death of their infant. The wife, Amy, believes that her husband does not share her grief, yet in fact he does. He simply cannot express it in the same manner as she. Rather than speaking specifically about the death of the baby, the husband laments the loss of a good fence, which nature, in its indifference to the care and craft of human hands, can swiftly destroy. During the wake, when the infant's body is laid out in the parlor of their home, the husband says, "'Three foggy mornings and one rainy day / Will rot the best birch fence a man can build'" (Frost, "Home Burial" 92–93). In this instance, the ruined fence becomes the objective correlative for the husband's feelings of powerlessness and grief. He knows that nature, whose forces are for him random and indifferent to human suffering, can quickly undo his labors, despite his best efforts. For the reader, the image of the ruined fence evokes feelings of loss, isolation, and despair; in other words, the external image telegraphs the husband's internal state, allowing the reader to feel what the husband is feeling. The wife, on the other hand, is unable to make the connection between the loss of the fine birch fence and the loss of the baby. To her husband's sad declaration, "'A man can't speak of his own child that's dead,'" the wife replies, "'You can't because you don't know how to speak'" (Frost, "Home Burial" 70–71). Amy is unable to make a sympathetic connection with her husband, who is in fact experiencing the same profound anguish as she.

This example of an objective correlative points to two major aspects of modernist thinking: first, the universe is marked by randomness and indifference; second, we have become so isolated and alienated from one another, that communication is empty and meaningless, thus precluding the possibility of genuine reciprocity, or community. The work of the literary modernists therefore was transformative, as they attempted to put together the fragments of their experience so as to construct an order and meaning which they believed did not inhere in the world. In his 1939 essay, "The Figure a Poem Makes," Robert Frost explains that the figure of a poem is not "static." It is quite the opposite, he argues, comparing it to love's "ecstasy," in that "it begins in delight, it inclines to the impulse, it assumes direction with the first line laid down, it runs a course of lucky events, and ends in a clarification of life—not necessarily a great clarification, such as sects and cults are founded on, but in a momentary stay against confusion" (Frost, "The Figure a Poem Makes" 132). That "confusion" may be likened to feelings of disorientation and dislocation that arise when one perceives modern life as incoherent and fundamentally unstable. For Frost, freedom exists in the making of poetry itself, that is, in the process of creating order from "the vast chaos" of his experiences ("The Figure a Poem Makes" 132). Frost indicates that for him the poem has taken the place of religion

ONE. Rekindling an Old Light

("sects and cults") in supplying a sense of meaning or purpose, in other words "clarification," of human existence. In this way, he encapsulates the prevailing literary sensibility of most of the first half of the twentieth century when he asserts that the work of art is "a momentary stay against confusion."

* * *

The Lord of the Rings appeared in print just as the modern period was evolving into postmodernism. It was first published as three separate books over an eighteen-month period beginning in England in July of 1954 and ending in America in January of 1956. Tolkien, however, composed the book between 1936 and 1949, that is, during the modern period. He was a contemporary of writers like T.S. Eliot, Virginia Woolf, and Robert Frost, and he emerged from the same intellectual atmosphere and cataclysmic events as they did. Like the modernists, Tolkien inherited an increasingly secularized and mechanized world. He shared with them apprehensions about industrialism and the loss of the pastoral world. For their part, the modernists followed the intellectual trajectory of the nineteenth century, creating characters that are deeply self-absorbed and addressing themes of profound loss, faithlessness, disaffection, loneliness, and alienation. While Tolkien certainly addresses themes of loss and despair, many of the characters he created are not self-absorbed but selfless, sometimes to the point of complete self-sacrifice. He incorporates in his work "the old values of love, kindness, and humility," those values which, as Clyde Manschrek notes, Nietzsche denigrated. Largely because Tolkien's work emphasizes traditional values such as faith in a divine will that supports human existence as well as self-sacrifice for the greater good, *The Lord of Rings* in particular is ultimately a story about hope and human goodness and strength in the face of despair.

Unlike his contemporaries, so many of whom seem to be trapped in the present moment, Tolkien appears not to have felt disconnected from the past and its values, for those values were to him enduring and derived largely from his faith. In an often-quoted letter of December 1953, Tolkien states that *The Lord of Rings* is "fundamentally religious and Catholic" (Tolkien, *Letters* 172). Those of the story's characters who are admirable make choices based on values of kindness, charity, and concern for the welfare of all of Middle-earth and those who dwell there. Although they may stumble, as people in the real world of the storyteller sometimes do, they very often make amends for their poor choices. In Tolkien's invented world, overriding values of mercy and forgiveness make possible the reclamation of the nearly lost. The inhabitants of Middle-earth exist in a world where angels take the form of old men who carry with them the divine light of Creation, a world where the hand of God intervenes for the ultimate benefit of the good, and where success depends not on physical might or military prowess, but on humility, charity, and generosity of spirit, even at the cost of one's life. In light of Tolkien's letters, essays, and fiction, it is difficult to imagine that *The Lord of the Rings* could be anything *but* "fundamentally religious." His thinking appears always to have worked on two levels: the temporal and the eternal.

In December of 1944, Tolkien wrote to his son Christopher about the relationship between the temporal and the eternal worlds, locating our own essential existence, it seems, at the place where they intersect. He explained that the stories that come down to us through the ages demonstrate that all human beings possess "an eternal element" and that from the vantage point of heaven, we will see and understand our own lives as part of the "Whole Story" that is God's providence (Tolkien, *Letters* 106–07). Certainly, we are physical beings, subject to the laws of the material world, he reflects, yet at the same time we also have a spiritual nature that aligns with the eternal world and therefore cannot be touched by the world as we know it in time. In the letter, Tolkien refers to our earthly life in the temporal world, the world where evil can exist and indeed flourish (by its own standards). This he sets apart from our spiritual life in the unseen eternal world in which evil cannot triumph over the power of God (Tolkien, *Letters* 106–07). The Catholic's faith in God, including the belief that through Holy Communion human beings are in unity with Christ, brings him together with his fellows as part of the human family.

That community is not just the present earthly community of the church; it is much more insofar as it simultaneously stretches back into the past and forward into the future. For Tolkien, this is one of the essential lessons that literature can impart: we are more than ourselves at any given moment because our stories are part of the larger narrative that

ONE. Rekindling an Old Light

is God's plan for humanity. And because that story contains the whole of history, we must have a care now for the well-being of the future. This concept appears throughout *The Lord of the Rings*. For example, during the council of Elrond, the participants explore all possible alternatives for preventing Sauron from ever regaining the One Ring. Glorfindel, one of the Elf lords, suggests that the Ring be cast into the sea, thinking it thus would be forever beyond the reach of Sauron. Gandalf, however, knows that such a solution would ultimately be ineffective. He knows that God has changed the shape of the world once already and that time and nature bring about changes as well. The wizard alludes to the fact that there may well be evil creatures living in the deeps of the ocean, and across great distances of time the geography of the world is bound to change. Therefore, he reminds the others that they must think far beyond the scope of their own years, beyond even an "age of the world" (Tolkien, *The Fellowship of the Ring* 267). It is for this reason that Gandalf will support no other resolution than the destruction of the Ring, even if they should fail in the attempt, since this is the only sure way to free Middle-earth of Sauron. The Council's subsequent agreement that the Ring must be returned to the fires of Mount Doom where it was forged demonstrates their sense of responsibility to the future: yes, one simple and easy solution would be to throw the evil device into the sea. Such a plan would certainly be less dangerous, but it would be neither wise nor morally right. The Council's resolve to entrust the Ring to a diminutive and reluctant hero who must undergo the most perilous journey imaginable—into hell on earth—constitutes a monumental act of faith. Such a decision could never have been made in the absence of hope and a belief in a benevolent power at work in the world.

Tolkien's Catholic epistemology, though deeply and deliberately embedded in *The Lord of the Rings*, points always towards ultimate hope. Here, Tolkien would very likely hasten to qualify such an assertion by pointing out that it is "hope without guarantees" (Tolkien, *Letters* 237), for we cannot, while we exist in the world of time, fully understand the narratives that are our earthly lives. Nevertheless, we must not fall into despair. As Gandalf tells another Elf lord, Erestor, at the Council of Elrond, "despair is only for those who see the end beyond all doubt" (Tolkien, *The Fellowship of the Ring* 269). Neither wizards nor Elf lords can see as far as the story's end: only from the vantage point of the Eternal can the "Whole Story" be seen. Thus the leaders of the free peoples of Middle-earth must not give up hope.

In a letter to Christopher, Tolkien points out that when Sam finds Frodo after his struggle with Shelob, the Ringbearer appears to his companion as though he is dead, but this happens at the very moment when Sam loses "*hope*" (Tolkien, *Letters* 101). It is Sam's despair that convinces him that Frodo is dead, not the other way around. The loss of his most beloved friend is more than Sam can endure, and his greatest fear becomes his reality. Of course, Frodo has not been killed, but only sedated by the malevolent Shelob. Had Sam not given up hope, he might have realized that Frodo was still alive and thus saved him from capture by the Orc captains. But even hobbits are only human, and it is human frailty that makes Sam succumb to hopelessness and therefore misjudge Frodo's condition. In the face of his despair, however, Sam will find the courage in himself to carry on the quest because he knows that the destruction of the Ring is more important than his love for Frodo, more important even than Frodo himself. Ultimately, it is through faith and love that Sam finds the strength to carry on the quest.

At the very moment of the devastating loss of Frodo, the fate of Middle-earth depends on Sam's conviction that his actions have meaning and importance beyond the present moment to a reality and a future beyond his earthly perception. Tolkien underscores the importance of dedication to the greater good in this instance in which, in essence, the fate of the world depends on the ability of one humble individual to maintain hope in the face of personal suffering and anguish. This perspective differs significantly from that of the modernists. The despair that the modernists experience occurs in part because their vision is myopic, focused predominantly on the individual within prevailing circumstances, the effect of which is to further atomize community. It is not surprising, then, that many characters in modernist literature express feelings of loneliness and isolation. In *The Lord of the Rings*, Tolkien puts forth characters who consider themselves to be part of a larger community, joined to others by both joy and suffering, and recognizing that each one has a place within a divinely ordered cosmos.

For Tolkien, despair is not only folly, but it may have disastrous outcomes; unchecked, it leads over and over again to a fall, as is most acutely demonstrated in the pride, madness, and suicide of Denethor.

ONE. *Rekindling an Old Light*

So while modernist writers captured in their work the profound sense of alienation of their time, Tolkien created a world of both alienation and community, of isolation and fellowship, of pervasive evil and dehumanizing mechanization set against goodness and the artistic expression of beauty. The world of *The Lord of the Rings* is a world of providence and grace in which the actions of individuals for good or evil play out within a transcendent order.

Bradley Birzer underscores the contrast between Tolkien's Christian belief and the secularism of the modernists in his book, *J.R.R. Tolkien's Sanctifying Myth*. Birzer writes that Tolkien believed that "God places each uniquely created individual in a certain time, in a certain place, with certain gifts, for a certain reason. For Tolkien, modernity was committed to the denial of God as the author of man and the world. And once a man denies God, he denies his true self" (110). Tolkien's Christian beliefs, therefore, were for him life-affirming, and they provided individuals with a moral compass by which to guide their actions. In the world of Middle-earth objective truth and moral absolutes do exist, and therefore moral choices, no matter how seemingly insignificant, can have a profound impact on present as well as future circumstances.

Modernist thinking rejects traditional morality, and so we find in its literature a number of amoral characters. Many modernist writers depict characters that cannot or will not choose—or simply choose carelessly—to take part in the moral work of their lives and their world. Tolkien, on the other hand, created characters for whom choice is crucial and ongoing. Those characters in *The Lord of the Rings* who succeed do so because they maintain a holistic view of history, and this helps to guide their actions. They remember the past and do their part in the present to preserve goodness for the future. Thus they do not exhibit that sense of fragmentation and alienation which permeates so much modernist literature. Those of Tolkien's characters who stumble or fail do so because their concerns are immediate and often political. The sins of Boromir, Denethor, and Saruman are sins of overweening pride combined with a perspective limited geographically and temporally. Their ill choices reflect a particularly modern kind of self-absorption that stands in opposition to characters such as Aragorn, Frodo, and Gandalf, all of whom understand that their decisions occur within a vast historical and providential framework, however distant or removed it may seem from themselves and their circumstances. These three members of the Fellowship in particular subordinate themselves and their needs to the quest to destroy the Ring. They understand that its success is more important than any one individual at any one moment in time. They understand that the safety and security of the free peoples of Middle-earth depends on their steadfast commitment to one another and to the quest.

In late November of 1943, Tolkien wrote to his son Christopher that they two "were born in a dark age out of due time" (*Letters* 64). Nevertheless, he believed that this circumstance only strengthened their devotion to all that they loved and their conviction to do their part to make the world better with their own God-given abilities. This articulation of a sense of displacement may seem pessimistic, but in fact it implies Tolkien's deeper sentiments of acceptance and hope, acceptance of his place in the flow of time and hope that his efforts as one of "God's instruments" would bring light into a dark world. Tolkien believed that by the early twentieth century the light of God's Truth had very nearly gone out of the world. In 1916 he wrote to his friend Geoffrey Smith that their group, the "TCBS," was meant to renew that light of truth in the modern world. This sense of destiny points to Tolkien's conviction that a providential order exists within the universe and gives meaning to all lives that pass in and out of the world.

When Frodo learns about the history of the Ring and of its true nature as a device of evil, he laments to Gandalf that the discovery came about during his lifetime (*The Fellowship of the Ring* 50). The wizard replies with characteristic compassion and wisdom: "So do I ... and so do all who live to see such times. But that is not for them to decide. All we have to decide is what to do with the time that is given us" (Tolkien, *The Fellowship of the Ring* 50). Like Tolkien, Frodo is likely feeling that he has been "born in a dark age out of due time." His inheritance of the Ring has blasted him out of the peaceful agrarian life of the Shire into the tumult of the wide world, and there's no going back to blissful ignorance. Nevertheless, were it not for his striking out into that world and all its evils, Frodo, as Tolkien says of himself and his son, would "not *know*, or so much love" (*Letters* 64) his home. Quite crucially, it is Frodo's abiding love for the Shire and its people that helps to sustain his faith and conviction as he carries out the task that has been appointed to him. In the passage cited above, Gandalf makes no explicit reference to the "Power" who *gives*, or appoints to us, our time, yet clearly our place along the continuum of history is assigned to us by a higher being; we do not choose it. We do, however, choose to follow or to turn away from the path that is set before us. The wizard's message is clear: not only is Gandalf a steward; we are all stewards, and if there is to be peace in our time, we must take part in bringing it about by using the abilities God has given us to preserve what light and goodness there is in the world.

Like the modernists, Tolkien was in some ways pessimistic. For example, in his letters he mentions that all throughout its history the world has been "'going to the bad'" (Tolkien, *Letters* 48). Like the Elves of Middle-earth, he viewed history as "the long defeat" (Tolkien, *Letters* 255). He looked at history this way because he believed in the Fall of humanity and the loss of a real Eden that once existed in our world. Like the Elves, exiled from Valinor, the uncorrupted country of the Uttermost West, Tolkien believed that fallen humanity is many generations removed from the pristine world that God created. Tolkien's Elves are bound to that world, and their ultimate fate is unknown even to the Valar, the angelic regents of Middle-earth. Human beings, in contrast, are bound to die and thus escape from the world in time. Aragorn has an awareness of the Eternal world, and this is why before his death he tells a grieving Arwen, "In sorrow we must go, but not in despair. Behold! we are not bound for ever to the circles of the world, and beyond them is more than memory" (Tolkien, *The Return of the King* 1074). This is the promise of the Resurrection, a promise that modernist literature in general does not embrace.

For the modernists, by 1918 the metaphorical bottom of the world seemed to have suddenly dropped out; their work therefore offers slim hope, if any. Indeed, it is most often marked by hopelessness and despair. However, for Tolkien, to look with ennui upon strife and destruction, to lament our losses but do nothing to stem their flow, to sink to despair, these are the choices of moral and historic myopia, an inability to recognize one's responsibilities to oneself, to others, and to generations to follow. Against "the old values of love, kindness, and humility" depicted in *The Lord of the Rings*, the maze of alienation in which so many modernist writers find themselves is the path of self-absorption. It leads nowhere. For Tolkien, the way out of that maze could be found through fellowship and faith, including the belief in a benevolent God who brings order and meaning to our experiences in the temporal and eternal worlds.

Two
Industrialism, Instrumentality and "antiquity so appealing"

"For, indeed, we should be too much ashamed of ourselves if we allowed the making of goods, even on a large scale, to carry with it the appearance, even, of desolation and misery." In 1890, two years before Tolkien's birth, William Morris published a utopian novel, entitled *News from Nowhere*, which dramatizes both his "hatred for modern civilization" (vii) and his hope for the future. The story tells of the adventure of William Guest, a nineteenth-century socialist who deplores the ugliness and inhumanity of his own time and who wishes to witness just one day of the utopian society that had been the subject of discussion among the "Hammersmith Socialists" that evening. Guest emerges from the train, "that vapour-bath of hurried and discontented humanity," strolls home through an unexpectedly serene moonlit night, and falls asleep amidst thoughts of "days of peace and rest, and cleanness and smiling goodwill" (*News from Nowhere* 1–2). Guest wakes the next morning to find that his wish has come true as he discovers himself in twenty-second-century England, which has been elevated to such a state of pastoral beauty, agrarian simplicity, flourishing craftsmanship, and abounding fellowship as to be an earthly paradise. In this England of the future there are no ugly factories or dismal suburbs; men and women enjoy equal status and opportunity, and every person works at whatever vocation best suits him or her. Indeed, in Morris' utopian society, the word "work" is linked to concepts such as enjoyment, energy, pride, and self-fulfillment. Along with the factories and railways, virtually the entire infrastructure of Morris' own nineteenth-century England has disap-

peared: gone are the country's schools, police stations (and prisons, for crime is virtually nonexistent and easily dealt with), and churches. The Houses of Parliament have become an indoor dung-heap and marketplace, and the word "poor" has dropped out of the lexicon. The phrase "National Gallery" has come to signify any "place where pictures are kept as curiosities permanently" (*News from Nowhere* 39), though the word "national" is puzzling, since in this society the concept of "nation state" does not exist.

In *News from Nowhere*, Morris systematically dispatches the major components that made up nineteenth-century England—economy, education, national history, religion, government and the military, class distinctions, high art, and factories, the means of mass production. In the future that Morris invents, individuals, while abiding within a well ordered community, enjoy an unprecedented degree of freedom to achieve self-fulfillment and, consequently, happiness. So-called labor-saving mechanization has been replaced by craftsmanship, freeing robotic workers to become artisans, as they once were before the bad old days of industrialism. The old gaffer, Hammond, summarizes for Guest the nineteenth-century's corruption and exploitation of pre-industrial England's resources when he says:

> England was once a country of clearings amongst the woods and wastes, with a few towns interspersed, which were fortresses for the feudal army, markets for the folk, gathering places for the craftsmen. It then became a country of huge and foul workshops and fouler gambling-dens, surrounded by an ill-kept, poverty-stricken farm, pillaged by the masters of the workshops. It is now a garden, where nothing is wasted and nothing is spoilt, with the necessary dwellings, sheds, and workshops scattered up and down the country, all trim and neat and pretty. For, indeed, we should be too much ashamed of ourselves if we allowed the making of goods, even on a large scale, to carry with it the appearance, even, of desolation and misery [Morris, *News from Nowhere* 64].

Hammond's brief catalog of the state of England before, during, and after the Industrial Revolution underscores Morris' own disgust with the forces of industrialism and capitalism. Much of his concern was with the exploitation and abuse of nature that gave rise to a proliferation of factories as well as dirty, overcrowded cities, which in their turn destroyed the landscape.

Caught within this cycle of mass production and the unprecedented

Two. Industrialim, Instrumentality and "antiquity so appealing"

consumption of natural resources were human beings, both as the exploiters and the exploited. Disaffected with the outcomes of industrialism, including, among other things, workers alienated from their work and thus unable to derive enjoyment from it, Morris believed that mass produced objects lacked the quality, beauty, and uniqueness that could be conferred only by the craftsman's or artisan's hand. He thus strove to create by hand everyday objects and to reintroduce to his society medieval motifs in art and literature. The passage above is indicative of Morris' preoccupation with England's agrarian, feudal past. For example, Hammond describes pre-industrial England as primarily forests and "wastes," such as moors. It is notable that he lists these first: they were there, of course, before any human community, represented in this context first as "towns," which harbored those men who protected the "folk" on the lord's land, then as "markets" where people gathered not just to procure goods but to exchange news. Also included are the gathering places of craftsmen where likeminded men could exchange ideas and keep alive the skills of their trades. All of Hammond's examples show how Morris valued fellowship and a system of social organization whereby people are left largely to their own devices. In Morris' idealized English future-past there is no government to interfere in the private lives of individuals: note the absence of government agencies, of even well intentioned bureaucrats, whom Tolkien sometimes referred to as "planners" (*Letters* 235). There is a kind of simplicity suggested in Morris' examples: they underscore the worth of nature, the even exchange of goods, the importance of fellowship and community, and the value of knowledge and craftsmanship passed down from father to son through many generations.

The images in Hammond's catalog are at first peaceful and suggestive of harmonious order, but a shift in the tenor of the passage suggests the changing landscape of nineteenth-century England. Gaffer Hammond's descriptive language reflects the negative effects of industrialism: first, "huge and foul workshops" refers to the many factories; next, "fouler gambling-dens" ostensibly signifies the urban areas (Morris often speaks of nineteenth-century England as "filthy"); and, finally, where the forests and wastes have not been consumed by factories and cities, the countryside—he refers to it as an "ill-kept, poverty-stricken farm"—is in ruins from the exploitation committed by the "masters of the workshops," in other words, those who make profit as opposed to those who work so that others can become rich. Hammond's description shows not only Morris' disgust with the ruined landscape, but with the forces that caused the ruination. As Hammond describes it, the world of the nineteenth century is one of "desolation and misery": the desolation of the land and the misery of the people, the workers, whose forefathers were once "craftsmen." Much to Morris' despair, the craftsmanship that flourished in the past has been lost. It is a theme he will address elsewhere in the novel: Guest will learn that by the twenty-second century, no one will have remembered how to make objects for themselves, since machines had taken over completely work that was once done by hand.

Hammond's speech presents the reader with Morris' vision for the future: in his utopian England of the future people would be ashamed to show even a hint of such dire circumstances. Indeed, they can barely conceive of such a state of affairs, so foreign is it to their way of life, for they have returned England to its pre-industrial state, which Morris describes in edenic terms: their world is a garden. In the fashion of the medievals, all is "trim and neat"—a phrase Morris uses repeatedly in *News from Nowhere* as well as his in his quest romances, *The Wood Beyond the World* and *The Well at the World's End*. In the passage, Hammond tells Guest that England "is now a garden, where nothing is wasted and nothing is spoilt, with the necessary dwellings, sheds, and workshops scattered up and down the country, all trim and neat and pretty." In this depiction of a future pastoral England, people exist in harmony with nature, and there is an almost sublime order aesthetically and in terms of the use of natural resources: no waste implies the opposite of exploitation, which is respect for nature as well as for humanity. Morris contrasts this ethos to his own time in which so much of England's green space, as Hammond tells Guest, gave way to "factories for making things that nobody wants, which was the chief business of the nineteenth century" (*News from Nowhere* 66). In Morris' utopian world, human beings work in accordance with nature to create order and beauty, not only in the landscape, but also in manmade artifacts, from the largest building to the smallest table fork.

This harmony permeates their relationships as well, for despite any idiosyncratic differences among the "neighbors," there exists a standard of respect and acceptance that appears not to be breached. Even death doesn't disturb those who dwell in this happy valley. They simply accept it with equanimity: they neither fear it nor seek to postpone it. Like children, they appear to live in a world insulted from the harsh realities of life that arise either from nature, such as illness and disease, or human nature, such as jealously, greed, and selfishness. In his essay, "The Meeting of Past and Future in William Morris," Northrup Frye refers to this "curiously childlike quality of the people ... who sometimes seem to be living in a gigantic kindergarten" (313). This characterization corresponds to the notion that Morris would have England begin again, returning to its childhood, so to speak. Frye goes on to explain that history moves through cycles from youth to age, and amidst these cycles occurs revolution, largely around changes in technology. At such moments in history, the creative mind goes back to the "youthful" stage of pre-industrial times, since "the creative tendency is toward the pre-revolutionary" (Frye 316). During periods of rapid technological change, according to Frye, "cultural movements" tend to look for "a congenial period in the past, very frequently the distant past. Thus while political and economic movements go forward into the future, which in the twentieth century means carrying an increasing amount of technological baggage with them, cultural movements tend to rediscover neglected or forgotten earlier times in our tradition" (315).

For Morris, this means a return to the medieval in terms of both lifestyle and values. It is evident not only in *News from Nowhere*, but in Morris' romance tales as well, in which Morris embodies in his heroes and heroines the ancient values of honor, bravery, and devotion to the community even to the point of self-sacrifice.

Gaffer Hammond's little speech, then, tells us a great deal about William Morris' longing for the recovery of England's imagined golden past and his desire to repair the damage done in his own time. The damage of the nineteenth century is threefold: it is damage to the natural world, to the individual, and to the human community, all of which are diminished by industrialism and materialism. Thus, as Frye explains, Morris imagines a world where nature, individuals, and society itself are restored to a healthy vibrant state. However, in reading the work of Morris one cannot help but feel that he wants an actual return to the past rather than simply looking to the past as a way to rescue the present and future from the wasteland fate for which the Western world seemed to him to be destined.

Frye's remarks may be applied to Tolkien's work, especially in regard to the highly insulated and agrarian world of the Shire. Hobbits share many qualities with Morris' "neighbors": for example, above all they value tranquility as well as "a well-ordered and well-farmed countryside" (Tolkien, *The Fellowship of the Ring* 1). This sounds quite a bit like Morris' twenty-second-century England: lovely tidy farms that make up a pristine bucolic world where everyone gets along so well that there is virtually no need for a police force. Notably, when Lotho Sackville-Baggins forcibly takes over the Shire during the War of the Ring, he imprisons its mayor and declares himself to be "Chief Shiriff," thereby establishing a corrupt police force. In the industrialization of the Shire, Tolkien presents one vision among several in *The Lord of the Rings* of the destructive aspects of the machine age.

When they return to the Shire after the War of the Ring, the hobbits find their pleasant homes deserted, their gardens destroyed by weeds, and, perhaps most distressing, their beautiful trees replaced by a housing tract. The narrator explains that the hobbit homes have been abandoned, their lovely gardens neglected. In their place can be seen a row of "ugly new houses all along Pool Side.... An avenue of trees had stood there. They were all gone. And looking with dismay up the road towards Bag End they saw a tall chimney of brick in the distance. It was pouring black smoke into the evening air" (Tolkien, *The Return of the King* 1016). In his description of the modernized Hobbiton, Tolkien may well be incorporating elements of twentieth-century suburban housing tracts, a so-called modern improvement that he found most unappealing. In this case the new buildings are especially offensive because they have come at the cost of traditional hobbit homes as well as a number of cultivated trees. Thus the destruction of this one part of the Shire alone represents the loss of heritage and craftsmanship that comes with modernization. Beyond this degradation Frodo and his companions see the iconic image of the smokestack, poisoning the air just as the servants of Saruman have ruined the land.

The story of *The Lord of the Rings* is as far reaching in its scope as Middle-earth itself. Within the narrative there are stories within stories and echoes of tales from the most ancient ages of Tolkien's invented Sec-

Two. *Industrialim, Instrumentality and "antiquity so appealing"*

ondary world. The story of the corruption and reclamation of the Shire is a cautionary tale that guides the reader's vision toward the future while at the same time underscoring the value of the past. Whereas in *News from Nowhere* William Morris takes the reader from an industrialized England to a pre-industrial future England; Tolkien begins his tale with a pre-industrial society in order to instill feelings of pathos in his readers. Throughout their journey, both Frodo and Sam often think of the Shire and of the simple country life and folk that they left behind. To a significant degree, the success of the quest depends upon the hobbits' devotion to their homeland, and their memories of it and references to it help to keep that world in the reader's mind as well. When beyond all hope they succeed in their quest, they rightly deserve to return to the life they left behind. To find that such a world no longer exists would seem to be a terrible injustice. Like Frodo and his companions, we as readers are shocked by the transformation of the Shire, and we feel the loss more keenly because Tolkien has collapsed the time frame such that the change takes place in a matter of months rather than decades. In the real world, of course, there is no going back to the past via the future, and even in Morris' *News from Nowhere*, Guest must wake up from his dream of a utopian England. However, in Tolkien's imagined world, the Shire can, and in fact will, be restored to its pre-industrial state, and the shocking "desolation and misery" caused by Saruman's machines will be overcome.

* * *

Writers of the second half of the nineteenth and the first half of the twentieth centuries demonstrate a preoccupation with the past, particularly in terms of literature and culture. This preoccupation had much to do with the effects of the Industrial Revolution and the changing nature not only of society but of the natural world as well. In the face of such profound and widespread changes, writers took stock of contemporary life and found it to be in a state of distress. In confronting the harsh realities of industrialism and, later, world war, writers on both sides of the Atlantic looked to the past, to a time that seemed more humane. What they found there, according to Van Wyck Brooks in his essay, "On Creating a Usable Past," was of varied worth. Brooks argued that the English or European writer had a richer, more imaginative tradition to sustain him, whereas the American writer had virtually nothing of value to draw upon. What at that time made up the American literary tradition that was of any worth—the work of Melville, for example—had been overlooked, according to Brooks, in favor of lesser works, such as those of the local color writers.

From the vantage point of 1918 Brooks writes: "The present is a void and the American writer floats in that void because the past that survives in the common mind is a past without living value. But is this the only possible past? If we need another past so badly, is it inconceivable that we might discover one, that we might even invent one?" (339). Brooks is writing at the end of World War I, a time when many people felt a sense of profound disenchantment and disillusionment with virtually every aspect of Western culture. It was a time of collective shell shock on both sides of the Atlantic, not only literally for the soldiers who fought in that war but also figuratively for those who stayed at home. The literary critic Brooks, like so many other artists and intellectuals of the time, called upon his contemporaries to search beyond the immediate past in order to find something to help guide individuals through a time of insupportable tragedy and loss. His essay expresses the need for America's "spiritual history" to have real significance (340). Literature can accomplish this for us, according to Brooks, but it must connect imaginatively to a past whose meaning embodies a truth relevant to the present. Brooks is writing at a pivotal moment in the history of Western civilization, and, just as Frye describes, he is reaching beyond the immediate past, at least beyond the one "that survives in the common mind." The past that endured in 1918 America's collective consciousness would have been fraught with memories of the Victorian "progress" that led ultimately to modern mechanized warfare, a past of the worst imaginable "desolation and misery," to borrow a phrase from William Morris' Gaffer Hammond.

Van Wyck Brooks wrote in regard to the American past, but his remarks can be applied to English writers of the period as well. No matter how many centuries of great literature stood behind them, they, too, experienced that sense of loss and alienation that engendered the same impulse that took hold of Brooks: to cast their imaginations back to a more distant past in order to bring meaning and worth into a present that seemed to be failing on so many levels. Clearly, nineteenth- and

Two. Industrialim, Instrumentality and "antiquity so appealing"

twentieth-century writers were deeply engaged with the past in an effort to salvage the present, and the quest to find or create a "usable past" takes on many forms, especially during the modern period. In the face of industrialism and world war, both English and American writers of the nineteenth and twentieth centuries expressed concern for the future of Western Civilization. In short, in an effort to forge a path into that future, these writers engaged in various ways with the past.

William Morris' *News from Nowhere* is one example of how nineteenth-century literature portrays a growing sensibility regarding industrialism: it was comprised at best of feelings of disenchantment and loss; at worst, of downright disgust and horror. While mid-nineteenth century writers very often wrote about the intrusion of the mechanical into the pastoral, *News from Nowhere* laments the aftermath of that intrusion and articulates, well before the First World War sundered the Victorian past from the "modern" present, some of the first longings for the old pastoral world. For Morris this means not only pristine nature, but simplicity in living. Of course, such an ideal past never existed, but on both sides of the Atlantic we see this backward glance. It can take many forms: a simple statement of longing for the past, a recalling of past values to restore the present, or a study of the past as a model in the hope of creating a better future.

Almost as soon as it began in the late eighteenth century, poets and other writers responded to the effects of industrialization. As early as 1806, for example, the English Romantic poet William Wordsworth addressed the problem of materialism in his poem, "The World is Too Much with Us." For the speaker of the poem, humanity has lost its connection to nature, represented metonymically as the "Sea," "moon," and "winds" (Wordsworth 5–6). In the pursuit of wealth, of worldly things, the speaker and his fellow human beings "have given our hearts away" (Wordsworth 4). In other words, individuals are so consumed by work that they can give little thought or care for the natural world, which provides nourishment for the imagination and, indeed, the soul. The speaker makes the distinction between pre–Christian pagans, whose imaginations interacted with nature to create mythological figures such as the sea-gods Proteus and Triton, in contrast to nineteenth-century individuals, who are "out of tune" (Wordsworth 8) with the natural world and thus can no longer inhabit it imaginatively. This loss of enchantment with nature—"It moves us not," he laments—makes the speaker feel "forlorn" (Wordsworth 9, 12).

In "The World is Too Much with Us," Wordsworth points to the impoverishment of the humane as one cost of materialism in the early nineteenth century. However, even as early as 1794, another English romantic poet, William Blake, wrote prolifically about the other costs of emerging industrialism: pollution, poverty, and the exploitation of laborers, especially children. T.S. Eliot's post–World War I *isolato*, J. Alfred Prufrock, dwells in a dirty industrialized London, the origins of which reach back to the time of Blake. In his poem, "London," from the collection *Songs of Experience*, Blake puts forth images of human misery, sickness, and death amidst the soot-stained buildings, where "Chimney-sweepers cry," each "blackning Church appalls," and "the youthful Harlots [sic] curse ... plagues the Marriage hearse" (37). This tendency in literature, both American and English, to articulate a kind of alarm with or despair about worsening conditions in the country and the city as well as the effects of industrialism on humanity becomes even more pronounced as the nineteenth century progresses. The idea takes on many forms, including, as noted, William Morris' quest romances and utopian fiction, all of which resonate with the socialist beliefs that so many writers and intellectuals adopted as a response to the abuses of capitalism.

Prior to the work of Morris, the novels of Charles Dickens depict nineteenth-century poverty, filth, and the exploitation of laborers, among them children. His 1853 novel *Bleak House* opens with a description of a crowded and filthy London. "As much mud in the streets," the narrator tells us,

> as if the waters had but newly retired from the face of the earth, and it would not be wonderful to meet a Megalosaurus, forty feet long or so, waddling like an elephantine lizard up Holburn Hill. Smoke lowering down from chimney-pots, making a soft black drizzle, with flakes of soot in it as big as full-grown snowflakes—gone into mourning, one might imagine, for the death of the sun [Dickens 1].

Like so many writers, including Tolkien, Dickens emphasizes the image of dark smoke obscuring the natural world, in this case represented by the sun. Dickens anthropomorphizes the black "snowflakes," which "mourn" for the sun, in order to evoke in the reader a feeling of pathos over the damage to nature. In Dickens' London, even the fog is contaminated: "Fog everywhere. Fog up the river, where it flows among green aits and meadows; fog down the river, where it rolls defiled among the tiers of shipping, and the waterside pollutions of a great (and dirty) city" (1).

T.S. Eliot's world, the modern world, is a culmination of the effects of industrialization that began in the nineteenth century. Just over sixty years after the publication of *Bleak House*, Eliot would describe in "The Love Song of J. Alfred Prufrock" a dirty London under the pall of a curling, ubiquitous fog:

> The yellow fog that rubs its back upon the window-panes
> The yellow smoke that rubs its muzzle on the window-panes
> Licked its tongue into the corners of the evenings,
> Lingered upon the pools that stand in drains,
> Let fall upon its back the soot that falls from chimneys [130–31].

In this urban landscape, Eliot portrays nature as diseased, dirty, and suffocating, and it found its counterpart in the psychologically damaged inhabitants of the modern wasteland. The effects of industrialism on the country and the city were obvious and alarming; the effects on individuals were less observable but perhaps even more profound and disturbing.

The same year, 1853, that Dickens' *Bleak House* was published in England, Herman Melville's short story "Bartleby, the Scrivener: A Story of Wall-Street" appeared in *Putnam's Monthly Magazine* in America. In the tale of the pallid and passively resistant Bartleby, Melville looks critically at the effects on the individual of capitalism and its reliance on the industriousness of workers, that is, its reliance on America's Protestant work ethic. Melville's story puts forth early metaphors of the individual as robot, or machine, in the pursuit of wealth—if not his own, then, as is more often the case, his employer's, whether the business enterprise involves either goods or services, as in this case the transcription of legal documents.

At first Bartleby is a boon to his employer, the narrator of the story. The clerk works placidly and productively, virtually without ceasing. However, his employer comes to find Bartleby's quiet calm to be somehow disconcerting. "There was no pause for digestion" the narrator says of Bartleby, "He ran a day and night line, copying by sunlight and by candle-light. I should have been quite delighted with his application, had he been cheerfully industrious. But he wrote on silently, palely, mechanically" (Melville 46). Significantly, what so disturbs the narrator is Bartleby's dispassionate affect: the clerk's manner is machine-like, robotic. There is something inhuman about Bartleby's "incessant industry" (Melville 53). While the narrator does not yet realize it, he is beginning to see one of the negative effects of industrialism: the depersonalization and instrumentality of the individual. Ironically, Bartleby's isolation makes the narrator more aware of the need for brotherhood and compassion as part of the human condition. When Bartleby stops working completely, and his employer realizes that his new clerk will under no circumstances resume his industrious activity, the narrator begins to lose his temper. At first he is angry about the loss of productivity, but he soon recovers himself by recalling Jesus' Great Commandment: "love one another" (Melville 64). For the moment, at least, traditional Christian values of kindness and concern for others have won out over ever-present worries about what William Wordsworth referred to as "getting and spending."

Melville's narrator is caught in a struggle endemic to nineteenth-century life: the insidious substitution of instrumentality for any other value, such as human compassion and generosity, both of wealth and of spirit. The story is full of such dichotomies. For example, the more the clerk isolates himself, the more his employer feels the need to forge a connection with him. Despite Bartleby's refusal to work, the narrator feels not anger but sympathy. As an employer, he knows such obdurate and insubordinate behavior calls for dismissal; however, on some less conscious level he is drawn to the clerk. He explains that "there was something about Bartleby that not only strangely disarmed me, but, in a wonderful manner, touched and disconcerted me" (Melville 48). The narrator's perception of Bartleby is also dichotomous: as an employer he requires uninterrupted industriousness; as a fellow human being, he is compelled to sympathy by the clerk's "loneliness" and "miserable friendlessness" (Melville 54). The latter response in the narrator puts him in touch with his own humanity, which is at odds with his materialism. Thus Melville presents his reader with yet another dichotomy. Ultimately, the narrator's Christian charity fails, since Bartleby ends up in the Tombs, a Manhattan prison, and dies of starvation.

Two. *Industrialim, Instrumentality and "antiquity so appealing"*

In the end, Bartleby's agency is little more than the negation of industriousness: he won't do anything at all, not even eat. The narrator's capacity for *caritas*, his ability to love one who is "unlovable," proves finally to be insufficient: he has failed to rise above his own materialism. Since in death Bartleby is beyond the reach of his employer's half-hearted attempts to support him, physically and emotionally, the narrator shifts his position to look upon Bartleby not as a person in need of Christian charity, but as an object of pity. His ability to recognize the pathos of Bartleby's situation, and its representativeness of human frailty more generally, comes too late. In his frustration the narrator cries out finally, "Ah Bartleby! Ah humanity!" (Melville 74).

As readers, we may well ask ourselves, what is the narrator's responsibility to Bartleby? Certainly it is to look upon his clerks—all three of his clerks—as more than robots or machines. In "Bartleby, the Scrivener," Melville implicitly takes issue with the ethic of industriousness that facilitated the machinery of capitalism to the detriment of the individual. It is a model whose origins extend back even beyond the iconic image of Benjamin Franklin arriving as a young man in Philadelphia with a penny-loaf of bread tucked under each arm. In his chapter on Franklin in his book, *Studies in Classic American Literature*, D.H. Lawrence takes issue with Franklin's prescription for the development of the industrious individual. "I am a moral animal," Lawrence writes, "But I am not a moral machine. I don't work with a little set of handles or levers. The Temperance-silence-order-resolution-frugality-industry-sincerity-justice-moderation-cleanliness-tranquility-chastity-humility keyboard is not going to get me going. I'm really not just an automatic piano with a moral Benjamin getting tunes out of me" (Lawrence, *Studies in Classic American Literature* 22).

Franklin's rag-to-riches-success-through-industriousness ideal is a foundational aspect of the American national consciousness. For Lawrence, however, this "unlovely, snuff-colored little ideal, or automaton" (*Studies in Classic American Literature* 27) is damaging rather than life affirming, insofar as it gives primacy to the forces of materialism while stripping away individuality. Lawrence writes, "Either we are materialistic instruments, like Benjamin, or we move in the gesture of creation, from our deepest self, usually unconscious" (*Studies in Classic American Literature* 26). Lawrence's assertion calls to mind Wordsworth's lamentation that in our pursuit of material things, "we have given our hearts away." So completely have we cut ourselves off from our own humanity that we have lost the ability to enchant the world around us, thereby nourishing our souls through imaginative activity. Rather, we have become "automatons." Herman Melville's lonely clerk, Bartleby, like Lawrence, though rather less aggressively, resists the forces that would make him a useful cog in a massive machine.

By 1890, when William Morris published *News from Nowhere*, not one but two industrial revolutions had taken hold of the Western world. The nineteenth-century "desolation and misery" that Gaffer Hammond speaks of had become ubiquitous. By 1923, D.H. Lawrence was railing against "Americanizing and mechanizing … for the purpose of overthrowing the past," which in fact, he asserted, proved mainly to trap individuals in so-called "'productive' machines like millions of squirrels running in millions of cages" (*Studies in Classic American Literature* 27). Lawrence's dispute with the American past is twofold: on the one hand, he rejects the American cultural tradition of success through industriousness as a dehumanizing process that serves the interests of a capitalist machine; on the other hand, he rejects American literary tradition as promoting an ideal of democracy that does not in truth exist, since the "will of the people" is no more than a "figment," according to Lawrence (*Studies in Classic American Literature* 14).

Unlike the other writers in his study, whose work had by then been canonized, Lawrence points to the work of Herman Melville as an example of American literature worth building a tradition on. Van Wyck Brooks, in his essay "On Creating a Usable Past," also points to Melville as having been wrongly overlooked by the arbiters of literary taste (340). Both critics were concerned with the past and American literary tradition; both were also concerned with the future of Western civilization. Lawrence believed that art had the potential to be a "mine of practical truth" (*Studies in American Literature* 8). Brooks concluded his 1918 essay by calling for a re-examination of American literature that would unify Americans in the present moment by showing their common humanity with those who had gone before them. He writes:

> Knowing that others have desired the things we desire and have encountered the same obstacles, and that in some degree time has begun to face those obstacles down and make the way straight for us, would not the cre-

ative forces of this country lose a little of the hectic individualism that keeps them from uniting against their common enemies? And would this not bring about, for the first time, that sense of brotherhood in effort and in aspiration which is the best promise of a national culture? [Brooks 341].

In the aftermath of World War I, according to Brooks, it is of practical and spiritual importance to understand that others have endured the same adversity and shock, and they survived and found a successful path into the future. Brooks implies that Americans of 1918 can do the same; however, in order to build a smooth road into the future, one must look to the past.

The First World War gave the lie to the Victorian belief that history progressed smoothly and without interruption into a brighter future. In his essay, "Tolkien's Catholic Imagination: Mediation and Tradition," Thomas Smith argues that after World War I people began to understand "the implications of the modern project" which promised to improve life "through the harnessing and application of various kinds of power," including scientific, technological, economic, military, and political power (80). However, the long term result of the "modern project" was not the enrichment of life but rather the "degradation and suffering" of individuals (Smith 80). "A project that sought to improve on the stinginess and indifference of nature," Smith writes, instead

> ruined nature. A project that claimed it would create rational, stable, secure, political organization, created states that were criminally stupid, murderous, insecure and unstable. In short, people began to suspect that the project that aimed to liberate, also enslaved. Many experienced this senseless, violent mechanized war between modern nation states not as a deviation from modernization, but as its culmination. If a vision of life that promises to make life more human, makes life more inhuman, disillusionment will result [80].

Even before the war, the modern captain of industry had, as E.M. Forster wrote in his 1910 novel *Howards End*, "split the precious distillation of the years, and no chemistry of his can give it back to society again" (137). For Brooks' generation, new thinking and new ideals were required, but their foundation was to be found in a less immediate past. For Brooks, as for Lawrence, the literary past that could help society move into the future was one that moved society away from widespread individualism. Brooks called upon Americans in 1918 to rise above the idea that they were are a nation of industrious individuals each out to achieve his own personal success. Modern literature, however, does not focus on fellowship and community; rather, it tends to look intently at the isolated self in a world that is at best indifferent and at worst hostile to the individual and the humane.

As were so many nineteenth- and early twentieth-century writers, Tolkien was alarmed and often disgusted by the effects of industrialism. He, too, engaged with the past as a way to restore the present and forge a straight path into a more humane future. He, too, was profoundly disturbed by the instrumentality and depersonalization brought about by technologies that increasingly found their way into everyday life, in both the private and public spheres. William Morris, in *News from Nowhere*, explicitly asserts his belief that nineteenth-century mechanization, rather than improving life, caused men misery insofar as it deprived them of the ability to create with their own hands and compelled them to work in unhealthy and often unsafe conditions. When the novel's time-travelling protagonist, William Guest, attempts to defend his own century by citing the "labour-saving machinery" that was created during the Victorian Age, the old Gaffer responds hotly: "'Yes, they were made to 'save labour' ... on one piece of work in order that it might be expended—I will say wasted—on another, probably useless, piece of work. Friend, all their devices for cheapening labour simply resulted in increasing the burden of labour'" (Morris, *News from Nowhere* 85). For Morris, the use of machines did not result in more leisure time for workers, or even in more time to create better quality goods; rather, it resulted simply in greater output of goods that were lower in quality than those produced by artisans and craftsmen.

Tolkien makes a very similar assertion when he writes, "Labour-saving machinery only creates endless and worse labour" (*Letters* 87). Although Tolkien stated unequivocally that he was not a Socialist (*Letters* 235), he shared many of the same concerns as William Morris, including the loss of craftsmanship, that is, the human potential for creating aesthetic beauty in objects meant not only as ornamentation but for everyday, practical use as well. This ability derives from what is most humane about us: Wordsworth might have called it "our hearts"; Lawrence might have called it "our deepest self." Either way, such creation is an act of imagination, something that "robots" and "automatons" can never possess. Tolkien therefore gives us the Elves and Dwarves of Middle-earth, who create beautiful buildings and objects using the materials of the natural world. They may create those things through artistry and craft or through enchantment, but never with the use of machines, which in Tolkien's invented, or "subcreated," Secondary world are always associated with evil and the will to power over other sentient beings, from the smallest hobbit to the largest Ent.

Tolkien saw the modern age as a time when the ascendency of machinery and a concomitant decline in morals and wisdom were diminishing the quality of the average person's life. For just one example out of many, we may turn to Tolkien's comments in a letter he wrote to his son Christopher, at the time a pilot with the RAF, in July of 1944. In the letter, Tolkien differentiates between art and machinery: whereas art through the use of imagination strives only to emulate divine creation and thereby glorify God, machinery serves to confer power beyond the scope of natural human ability (*Letters* 87). According to Tolkien's Catholic epistemology, human beings are inherently flawed because of original sin. This fallen state of being makes humanity particularly susceptible, according to Tolkien, to the temptation to abuse technology in the service of, for example, the acquisition of various forms of power over others. Such technology might include anything from factory work to modern weaponry. Thus he explains to his son that the tendency to use technology in ways that ultimately harm human beings is "the tragedy and despair of all machinery" (Tolkien, *Letters* 87). Tolkien puts forward a frightening trajectory when he describes the progression from "Daedalus to Icarus to the Giant Bomber," lamenting that many people were either unfamiliar with such stories out of the past, or they didn't understand them (*Letters* 88). In Tolkien's work, the products of machinery are evil; they are always a degradation, both in themselves as well as to the person who makes things using machines.

In his book *Tolkien and the Great War*, John Garth underscores the contrast between things made by hand, by the God-given abilities of individuals, and things made by machines. According to Garth, Melko, the Prime Dark Lord, of whom Sauron was a protégé,

> represents the tyranny of the machine over life and nature, exploiting the earth and its people in the construction of a vast armoury. With a brutal inevitability, the Gnomes [Elves], with their medieval technology, lose the

contest. Tolkien's myth underlines the almost insuperable efficacy of the machine against mere skill of hand and eye. Yet it recognizes that the machine would not exist without the inventor and the craftsman. [...] In the Hells of Iron, the higher arts and sciences are subsumed or crushed in the service of mechanical industry—endlessly repetitious and motivated by nothing but the desire for more power [*Tolkien and the Great War* 223].

This is the frightening truth about machinery: it can and indeed is very often put to destructive uses. Rather than enriching humanity and enhancing the world, it has the power to corrupt the natural goodness of people and to unmake the natural beauty of the world.

In his remarks about technology, Tolkien reveals a great deal of his own sensibility, including his dislike for machinery, an antipathy that stemmed in part from his belief that in a fallen world human beings desirous of power may make or make use of objects that can unnaturally increase their abilities, thereby allowing them to exercise their will often instantaneously (*Letters* 145). This was the case of the weaponry of modern warfare, which allowed the politicians and their generals on both sides to direct campaigns of unprecedented violence with terrifying efficiency. In *The Lord of the Rings*, we see the fearful abuse of technology exemplified in the evil works of Saruman at Isengard and later in the Shire. Even more devastating and frightening is the use of technology by the satanic figure of Middle-earth, Sauron, who makes the Ring, itself a kind of machine, in order to dominate the wills of others and destroy any who would oppose him. In a 1951 letter in which he argues for the inseparability of *The Lord of the Rings* and *The Silmarillion*, Tolkien clearly relates "the Machine" to the misuse of "magic," when it relies on technology rather than a person's "inherent inner powers or talents" as well as the abuse of those abilities for the purpose of "dominating: bulldozing the real world, or coercing other wills" (*Letters* 145–46). Sauron, of course, engages in both of these activities in his attempts to gain mastery over all of Middle-earth.

Those who use magic may well begin with good intentions; however, their methods and creations often only serve to spur and accelerate their striving for power. Indeed, even Sauron began with good intentions, working with the Elves to restore the wastelands created by the war against Morgoth, the Prime Dark Lord (Tolkien, *Letters* 145–46). (In Tolkien's mythology, Morgoth, originally known as Melkor, is a

Two. *Industrialim, Instrumentality and "antiquity so appealing"*

Lucifer figure who sought to usurp God's authority at the time of the creation of the temporal world.) Although Sauron may have begun with thoughts of repairing the damage done to Middle-earth, the better part of his nature had been corrupted by Morgoth long before, and his desire to heal Middle-earth soon gave way to a greater desire to hold dominion over it. This he nearly accomplishes through the use of "machinery," that is, the Ring. Such lordship, however, would be a usurpation of divine authority.

This brings us to a second aspect of Tolkien's sensibility: his Catholic faith. For him, one *a priori* principle of our world is humanity's fallen state. Therefore, the use of "machinery," in the real Primary as well as in Tolkien's imagined Secondary world, is an evil insofar as it promotes and facilitates the will to power, a desire to which fallen humanity is particularly susceptible. Again, Tolkien's Christian beliefs dictated, and indeed he often stated, that ultimate power resides in God alone: any power that human beings attain is only derivative from Him. Most significantly, those individuals who do possess "authority," are called upon by God—who in reference to the tales Tolkien often calls "Authority"—to use it in a wise and just manner. For Tolkien, then, "machinery," which he links to the misuse of magic, subverts the natural order by enabling its owners to wield a power to which they have no God-given right. Tolkien provides his readers with several examples of individuals who exercise legitimate authority, including Aragorn. In their essay, "The Corruption of Power," Agnes Perkins and Helen Hill cite Aragorn as an example of a leader who has legitimate authority because of his lineage and his actions, arguing that he "earned the moral right which, of course, carries with it the responsibility to use his position justly and humanely. He is great because he has steadfastly fought against evil, not because he has set out to seek power" (65). Aragorn gains his kingship through his own inherent abilities, including his power to wield Anduril and command the Oathbreakers. Such powers, however, are his by right, and they are not devices of dark magic.

The most humble of the Free Folk of Middle-earth, the hobbits, live in a world whose limited technology, such as Ted Sandyman's mill, would have appeared rustic to Tolkien's twentieth-century readers. The narrator explains that hobbits prefer only simple machines such as "a forge-bellows, a water-mill, or a hand-loom" (*The Fellowship of the Ring*

1). The narrator is careful to point out that their ability to disappear so effectively is not due to magic but is due rather to the development of a skill that is inherent in their nature combined with "a close friendship with the earth" (Tolkien, *The Fellowship of the Ring* 1–2). In disappearing, the hobbits are only making use of a natural ability: they are not trying to acquire a power that exceeds their nature, as does Bilbo when he uses the Ring to vanish mysteriously from his birthday party. However, for Tolkien there is a moral difference between the stealthiness of a hobbit and the use of a magical ring.

Galadriel chides the hobbits for their use of the word "magic," but that is because she differentiates between magic as enchantment and magic as technology. In his letters, Tolkien refers to magic as "magia." Individuals use magia, he writes, to achieve virtually instant and effortless results (Tolkien, *Letters* 200). He explains that the Elves use magia, which we might in this sense call "good magic," to adorn, heal, and preserve the world whereas Sauron, and Saruman to a lesser degree, use it destructively in an effort to gain mastery. Tolkien argues that magic in itself is not evil, but it can be misused by those who would seek power, either to exploit the natural world or to control other beings.

In regard to *The Lord of the Rings*, Tolkien writes, the most significant abuse of power is the "domination of other 'free' wills" (*Letters* 200). In his book, *J.R.R. Tolkien: Myth, Morality, and Religion*, Richard Purtill discusses the role of magic in Tolkien's fiction, noting that it can be used either to enrich or harm the world and its inhabitants. Purtill writes that in Tolkien's story "the use of magic or technology to control free wills is always evil.... However, even the use of machinery or technology to control the material world is dangerous: it makes our action on the world more rapid and more powerful, thus enormously 'amplifying' mistaken or malicious choices" (141). In *The Lord of the Rings*, the most destructive characters, Saruman and Sauron, use machinery in their attempts to dominate others. Tolkien asserts that individuals and governments use *magia* in their attempts to realize a corrupt desire for control and power, that is, mastery over others. As John Milbank asserts in his essay, "Fictioning Things: Gift and Narrative," "The sinister magic is technology too slavishly deployed, and here [Tolkien] rightly indicates that we avoid noticing the fact that modernity threatens to be the triumph of this sort of magic" (27). Tolkien contrasts magic used in this way, as machinery,

Two. Industrialim, Instrumentality and "antiquity so appealing"

with art. Art, as Tolkien makes clear, aims to illuminate truth and beauty and to glorify God. In other words, art can be a means by which to "testify for God and Truth."

For Tolkien, the object of "Art" is not to create at the primary level, but rather to invent a Secondary world in which the artist attempts to convey truths about the world created by God and the condition of fallen humanity within a transcendent order. In other words, art connects humanity to truth, the truth of both the temporal and eternal worlds. For Tolkien, such an achievement cannot be attained through the use of machinery. In a 1944 letter to his son Christopher, he asserts that it is "the *man-made* that is abundantly daunting and insupportable" (*Letters* 96). The letter is highly reminiscent of Morris' complaints about nineteenth-century England in *News from Nowhere*. In Morris' novel, no one grumbles about the temperature on harvest day, nor are they bothered by their friend Boffin's fanciful appearance, since he is as good-natured and self-effacing as his Dickensian namesake. What they do find appalling are nineteenth-century buildings, particularly factories, which they have removed from the landscape of twenty-second-century England. Morris, like Tolkien, was repelled by the products of industrialism, finding them to be poorly made and artificial looking, if not downright ugly.

For Tolkien, individuals in the modern industrialized world have increased their knowledge, but the outcome of this in part is their production of machinery that leads to even worse evil, for knowledge and wisdom are not one and the same. Moreover, people have forgotten (or have never learned) the wisdom of the past which is for Tolkien, ultimately, God's Truth, either revealed through the Bible or demonstrated in natural law, abiding as it were in the honor-bound societies of his pagan ancestors. Tolkien regarded such truth as a guide for us in the present as we look toward the future. Such wisdom comes down to us through time in the form of legend and myth, including the revealed truth of the Gospel, which he called the "True Myth." Thus he includes in his letter the reference to Daedalus, the master craftsman who fashioned wings for himself and his son Icarus in order to escape from imprisonment in a tower. Daedalus has the wisdom and self-constraint not to fly too close to the sun, which would melt the wax that holds together his man-made wings, nor to the sea, whose spray would soak the feathers, thereby making them too heavy to remain aloft. The craftsmanship of Daedalus, however, becomes the technology that is his son's undoing: Icarus, in what may be interpreted either as overweening pride or mere youthful foolishness, ignores or forgets his father's warning, flies too close to the sun, and falls into the sea when the wax that held together his wings melts.

According to Tolkien, this ancient myth should act for us as both admonition and reminder. To our own detriment, however, we fail to understand the myth as a cautionary tale, the moral of which for Tolkien is to beware of the technology that gives us power beyond our human ability. Yes, Daedalus was capable of crafting wings that allowed him to accomplish an otherwise impossible task: to escape from his prison tower and cross the sea; however, without the wisdom and self-constraint that his father possesses, Icarus becomes the victim of this new "machinery." Tolkien, in his letter to Christopher, makes reference to the story in order to make the point that people have forgotten or turned away from the lessons, and thus the wisdom, of the past. The abandonment of ancient wisdom can affect life on multiple levels: it may lead eventually to something as devastating as modern technological and biological warfare, or as seemingly benign as the loss of craftsmanship itself, just as in the twenty-second-century England of *News from Nowhere* people had forgotten how to work with their hands, so completely had machines taken over the work once done by human beings.

Of course, Tolkien is referring to much more than artistry in woodworking or weaving. His admonition speaks to the loss of the lessons that have taught us through the ages about our own humanity. Like Morris, Tolkien looked to the very distant past for the models of community and personal dignity that would help his generation rise above the devastation of two World Wars. He turned to heroic literature, often oral and later transcribed, sometimes with the interpolations of their Christian recorders, as in the case of the Anglo-Saxon poem, *Beowulf*. Much of his thinking regarding the nobility of England's pre–Christian ancestors can be found in his 1936 essay entitled, "*Beowulf*: The Monsters and the Critics." Originally presented as a lecture, the essay would forever change the way scholars looked at the eleventh-century poem. Up until the time of Tolkien's essay, critics regarded the poem as having value only as "an historical document" rather than a work of art ("The Monsters and the Critics" 104). They took issue with its artistic elements, citing its narrative structure as weak and the story itself as merely simple and predictable. Most importantly, in terms of Tolkien's analysis, critics argued that the Anglo-Saxon *Beowulf* poet placed too much emphasis on the story's monsters, thereby leaving the serious, that is, historical, elements on the outskirts of relevance rather than at the very heart of it. Tolkien's groundbreaking essay refutes the accepted belief that the monsters, particularly Grendel and the dragon, are at the margins of the story and therefore are of marginal importance to it ("The Monsters and the Critics" 115).

For the fifth-century Scandinavians who inhabited the world of the Geat warrior Beowulf and the "God-cursed" monster Grendel, the center of life would have been the mead hall, the place of the highest culture and nobility of the community. The "great hall," rendered by Tolkien in his own fiction as Meduseld of Rohan, is the heart of the world of the Mark, and it is as important as any great hall of heroic literature. It was in such halls that society kept its most treasured possessions and practiced its most sacred rituals. It was in the great hall that the "scop," the storyteller in service to the king, created and sang the poetry that wove together history and legend to construct and preserve the identity of his people in the form of oral history. It was in the mead hall that individuals found shelter from the extremes of nature, food for the nourishment of the body, and fellowship for the nourishment of the soul.

In William Morris' *The House of the Wolfings*, the Romans' attacks on the mead halls of the Gothic tribes stir the men of the Mark to their most passionate battle frenzy. In the following passage Morris places great emphasis on the centrality of the mead hall. Just as holy as the meadows, woods, and rivers of their homeland is the "Roof of the Kindred." The great hall, Morris writes, was built by the forefathers of the Wolfings to protect their people from

> the fire and the lightening and the wind and the snow, and the passing of the days that devour and the years that heap the dust over the work of men. [The Wolfing warriors] thought of how it had stood, and seen so many generations of men come and go; how often it had welcomed the newborn babe, and given farewell to the old man: how many secrets of the past it knew; how many tales which men of the present had forgotten, but which yet mayhap men of times to come should learn of it; for to them yet living it had spoken time and again, and had told them what their fathers

had not told them, and it held the memories of generations and the very life of the Wolfings and their hopes for the days to be [*House of the Wolfings* 34].

Nothing in this world is lasting, but the great hall will endure through many lives of men. Through memory and narrative the mead hall connects the Wolfings to both their past and future. It represents the common humanity that all the tribes share, and this helps them to come together against a common foe. They must do so, or they will die, and their culture with them. In just this way, the diverse races of Middle-earth come together against Sauron. Stand they must, but if they stand alone, they will certainly fall.

Even John Gardner's postmodern monster, Grendel, from the novel of the same name, recognizes the importance of the mead hall as the center of community, when he shrewdly observes that "Hrothgar's whole realm was like a wobbly, lopsided wheel with spokes of stones" (39). For *Beowulf*'s pagan king Hrothgar and his people, the mead hall was not only the center of community, but it represented the history and culture of the Danes. As portrayed by the Anglo-Saxon poet, the monster Grendel is a descendant of the biblical Cain, who murdered his brother Abel and thus was cursed by God. Grendel, like Cain, is literally an "outlander" who is doomed to exist beyond the pale of human community and fellowship. When the monster attacks the thanes in the mead hall, he is in fact striking at the very heart of the Danish community. However, even more profound than being a symbol of the human community, the mead hall is a symbol of the human condition.

In his *The Ecclesiastical History of the English People*, the Anglo-Saxon monk, Bede, compares the pagan's life on earth to the flight of a sparrow through a mead hall. In Bede's account, King Edwin's councilor explains:

> This is how the present life of man on earth, King, appears to me in comparison with that time which is unknown to us. You are sitting feasting with your ealdormen and thegns in winter time; the fire is burning on the hearth in the middle of the hall and all inside is warm, while outside the wintry storms of rain and snow are raging; and a sparrow flies swiftly through hall. It enters in at one door and quickly flies out through the other. For the few moments it is inside, the storm and wintry tempest cannot touch it, but after the briefest moment of calm, it flits from your sight, out of the wintry storm and into it again. So this life of man appears but

Two. Industrialim, Instrumentality and "antiquity so appealing"

for a moment; what follows or indeed what went before, we know not at all [*History of the English People* 95].

Bede's famous analogy makes the point that for the pagans, the fellowship, comfort, and glory of this world were overshadowed by the "outer darkness," but the advent of Christ brought light and hope to human existence beyond the earthly life represented by the light and warmth of the mead hall. The argument put forth by King Edwin's councilor offers hope for eternal life after death in the temporal world. In relation to the mead hall, which represents the human community and human mortality, that is, the human condition, the monster Grendel stands in for the outer darkness that encircles Hrothgar's hall, Heorot; in other words, the monster represents all of those forces in the universe that are hostile to man and threaten his extinction. Therefore, to face Grendel, as well as to face the dragon, who also promises the annihilation of the self, is to come face-to-face with one's own mortality and the black nothingness that exists beyond the walls of the mead hall. Such a confrontation is an act of the utmost bravery and nobility. For Tolkien, this is by far the most important aspect of the Anglo-Saxon poem.

To assert, as critics before Tolkien repeatedly did, that the eleventh-century poet placed too much emphasis on the romantic aspects of the story—the hero's struggles with and victories over the monsters—fails to recognize the meaning at the heart of the poem, and, in fact, Tolkien argues, "it is the poet himself who made antiquity so appealing. His poem has more value in consequence, and is a greater contribution to early mediaeval thought than the harsh and intolerant view that consigned all the heroes to the devil" ("The Monsters and the Critics" 124). What are the ancient aspects of the poem that have such worth and appeal for the poet's eleventh-century audience as well as today's readers? Of course they are the historic events themselves, but they are, more abstractly, the noble qualities of the fifth-century characters who inhabit the Northern world of England's Teutonic ancestors. Rather than dismiss these ancient warriors as unenlightened, unregenerate heathens bound for hell, the Anglo-Saxon Christian poet, according to Tolkien, took a more generous, one might even say a more Christian, view by emphasizing their courage and commitment to one another in their willingness to sacrifice themselves for the welfare of the community. *Beowulf* presents its twentieth-century readers with a past that Van Wyck Brooks might characterize as having "living value": in this case the Northern heroic values of bravery and honor in the face of ultimate defeat.

"*Beowulf*: The Monster's and the Critics" goes a long way to demonstrate Tolkien's engagement with the past. He read closely the stories that ancient peoples told about themselves, the aspects of their culture that they chose to preserve, and there he found meaning that transcends time. In "The Monsters and the Critics," Tolkien argues that the goal of the Anglo-Saxon poet was "to depict ancient pre–Christian days, intending to emphasize their nobility, and the desire of the good for truth" (123). This is consistent with Tolkien's goal for his own writing: to "testify for God and Truth." Other critics examined *Beowulf* for what it could tell them about technical matters; Tolkien looked at it and saw what it could tell us about ourselves. He found that this story that originated fifteen centuries before his own had much to say about our humanity: our frailty and weaknesses as well as our courage and dignity. Much of the essay conveys a tone of admiration, it seems, for the Beowulf poet for raising up his pagan ancestors to a level of Christian exemplum so that his own eleventh-century audience could admire them as well. By putting their struggle in the context of Christianity, the Anglo-Saxon poet made them more than acceptable: he made them praiseworthy.

For Tolkien the heart of the story follows the pattern of Beowulf's youth and age, arcing from his young man's contest with Grendel to his old man's struggle with the dragon. The hero is victorious in both, but like all heroes, pagan and Christian, he is doomed to defeat in the final earthly battle, which in every case is against time itself. For the Christian hero, however, that defeat is only temporary. Christ will achieve final victory, unlike the monsters of Norse mythology, which are destined to win in the end over the forces of men and gods during Ragnorok. Tolkien's essay demonstrates that against the arc of Beowulf's career from warrior to king, from battling Grendel to battling the dragon, are the historical events of the poem. These events are the backdrop that gives the reader the sense that Beowulf's struggle was somehow more real, his invented life more anchored in the ongoing story that is human history. In interpreting *Beowulf*, Tolkien engaged the past in a way that no other of its critics before him had: he recognized that the *Beowulf* poet cast his imagination back over hundreds of years to consider the world of his distant ancestors, to see their fated struggle in the world of

Two. Industrialim, Instrumentality and "antiquity so appealing"

time. All great kings, along with their empires and their monuments, will come to dust in the end; this is the tragedy of the human condition. In the face of it, the pagan warrior sought an honorable death: to die with the bodies of his enemies all around him and with his own body covered in wounds.

William Morris portrays just such an heroic end in his romance tale, *The House of the Wolfings*. The Goth warriors, far outnumbered by the Romans, fight desperately; none dies without killing at least one enemy soldier. The oldest warriors of the kindred "fought as if they and the few around them were all the host that was left to the folk, and heeded not that others were driven back, or that the Romans gathered about them, cutting them off from all succor and aid, but went on smiting till they were felled with many strokes" (*House of the Wolfings* 123). This is death that Tolkien gave to Boromir, thereby elevating him to a place of the utmost dignity within the context of honor-bound warrior society and, indeed, within the world of Middle-earth. When his companions find Boromir after his defense of Merry and Pippin near Parth Galen, he is "sitting with his back to a great tree" (*The Two Towers* 416). Such a posture may symbolize the final and most honorable defeat of the warrior who fought with his back to the proverbial wall. Certainly, Boromir's death is a most honorable one, as evidenced by the many fallen enemies around him. When his companions find him, Boromir appears to be sitting peacefully, but as they come closer they can see that he had been impaled by many Orc arrows. There are other indications that Boromir fought until his very last breath: "his sword was still in his hand, but it was broken near the hilt; his horn cloven in two was at his side. Many Orcs lay slain, piled all about him and at his feet" (Tolkien, *The Two Towers* 416). Like Beowulf, Boromir fought until all the strength had bled out of him. This was his greatest achievement and the warrior's greatest hope.

Unlike the warrior Beowulf of the original fifth-century story, however, Boromir existed in what Tolkien referred to as a "pure monotheistic world" (*Letters* 204) in which the immortality of the spirit was acknowledged, at least by the learned. Tolkien imagined the Beowulf poet engaging with the past by contrasting the fate of the pagan with that of the Christian. The Anglo-Saxon poet interpolated Christian beliefs into *Beowulf*, thereby overcoming the limitations of the "pagan creed," by virtue of which, Tolkien writes, "all glory (or as we might say 'culture' or 'civilization') ends in night" ("The Monsters and the Critics" 119). The Beowulf poet was aware that the pagan stories do not offer "the solution of that tragedy" because, for Tolkien as for the Anglo-Saxon poet, the only solution is the eternal life of the soul through Christ's redemption of humankind. We therefore have in *Beowulf*, Tolkien writes,

> a poem from a pregnant moment of poise, looking back into the pit, by a man learned in old tales who was struggling, as it were, to get a general view of them all, perceiving their common tragedy of inevitable ruin, and yet feeling this more poetically because he was removed from the direct pressure of its despair. He could view from without, but still feel immediately from within, the old dogma: despair in the event, combined with faith in the value of doomed resistance ["The Monsters and the Critics" 119].

The Anglo-Saxon poet, from his vantage point of Christian faith, according to Tolkien, was able to imagine a world in which the pagan hero Beowulf and his thanes could battle against evil with the assurance that there was more than the outer darkness beyond the walls of the mead hall. At the same time, the eleventh-century poet admired "doomed resistance": faith in the warrior ideal that encompassed enduring values of courage in the face of despair, devotion to the greater good, and self-sacrifice on behalf of the welfare of the community. The old King Beowulf faced the enraged dragon, the most deadly enemy he had ever faced, with the help of only one of his thanes, Wiglaf. Of all of Beowulf's company, only Wiglaf possessed the level of devotion to his king that could help him overcome his fear of the dragon. The dying Beowulf rewards this loyalty and bravery by passing his kingship on to Wiglaf, who exemplifies both warrior and Christian values.

In his loyalty to the hobbits Merry and Pippin, demonstrated by his courage in standing virtually alone against an onslaught of orcs and his self-sacrifice for the greater good, Boromir, too, exemplifies warrior values. After his confession to Aragorn and his expression of regret for his attempt to take the Ring from Frodo, he exhibits humility in his final wish that Aragorn claim lordship over Gondor for both its defense and the restoration of its glory. Just as Wiglaf oversees the solemn and dignified funeral rites for Beowulf, Aragorn and his companions give to Boromir the ritual funeral that confers the greatest honor. Boromir, like

Two. *Industrialim, Instrumentality and "antiquity so appealing"*

Beowulf, knows he cannot overcome his opponent, but he fights with as much passion and strength as though he hoped for victory. C.S. Lewis, in agreement with Tolkien, believed that any victory humanity might achieve against the forces of darkness was only temporary. "If we insist on asking for the moral of [The Lord of the Rings]," Lewis wrote, "that is its moral: a recall from facile optimism and wailing pessimism alike, to that hard, yet not quite desperate, insight into man's unchanging predicament by which heroic ages have lived" ("The Dethronement of Power" 14).

Tolkien imagined the Beowulf poet surveying the past in order to understand his predecessors and to perceive through their literature their contribution to the store of human knowledge and understanding. He maintains that the poet did not simply translate an ancient tale that told of the history of a people and their struggle against the enemies of their kingdom, both human and non-human. Rather, according to Tolkien, the Beowulf poet re-imagined the world in which that struggle took place, altering the context of the fight from pagan to Christian and portraying Grendel as a demon from hell so as not to diminish the power and terror of the monster. The hero's willingness to confront that evil ennobles him for the Anglo-Saxon poet's audience, thereby showing them one way of existing in the world.

In regard to William Morris' preoccupation with heroic romance, Northrup Frye explains that "the stories" of the past are "imaginative projections of life that humanity at present can see no use for, and yet are the sources of all the styles of living, past, present, and future, that it has set up. They are myths that form a mythology, and a mythology is the world man builds as distinct from the world that surrounds him, so far as the former can be presented in words" (Frye 318). The sub-created world of Tolkien, like those of William Morris before him, and the *Beowulf* poet long before them both, engages with the past by distilling truth from the ancient tales and creating a fictional world that is informed by moral absolutes. Through an act of imagination that forges a connection with other minds, each man created a vision of life that offered hope to his readers, hope in the author's own time and long after his death. In 1918 the American critic Van Wyck Brooks wrote, "Unhappily, the spiritual welfare of this country depends altogether upon the fate of its creative minds. If they cannot grow and ripen, where are we going to get the new ideals, the finer attitudes that we must get if we are ever to emerge from our existing travesty of a civilization?" (339). On the other side of the Atlantic, unknown to Brooks, a young creative mind was flourishing amidst the ruins of the Great War, perhaps even in spite of them. John Ronald Reuel Tolkien was creating a mythology, indeed a chronicle of several millennia of Middle-earth, our earth, and the stories it contains bring forth for posterity the lessons of the past, lessons of courage and kindness, and of faith in humanity and the benevolence of its Creator. In this way he sought to achieve the goal of the TCBS: to "rekindle an old light" in the world. That light has many aspects: it is the light of God's creation, the Imperishable Flame which is the divinely powerful "secret fire" of which Gandalf is the guardian; it is the light of the Gospels, which Tolkien called "true myth"; and it is also the light of human goodness and strength, as old as human memory. To recognize that light in its ancient embodiments and bring it into the present is to profoundly engage with "antiquity so appealing."

Three

The Lord of the Rings: "Insubstantial dream of an escapist"

"*The goblins were right.*" These words are spoken by a young Helen Schlegel in E.M. Forster's 1910 novel, *Howards End*. While attending with her family a performance of Beethoven's Fifth Symphony, Helen is particularly moved by what she visualizes as the "heroes and goblins" of the third movement. As she listens, Helen envisions a line of goblins making their way across the universe. The goblins terrify her, not because they are menacing; rather, they are disturbing in their calm indifference to the triumphs and agonies of humanity. She imagines that the goblins "merely observed in passing that there was no such thing as splendour or heroism in the world … once at all events, she had felt the same, and seen the reliable walls of youth collapse. Panic and emptiness! Panic and emptiness! The goblins were right" (Forster 30). *Howards End* speaks to us from the Edwardian period of English history, itself the end of a long era of "splendour," a time of noble families who lived in great houses and possessed enormous wealth and social status. After the Great War, it became impossible in a world of austerity to return to the opulence of the past. Even before the war, however, people were starting to question the morality of such wealth and luxury in the face of growing poverty and deprivation. The notion of a great chain of being, a natural order of society from God to monarch to nobility to common people, had been challenged throughout the nineteenth century, as people began to reject traditional paradigms of social determinism.

Helen's ruminations on Beethoven's Fifth symphony reflect this growing disbelief that the universe is divinely ordered and that the actions of men for good or ill within that order have eternal meaning and value, or at least have the potential for such things. Helen's goblins also provide a glimpse into the feelings of disenchantment and loss that would be expressed by so many of the post-war writers who would follow Forster, those who perceived modern life to be without any sort of transcendent meaning. Forster's image of the goblins, therefore, moves both backward to Bede's metaphor of the outer darkness that surrounds the mead hall and forward to the Dragon of John Gardner's postmodern novel, *Grendel*, whose nihilism reveals itself as a kind of ultimate ennui whereby the eye of the beholder can no longer perceive meaning in anything it sees. This is the truth that Helen's goblins "merely observed in passing."

For Forster's Helen Schlegel, belief in ideals such as true love's ability to overcome any obstacle, such as a lack of wealth or social standing, is maintained by the ingenuousness of youth. In the passage above, the phrase "reliable walls of youth" can be interpreted on two levels: first, it may relate to the disenchantment that comes with the loss of childhood innocence. Helen had fallen in love with Paul Wilcox less for himself than for what he represented: the Wilcox family, about whom she had created a fantasy of perfect domestic harmony and happiness. This vision was enhanced by the enchantment of the bucolic Howards End, the ancestral home of Mrs. Wilcox. After knowing the younger Wilcox son for only a few days, Helen writes to her sister, Margaret, to declare that she and Paul are in love, but the youthful impetuousness of an evening is followed by the sobering reality of the next morning and with it another hasty message to her sister to say that the romance was over before it had properly begun. That morning at breakfast she had seen the young man's terrified expression at the thought of losing his place in the materialistic world of the Wilcoxes. In that moment Helen realized the difference between the "prose" of materialism and the "poetry" of the life of the mind, which is the world that the Schlegel siblings inhabit. She tells her sister, "I felt for a moment that the whole Wilcox family was a fraud, just a wall of newspapers and motor-cars and golf-clubs, and that if it fell I should find nothing behind it but panic and emptiness" (Forster 23–24). For Helen, then, this realization brings with it the collapse of "the reliable walls of youth" that in the past had insulated her romantic imagination.

The phrase may be interpreted more generally in relation to the

THREE. The Lord of the Rings: *"Insubstantial dream of an escapist"*

"youthful" phase of the history of Western culture. As noted earlier, Northrup Frye, calling upon Oswald Spengler's 1918 book, *The Decline of the West*, argues that societies pass through various ages, from youth to maturity. E.M. Forster was writing during that liminal period when the benefits of Victorian progress into an ever brighter future would reach their peak with the twentieth-century luxuries of Edwardian life, only to come finally crashing back to earth with the devastation of World War I. The fictional character, Helen Schlegel, occupies a pivotal moment in history in which she may look both backwards and forward to see that the old beliefs which made sense of the world are crumbling as though they were little more than facades to begin with, nothing more than youthful romantic illusions of "splendour or heroism." In their place is a void so appalling that her immediate response is one of alarm: "Panic and emptiness!" (Forster 30). Later writers would go on to locate this emptiness, and the feelings of dislocation and alienation to which it gives rise, within individuals themselves as well as in modern society.

Howards End is a pre-war novel, so it sets the stage for the break that is about to occur when the cataclysm of World War I fractures the ostensibly smooth continuum of Western history. Specifically, the book portrays the intellectual atmosphere of disaffection with Victorian and Edwardian tradition and ideals that would soon spread to the larger culture, becoming the disaffection not only of intellectuals, whose business it is to deal in abstractions, but of laborers, clerks, and all manner of people concerned with the everyday business of life. More than this, though, *Howards End* puts in human terms the gulf between the old world that was passing and the modern world that would take its place. In this respect, then, the goblins are both harbinger and symbol of the new era.

Helen's goblins do not act beyond walking and observing. They do not bring about but merely bear witness to the world as wasteland; their presence is a reminder that something has been lost to—or forsaken by—Forster's generation. Beethoven's Fifth Symphony, called up from a past that spoke for "splendour and heroism," acts to the modern sensibility, as represented by Helen Schlegel, as a defense against the disillusionment of the early twentieth century, temporarily staving off the panic of individuals who found themselves disconnected from one another, from tradition, and from nature. This disconnect arose in part from differences in social class, but it also found its source in the ideological differences of mainstream Victorians and Edwardians on the one hand and the younger generation who rejected those ideals on the other. What was left in their place was a kind of anxiety: the fear that results from the conviction that, as the goblins remind us, the universe is vast but empty. By constructing "ramparts," the artist can keep the goblins at bay: to Helen's mind, Beethoven can dispel them, but he cannot destroy them, for such is the state of Helen's—and Forster's—world. The artist, whether it be through music or painting or literature, attempts to create beauty and meaning where he perceives barrenness and meaninglessness, to bridge the divide that separates the materialistic and the aesthetic worlds and thereby stave off "panic and emptiness."

Forster gave to *Howards End* the epigraph, "Only connect...." In a talk that she gave at the Library of Congress on Halloween of 1966, P.L. Travers says that Forster's epigraph may well be "the theme of all Forster's writing, the attempt to link a passionate skepticism with the desire for meaning, to find the human key to the inhuman world around us; to connect the individual with the community, the known with the unknown; to relate the past to the present and both to the future" ("Only Connect" 233). To this end, in part, Forster gives us Mrs. Wilcox, who represents an awareness of and continuity with the past as well as a living connection with the human community and the natural world. Howards End, the home where Mrs. Wilcox was born and raised, represents a necessary element in the balance between Victorian materialism, or "prose," and the aesthetic sensibility, or "poetry." The central character of the novel, Margaret Schlegel, comes to realize that such a balance must exist in order for individuals to find peace in their time and to restore community. Indeed, it is not to her own children but to her spiritual heir, Margaret Schlegel, that Ruth Wilcox bequeaths her ancestral home. This break in the traditional continuity regarding the ownership of the land mirrors the less tangible cultural fracture that takes place during the early part of the twentieth century.

In Mrs. Wilcox, Forster puts forth an example of human dignity, derived not from social or economic class, but from an almost mystical connection with the land and the people who cultivate and cherish it from one generation to the next. Mrs. Wilcox herself occupies a liminal place in the world of the novel: she exists neither in the realm of mate-

THREE. The Lord of the Rings: *"Insubstantial dream of an escapist"*

rialism, like the other Wilcoxes, nor of aesthetics, as do Margaret and Helen Schlegel and their brother, Tibby. Among all of the characters of *Howards End*, Ruth Wilcox is unique insofar as she is more a part of nature than of society. After her death, her husband, Henry, recalls her as childlike, ingenuous: "Ruth knew no more of worldly wickedness and wisdom than did the flowers in her garden or the grass in her field. Her idea of business—'Henry, why do people who have enough money try to get more money?' Her idea of politics—'I am sure that if the mothers of various nations could meet, there would be no more wars'" (Forster 82). One imagines that she would fit well into the "gigantic kindergarten" to which Frye likens William Morris' future utopian England. The future that Morris constructs rests on a distant past that can never be recovered, for it represents an idealized England of long ago that never existed in the first place. In what Tolkien would call the "Secondary world" of the novel, however, there is an implicit value in this childlike innocence: it provides a model of one particular way to be in the world. Morris' "neighbors" and Forster's Ruth Wilcox provide readers, as Northrup Frye writes, with "imaginative projections of life." As such, each acts as an exemplum of human life lived in harmony with nature and with other people. Such individuals seek nothing more than to exist alongside others for the joy and enrichment their company brings, rather than to exploit what is other than themselves in order to achieve power for themselves. In the character of Ruth Wilcox, Forster imagines for his readers an uncorrupted individual who seeks neither material wealth (her family's estate was nearly bankrupt when Henry Wilcox took over the management of it) nor mastery over the land or its caretakers.

The childlike innocence and purity of spirit that Ruth Wilcox represents as well as the pastoral England to which she is linked cannot endure in the real, or Primary, world of the novelist; like Mrs. Wilcox they will pass out of existence almost parenthetically. In his own sub-created world of Middle-earth, Tolkien puts forth the character of Tom Bombadil, who personifies the pastoral England of the author's youth. Tom Bombadil represents unfallen humanity: he peacefully coexists with nature, enjoying it but never using it for his own gain. He helps others and has no interest in achieving even the slightest degree of mastery over other free wills. In answer to Frodo's question as to whether Bombadil is the master of the country surrounding his home, Goldberry tells the hobbits that the land certainly does not *belong* to Tom Bombadil. Ownership of so many other living things would be burdensome, for "'all things growing or living in the land belong each to themselves'" (Tolkien, *The Fellowship of the Ring* 124). Goldberry's response to Frodo's question goes a long way to explaining why the One Ring has no power over Tom. The Ring enslaves its wearer through the desire for power over others, depriving the wearer of his God-given free will. Since Tom has no wish to dominate others, the Ring has no effect on him at all: when he puts it on he does not disappear, much to the astonishment of the hobbits.

Through the example of Tom Bombadil, Tolkien, in his imagined world, shows his readers how to be in the real world: kind, generous, respectful of nature and of other people, and content to be master of oneself and no one else. Forster gives such qualities to Ruth Wilcox and Margaret Schlegel. In these characters Forster presents a more muted kind of heroism than is first imagined by Helen, though perhaps it is more enduring. In the end, Helen tells her sister that it was she, Margaret, who "picked up the pieces, and made us a home" (Forster 308). That is, from the fragments of the Wilcox's and Schlegels' tragedies—Henry Wilcox broken in spirit, his son Charles imprisoned, and Leonard Bast, the impoverished father of Helen's illegitimate child, dead—Margaret has re-established community and tied it to a place of meaning and worth. Helen asks her sister, not without some astonishment, "Can't it strike you—even for a moment—that your life has been heroic?" (Forster 308). Helen has come to understand that ordinary women with the extraordinary power to forge connections across lines of class and gender can also stand against the nihilism of the goblins.

For Helen, Beethoven has the power to overcome the goblins, yet the monsters of the outer darkness are bound to return. Despite the Victorian optimism of industrialists like Henry Wilcox, Helen knows that regardless of humanity's ability to achieve greatness and to express truth and beauty, the goblins are a permanent part of human existence. She thinks:

> Panic and emptiness! Panic and emptiness! Even the flaming ramparts of the world might fall.
> Beethoven chose to make it all right in the end. He built the ramparts up. He blew his mouth for the second time, and again the goblins were

THREE. The Lord of the Rings: *"Insubstantial dream of an escapist"*

scattered. He brought back the gusts of splendour, the heroism, the youth, the magnificence of life and death, and amid vast roarings of superhuman joy, he led his Fifth Symphony to its conclusion. But the goblins were there. They could return [Forster 31].

To Helen's mind, Beethoven conveys truth. Her interpretation of his Fifth Symphony as a portrayal of humanity's struggle for meaning and transcendence against the vastness and indifference of the universe is in keeping with the modernist sensibility that at best one may attempt to construct meaning, but ultimately one is more likely to be haunted by feelings of profound anxiety and futility. The goblins can and do come back; though they may recede behind human achievement, they are never far away.

Just as the figure of the dragon can be used as a foil for an ancient hero, such as the dragon in *Beowulf*, or a representation of twentieth-century nihilism, such as John Gardner's Dragon in *Grendel*, the image of the goblin can be put to multiple uses. Forster's goblins are figurative reminders that the cultural traditions and ideological foundations that once held up and held together the old world had been cut away by the forces of industrialism and the science and secularism that drove it throughout the nineteenth and early twentieth centuries. These forces would soon find their culmination in the First World War, leaving in their wake a greatly damaged human community and a Western culture in fragments. Tolkien's work, too, responds to the trauma of the first decades of the twentieth century. The goblins of *The Lord of the Rings*, the Orcs, are both figurative and literal: within the story they are quite real: they have their own agency, and they act upon the world in damaging ways rather than merely observe it. At the same time, they fulfill the role of the monster Grendel insofar as each represents the darkness that surrounds the mead hall. They also represent Gardner's Dragon, who in his nihilism perceives of the world as a moral and spiritual wasteland. Tolkien's orcs delight in their part as cogs in the machine that would systematically strip the world until it is, like Mordor, the most striking of Tolkien's wastelands, little more than bare rock. In the process they would help to enslave, just as they themselves are enslaved, the inhabitants of Middle-earth. The end result of these forces is a wasteland world in which individuals are alienated not only from the natural world and each other but also from themselves.

For Forster, the alternative is connection: connection to others and to the natural world through the resolution of the opposing forces of materialism and aesthetic sensibility, that is, "prose" and "poetry." Tolkien, too, places great importance on connection. Indeed, the survival of Middle-earth depends on the unity of its free peoples, on their rising above old animosities and perceived transgressions against one another in order to gather the fortitude and strength necessary to face a virtually invulnerable enemy. For Tolkien, however, unlike Forster, there is always a benevolent power beyond the world that mitigates against evil. For him there was no doubt, no ultimate despair. *The Lord of the Rings* bears witness finally to the conviction that the universe is not empty. Tolkien was not panicking.

* * *

The modernists' response to the intellectual, social, and political circumstances of the early twentieth century is marked largely by a rejection of tradition and the attempt to create new ways to transform what they perceived to be chaotic and fragmented experience into ordered wholes. At the same time, modernist literature looks closely at the self in the context of a new "modern age" reality. Like his contemporaries, Tolkien responded to the profound changes that took place in the early twentieth century; however, he chose as his preferred genre what he called "fairy-story," and for this he was often criticized as writing "escapist" (read "non-serious") literature. Tolkien's friend and most enthusiastic supporter as he drafted *The Lord of the Rings*, C.S. Lewis, wrote a review in which he argued that one of the book's greatest strengths is its realism. As an example, Lewis points to Tolkien's portrayal of global war. The War of the Ring, Lewis argues, is fundamentally similar to World War I. "It is all here," Lewis writes: "the endless, unintelligible movement, the sinister quiet of the front when 'everything is now ready,' the flying civilians, the lively, vivid friendships, the background of something like despair and the merry foreground, and such heaven-sent windfalls as a cache of tobacco 'salvaged' from a ruin" ("The Dethronement of Power" 13). In Tolkien's subcreated world, massive armies march across lands unknown to them to confront their enemies on multiple battlefields; soldiers wait anxiously before the battles of Helm's Deep, the Pelennor, and the Morannon; and the people of Rohan

THREE. The Lord of the Rings: *"Insubstantial dream of an escapist"*

flee before the Hun-like invaders of Saruman's legions. Amidst all of these martial nightmares, old friendships are strengthened even as new friendships spring up, as for example, Merry and Pippin cleave to one another while at the same time forge strong connections with individuals from other races, including Théoden and Treebeard. Lewis' remarks also call to mind, of course, the image of Merry and Pippin atop a pile of rubble, serenely enjoying the Shire tobacco they'd found in one of the guardhouses of Isengard. Apart from the fantastic nature of some of these characters, all of these circumstances could take place in the Primary, or real, world.

In both *J.R.R. Tolkien: Author of the Century* and *The Road to Middle-earth*, Tom Shippey discusses critical responses to Tolkien. In the latter book, he notes that Tolkien's critics were "dead sure his writing could not possibly have any relevance to the century he and they lived in" (Shippey, *Road to Middle-earth* 329). Nevertheless, Shippey argues, "*The Lord of the Rings* in particular is a war-book, also a post-war book, framed by and responding to the crisis of Western civilisation, 1914–1945" (*Road to Middle-earth* 329). Shippey includes Tolkien with his contemporaries, William Golding, T.H. White, George Orwell, and Kurt Vonnegut, all of them canonized writers. "All of these men," according to Shippey, "were writing obviously, or even self-declaredly, about the nature of evil, which they thought had changed in their time, or about which the human race had gained new knowledge" (*Road to Middle-earth* 329). While modern war had brought evil to the forefront of the minds of all these writers, Tolkien would have considered the question of evil in the context of Christianity. A prevalent theme in his work is that evil has existed since the world began: in *The Silmarillion*, for example, Melko, a proud and rebellious angel, introduces evil as discordant notes in the divine music out of which the world is created. John Garth describes the parallels between Milton's Satan and Tolkien's fallen angel. "The primal rebel Melko," Garth writes, "covets Ilúvatar's creativity where the Satan of Milton's *Paradise Lost* coveted God's authority, a distinction reflecting Tolkien's aestheticist anti-industrialism and Milton's puritan anti-monarchism. Melko enters the void to search for the Secret Fire, yet having failed to find it he nevertheless introduces his own discordant music" (255). The notion of the introduction of evil into the world from its earliest days is consistent with Tolkien's Catholic beliefs, according to which only God can finally and completely achieve victory over such fundamental evil.

Tolkien's own feelings about the modern age are evident not just in the literature he crafted, but in a number of scholarly essays and a substantial legacy of letters written by him as a young man until shortly before his death at the age of eighty-one on September 2, 1973. These letters, which have been collected and edited by Humphrey Carpenter with the help of Tolkien's youngest son, Christopher, provide substantial insights about his responses to the rapidly changing world of the twentieth century. In one of his most important scholarly works, the 1947 essay "On Fairy-stories" (drafted in 1938), Tolkien addresses the charge of escapism, lays out his own theory of the nature of fairy-story, and argues that fairy story, or romance, does in fact treat very serious matters.

From the time of his youth, Tolkien had been creating languages and writing the mythology that would ultimately be published as *The Silmarillion*, *The History of Middle-earth*, and, in the early twenty-first century, *The Children of Hurin*. As most readers are aware, *The Hobbit* and *The Lord of the Rings* are relatively brief episodes within this much larger legendarium. As beloved as these two works now are, at the time of their publication (and even today among some arbiters of literary taste) they were not considered "serious" literature. Tolkien sometimes commented on such responses to *The Lord of the Rings*. For example, in September of 1954 he wrote that some critics' treatment of the story was reductive, interpreting it as merely "a plain fight between Good and Evil" without taking into account the complexity of human nature demonstrated on both sides of the struggle (Tolkien, *Letters* 197). Tolkien specifically makes note of Boromir, who is essentially noble and good but who falls to temptation through the combination of the Ring's power to corrupt and his own desire to protect his people and win victory over Sauron. Tolkien attributed the dismissive attitude of reviewers to their probable perfunctory or incomplete reading of the book as well as a lack of knowledge of the legendary matter that later came to be published as *The Silmarillion* and the multi-volume *History of Middle-earth*.

The negative response among critics is due in part to the fantastical nature of romance, a genre in which dragons, green knights, magical swords, indeed fairy-land itself, all find themselves very comfortably at home. In "On Fairy-stories," Tolkien addresses the charge that such sto-

THREE. The Lord of the Rings: *"Insubstantial dream of an escapist"*

ries are less real than "'serious' literature." He asserts, "The notion that motor-cars are more 'alive' than, say, centaurs or dragons is curious; that they are more 'real' than, say, horses is pathetically absurd. How real, how startlingly alive is a factory chimney compared with an elm-tree: poor obsolete thing, insubstantial dream of an escapist!" (81). For Tolkien, use of the fantastic allows the author to approach Truth, not escape from it. Fairy-stories, he argues, are concerned with "many more permanent and fundamental things" than "electric street-lamps" and the mass produced objects of the machine age. They may reasonably include fantastic worlds and creatures so long as the story itself maintains internal consistency: "Fairy-stories may invent monsters that fly the air or dwell in the deep, but at least they do not try to escape from heaven or the sea" (Tolkien, "On Fairy-stories" 81). For Tolkien, no matter how unreal events and characters within the author's Secondary world may be, the story itself may still maintain a strong connection to the Primary, or real, world. In his "Afterword" to George MacDonald's fairytale "The Golden Key," W.H. Auden explains the relationship between these two worlds:

> A Secondary world may be full of extraordinary objects (glass mountains and enchanted castles) and extraordinary events may occur in it, like a live man being turned into stone or a dead man restored to life; but, like the Primary world, it must, if it is to carry conviction, seem to be a world governed by laws, not by pure chance. Its creator, like the inventor of a game, is at liberty to decide what the laws shall be, but once he has decided, his story must obey them [83].

In Tolkien's Secondary world of Middle-earth, for example, the Nazgul on their fell beasts do not attempt to tunnel their way into Minas Tirith, but rather attack from the air and command Sauron's legions to batter the gates of the White City with Grond, itself a fantastical device, cast about with evil spells. The narrator says, "Long had it been forging in the dark smithies of Mordor, and its hideous head, founded of black steel, was shaped in the likeness of a ravening wolf; on it spells of ruin lay" (Tolkien, *The Return of the King* 837). That the battering ram should be a mechanism of evil, that is, of dark magic, is not an affront to the reader, who has come to understand that many forces, both natural and supernatural, are at work in Middle-earth, the author's invented Secondary World.

Tolkien and the Modernists

The danger of the Battle of the Pelennor is true danger within the world of the story. The faltering of the soldiers of Gondor upon confronting the atrocities of the armies of Mordor is understandable; only the most disaffected of men would not blench at the sight of the catapulted heads of his comrades rolling about his feet or the despair-provoking cries of the Nazguls' fell beasts in the air above his beloved city, for the voices that ride the air above Minas Tirith are "filled with evil and horror." So terrifying are these creatures that upon hearing them even the bravest of Gondor's warriors "would fling themselves to the ground as the hidden menace passed over them, or they would stand, letting their weapons fall from nerveless hands while into their minds a blackness came, and thought no more of war; but only of hiding and crawling, and of death" (Tolkien, *The Return of the King* 833). This exhibition of fear on the part of battle-hardened men who would have been ashamed to flee from an enemy helps to demonstrate the terrifying nature of the servants of Sauron.

Within Tolkien's invented world, as in the ancient Northern past of the real world, warriors on the side of good live by the values of honor-bound society. In such a community, like those of the Danes and Geats of *Beowulf*, warrior code demands that men fight no matter what the fear, no matter who or what the enemy, no matter how outnumbered they may be. Thus the aging King Beowulf fights the dragon, Boromir stands alone against a battalion of orcs, and Aragorn leads a battle-weary army to the very Gates of Mordor. All three men know that they cannot win, but they are prepared to die in the attempt. The soldiers of Gondor are descendants of the men of Númenor, whose ancient kingdoms and power once spanned Middle-earth from north to south. By describing, as the narrator does in the passage above, such brave and noble men blench rather than face their enemy, drop their weapons while there is still life in them, and even think of running from the battle, Tolkien signifies the depth and power of Sauron's evil. In the world of Middle-earth, such terror is real and *necessary*, for, as Tolkien writes, even in a fairy story there must be "a warp of fear and horror, if ... it is to resemble reality, and not be the *merest escapism*" (*Letters* 120; emphasis added). He makes a similar assertion in his response to a reader's interest in "the Necromancer" of *The Hobbit*, one of the menacing aspects of the tale that had stalked from the tumultuous and tragic world of his legendar-

THREE. The Lord of the Rings: *"Insubstantial dream of an escapist"*

ium into a land that lay far beyond the green and pleasant hills of Bilbo's Shire. Yet it is that very menace, abiding silently in the shadows of Mirkwood, which lends credence to the land of the hobbits. Just as *Beowulf's* Grendel represents all that is hostile to humankind, the Necromancer of *The Hobbit* represents the ineradicable existence of evil in the world of time.

In the absence of a being or force antithetical to the striving of humanity for goodness, The Shire would seem to be very much a "gigantic kindergarten" whose inhabitants are never touched by evil and, indeed, never even fear its touch. Like children unaware of the protection of their parents, the hobbits of Middle-earth are protected by the Rangers of the North, the last remnant of the Men of Westernesse. At the Council of Elrond, Aragorn tells Boromir that Middle-earth is kept safe not only by the strength of Gondor. There are many evil beings in the world that threaten communities like the Shire and Bree, but there are brave guardians against those monsters. "What roads would any dare to tread," Aragorn asks, "what safety would there be in quiet lands, or in the homes of simple men at night, if the Dúnedain were asleep, or were all gone into the grave?" (Tolkien, *The Fellowship of the Ring* 249). The image that Aragorn creates for Boromir recalls the image of the mead hall amidst the encircling darkness: the peaceful community of the Shire is ringed about by a desolation of darkness from which evil things come creeping. This juxtaposition of human fellowship against evil incarnate is evident in the eleventh-century poem *Beowulf*, in which the monster who attacks Heorot, the heart of Hrothgar's kingdom, is an outlander: Grendel exists beyond the pale of the human community, and he feels only animosity toward it. Similarly, many of Middle-earth's borderlands are liminal places where good and evil come into contact with one another: the ancient and hostile Old Forest, in which Frodo and his companions are threatened by Old Willow, thrives just on the other side of the Hedge that marks the eastern boundary of Buckland; Orcs harry the border guards of Lothlórien; and Gondor is caught between enemies to the north, south, and even the west, thanks to the treachery of Saruman. Overarching all of this danger is the ultimate threat of evil that seeks the enslavement or destruction of the free peoples of Middle-earth: Sauron.

Just as the Nazgul of Tolkien's heroic fairy-story have the power to instill paralyzing terror in the hearts of their enemies, Gandalf, the White Rider, Keeper of the Secret Fire, has the power to inspire them to screw their courage to the sticking place. When Denethor succumbs to despair, he tells Pippin, "Follow whom you will, even the Grey Fool, though his hope has failed" (Tolkien, *The Return of the King* 833). Of course Gandalf's hope has not failed; though it may be just the slightest of hopes, he will not forsake it. For Tolkien it is wrong to despair, as is clear in the case of Denethor and his abdication of his stewardship, subsequent to which, the narrator explains, Gandalf assumed leadership of Gondor's soldiers. It is Gandalf, an emissary of the divine Valar, who kindles courage and inspires at least some of the Gondorian soldiers to hold their ground, to stay at their posts in the face of unspeakable horror. Honor, courage, humility, dignity, fortitude in the face of overwhelming odds, these characteristics are not peculiar to fairy-stories, or romance; they are enduring human virtues that transcend time and culture. They are part of the "fundamental things" with which fairy-stories concern themselves. What could be more real or speak more poignantly to the human heart?

In the course of explaining that well-crafted "fairy-stories" are not mere escapist fiction, Tolkien contrasts the modern era with bygone days. He writes, "Many stories out of the past have only become 'escapist' in their appeal through surviving from a time when men were as a rule delighted with the work of their hands into our time, when many men feel disgust with man-made things" ("On Fairy-stories" 83). Nineteenth- and early twentieth-century progress had brought about extraordinary human achievements in science and technology, but along with these advances were the devastating effects of industrialism for both humanity and the natural world. Among the collaterally damaged were the vast numbers of poor, whose labor helped to generate enormous wealth for the few, and the world's natural resources, which were being consumed at an unprecedented and unchecked rate. Moreover, mass production's gift to humanity was not only the electric street lamp and the motor car, but the tank and machinegun as well. "It is," Tolkien writes, "part of the essential malady of such days—producing the desire to escape, not indeed from life, but from our present time and self-made misery—that we are acutely conscious both of the ugliness of our works, and of their evil" ("On Fairy-stories" 83).

Three. The Lord of the Rings: *"Insubstantial dream of an escapist"*

In *News from Nowhere*, William Morris expresses his belief that mass production has diminished rather than enhanced the quality of life. In one of his many indictments of the nineteenth century, Gaffer Hammond rails against this "horrible burden of unnecessary production" which drove people to consider their work and the products of it as repugnant. Hammond tells Guest, the novel's protagonist, that nineteenth-century mass production meant creating more and more objects of less and less quality. The cost of this "'cheapening of production,'" Guest says, is no less than "everything": "the happiness of the workman at his work, nay his most elementary comfort and bare health, his food, his clothes, his dwelling, his leisure, his amusement, his education—his life, in short—did not weigh a grain of sand in the balance against this dire necessity of 'cheap production' of things, a great part of which were not worth producing at all" (Morris, *News from Nowhere* 84). For Morris, escape from this terrible reality meant not only envisioning a better reality in the subcreated worlds of romance, but having a formative impact on the real world by creating workplaces where craftsmen and craftswomen could flourish. For Tolkien, the "desire to escape" is quite sensible. Any reasonable person would naturally attempt to escape from dire conditions. Such "grim and terrible" circumstances Tolkien lists as "hunger, thirst, poverty, pain, sorrow, injustice, death" ("On Fairy-stories" 83). The reader of fairy-stories, he asserts, can enter the world of "faerie," which is the world of romance where the natural and supernatural worlds intersect, thereby giving the writer (and thus the reader) greater scope to explore the fundamental truths of human existence.

Through the use of "fairy-stories," or romance, Tolkien hoped to bring the light of Christian truth into a world that seemed to have grown very dark indeed. As noted, Tolkien's letters show how ubiquitous in his thinking was his Christian faith, to which he returns again and again in letters ranging in subject from everyday personal, professional, and political events to explanations of his literary works. Tolkien's Catholicism was the lens through which he filtered his experience, and one need not be a theologian to understand the conceptual underpinnings of his work: Tolkien himself provided us with ample and lucid explanations. One might say that his overall assessment was that he was living in a time of the greatest mechanization in human history, and it had, in combination with the frailty of fallen humanity which left individuals highly susceptible to all manner of temptation, produced evils on an enormous and unprecedented scale. Fairy-story, Tolkien argues, can help us to regain a clear perspective on the truth that has been obscured. In "On Fairy-stories," he writes, "Recovery (which includes return and renewal of health) is a re-gaining—regaining of a clear view"; what we have a view of is no less than "the underlying reality or truth" ("On Fairy-stories 77, 88) within and beyond the universe. For Tolkien, that truth is the story of Christ.

In a 1944 letter to his son Christopher, Tolkien describes the essay and explains that at their best fairy stories achieve a moment of "eucatastrophe: the sudden happy turn in a story which pierces you with a joy that brings tears" (*Letters* 100). He goes on to explain that eucatastrophe allows the reader to perceive absolute Truth, which for him is the story of the life, death, and resurrection of Christ. Tolkien believed that the New Testament is the greatest fairy story ever told, and that it is true because its author is God, the Creator of all (*Letters* 100–01). For Tolkien, fairy stories at their best do what the Gospels do: they reveal truth. Eucatastrophe allows us a moment of clarity, a brief glimpse of the eternal. Such stories are not "mere escapism," and thus *The Lord of the Rings*, itself a fairy-story as well as heroic legend, is not mere escapism. What we escape *from* is the darkness and confusion of a fallen world; what we escape *to* is the clarity of God's truth.

Importantly, the creation of the world of "faerie," an imaginary world complete in and of itself, does not equate with the modernist impulse to use literature as a means of constructing unity and meaning in the actual, or Primary, world. Modernist writers perceive of the world as being marked significantly by fragmentation and alienation. For them, the world *is* a wasteland; Tolkien's sub-created world, in contrast, by no means displays these negative qualities as being the essence of the world; rather, they are a part of it, as are the grim realities of "pain, sorrow, injustice, and death." In a fallen world, evil and corruption will always exist; however, they exist alongside the beauty of the world and the joy, love, and fellowship that are to be found within it. For Tolkien, the world itself is part of God's Creation and is therefore *not* a wasteland. Thus whereas the modernists attempt to transform fragmented and chaotic experience into fictional wholes, Tolkien aims to create a Secondary

THREE. The Lord of the Rings: *"Insubstantial dream of an escapist"*

world in order to *illuminate* the Primary world, which to his mind is already unified and coherent, though profoundly flawed. Though we may not perceive it as such, we must have faith that all events and circumstances are subject to God's will.

In a 1954 letter draft, Tolkien parenthetically explains that the Primary world seems incoherent to our human perception; nevertheless, the actual world, like the eternal world, is "ultimately under the will of God" (*Letters* 191). Therefore, although in the temporal world corruptions and inconsistencies exist, and though we may not understand why, we must accept that God allows them to exist, and thus there is some reason and purpose for their presence in the world. In reference to Sauron specifically, Tolkien explains that evil, the existence of which God allows, must come into any story that strives to convey truth about the real world. "The indestructibility of *spirits* with free wills," he writes, must be a guiding principle in any story (*Letters* 280), whether real or imagined. Although they are corrupt and evil, Saruman and Sauron each possess a spirit that cannot be destroyed. Therefore, in accordance with the laws of Middle-earth, despite the victory of the West, consummate evil can and will return.

In contrast to the modernists, who very purposefully sought to create something new in art, literature, and music, Tolkien turned to ancient stories. He hoped to achieve through literature, specifically fairy-story, what he called "Recovery," a way of seeing the world that recaptures for us fundamental truths about the temporal and eternal worlds. He meant to restore our view of reality, as he believed that we have lost or failed to recognize truth, either because of our familiarity with the everyday world or because of the limitations of our own perspective. "Escapism" does this, he argues, by "transforming experience" (Tolkien, *Letters* 85). For Tolkien, we have become blind to the meaning of everyday life, and this, too, points to the value of fairy-story: the storyteller as subcreator of a Secondary world complete in itself can help us to move beyond our limited way of seeing. Tolkien argues that fantasy takes its materials from the Primary World, since only God can create *ex nihilo*, from nothing.

For Tolkien's sub-creator, success is achieved through the internal consistency of the story, which gives the reader a sense of reality, of being inside of the Secondary World rather than simply looking in on it as if through a window of the Primary World. Tolkien's assertions about the Primary and Secondary worlds as well as those regarding creation (accomplished by God) and subcreation (sometimes effectively accomplished by human beings) point to a crucial difference between himself and his modernist contemporaries. Tolkien's subcreated world reflects the meaning and design that in fact inhere in the world. The literature of the modernists, on the other hand, reflects the meaninglessness and randomness which characterize the world as they perceive it. For them there is a fractured story that can be retrieved; for Tolkien the story is not fractured but continuous.

What Tolkien does construct is the imagined history of Middle-earth, but the spiritual and moral truths of that Secondary world exist for Tolkien in a way they no longer do for the modernists. In his letters, Tolkien repeatedly asserts that the world of *The Lord of the Rings* (the world of his legendarium) is our world in a distant and imagined past. He states this most briefly in an apparently private commentary composed in 1956 in response to a review of *The Return of the King* written by W.H. Auden. Tolkien explains that Middle-earth is in fact our real world, but the historical events of the story are imagined (*Letters* 244). This is similar to the poem *Beowulf*, which has for its setting the real world, and which includes fragments of actual history but is primarily a wonder tale of an ancient warrior with superhuman ability who for the good of the community pits himself against virtually unconquerable monsters. Earlier in that commentary, Tolkien explains that Middle-earth is the world that God created in contrast to "imaginary worlds (as Fairyland) or unseen worlds (as Heaven or Hell)" (*Letters* 239). It is significant that Tolkien implicitly asserts that Heaven and Hell are real, as he characterizes them as "unseen," not unreal, and differentiates them from "Fairy-land," an "imaginary" world. Heaven and Hell are for him aspects of the Primary world, whereas fairy-land is derivative and exists only in the carefully crafted Secondary world of art.

Most avid readers of Tolkien's work are likely aware of his admission that he hoped to create a mythology for England, as it lacked one comparable to, for example, the Greek myths or the *Kalevala* and the *Eddas*, products of the northern imagination that he so admired. He felt that even the legends of King Arthur and the knights of Camelot could not serve the purpose, since they were not genuinely linguistically English

THREE. The Lord of the Rings: *"Insubstantial dream of an escapist"*

(Tolkien, *Letters* 144). Over forty years earlier, E.M. Forster had expressed a similar view in *Howards End*, as the main character, Margaret Schlegel, ruminates: "Why has not England a great mythology? Our folklore has never advanced beyond daintiness, and the greater melodies about our country-side have all issued through the pipes of Greece. Deep and true as the native imagination can be, it seems to have failed here" (Forster 243). Margaret's words are in keeping with Van Wyck Brooks' call for a "usable past" that would help to restore a sense of continuity with the past as well as revive feelings of brotherhood and solidarity that would help sustain individuals in the face of the terrible losses of World War I. Tolkien's persistent assertions that Middle-earth is our earth are therefore consonant with his desire to provide England with tales of its own heroic and noble, if oftentimes tragic, origins. Yet it seems quite possible that his purpose was more profound than filling in the literary gap that was created by the invasions and occupations of early England.

Tolkien often referred to his legendarium as his "private hobby," but in the process of writing it he had a point to make, and his tales, from his earliest poems to *The Lord of the Rings*, allowed him to make that point. Although in his letters Tolkien once wrote that he had "no didactic purpose" (*Letters* 297) in writing the story, he more often wrote of his intent to demonstrate right thinking and behavior in an age when these things seemed to him to have fallen by the wayside. In keeping with his belief that we often act as "God's instruments," he writes of *The Lord of the Rings* that "parts seem (to me) rather revealed through me than by me" and he believed that the tale is "didactic" (Tolkien, *Letters* 189). Middle-earth's being our earth connects us to an historical age, albeit an imaginary age, in which individuals like ourselves struggle with the same essential questions regarding good and evil, suffering and death, sin and redemption, and so forth. Tolkien wants his reader to be at home in Middle-earth and to recognize ourselves in his characters because they often demonstrate the wisdom and virtues that he felt were disappearing in his time.

In the Auden commentary, Tolkien begins to clarify the temporal aspect of Middle-earth, explaining that the reader does not feel like an alien there because it is our real world, albeit somewhat "glorified by the enchantment of distance in time" (*Letters* 239). That once-upon-a-time setting would be about 6,000 years ago, according to Tolkien's reckoning, which thereby places the twentieth-century reader at about the turn of the Sixth and Seventh ages of the real Primary world (*Letters* 283). In creating an imaginary age of our world Tolkien enables the reader to better enter into his Secondary world, largely through our familiarity with it, because we can love that world, he writes, with "the love of blood kin" (*Letters* 283). In his essay, "Folklore and Fantastic Literature," C.W. Sullivan explains the importance of the familiar in fairy story: "Some part of the creative process through which the mimetic and the fantastic elements are combined—or reconciled—into a logically-cohesive Secondary World must also include a strategy or strategies by which the reader will be able to connect with, be able to understand, and be able to decode that Secondary World itself" (281). Even if we do not hail from the northwest of Europe, we still recognize Middle-earth, in part because the fundamental truths we find there are not alien to us even today. We are here on common purpose with the characters of Tolkien's Secondary world: to live in the world that God, Tolkien's *Eru Ilúvatar*, has created and to play our part in its history within His divine plan. According to Tolkien's Catholic sensibility, that history is shaped by the interaction of free will and grace, that is, by our choices as actors in the Whole Story, accepting or rejecting the grace of God, who is the "Writer of the Story."

For Tolkien, the world has an "Author"; it is in fact structured and unified, and there is meaning and purpose within and behind it. In contrast to his modernist contemporaries, Tolkien was not using literature as a way to put together broken pieces to make a whole, and he was not building a barrier against a wave of despair arising from a hundred years of intellectual abstractions set into dizzying motion by the cataclysm of war. The articulation of the twentieth-century sense of hopelessness, of dislocation, alienation, and loss, and the anguished cries of the literary elite, of those who wrote and read "serious literature," against the disintegration of community and the self were not the business of Tolkien. His purpose is rather to redirect our vision to what already exists, and in the process show us a way of being in a world that is in danger of becoming a wasteland.

In the world as wasteland, the world as the modernists perceive it, individuals *feel* alienated because they truly *believe* that the world,

THREE. The Lord of the Rings: *"Insubstantial dream of an escapist"*

including our lives within it, is subject to random forces. In other words, their subjective feelings of alienation are underscored by their objective regard of the world as empty in those terms described above. In their alienation they are cut off from one another and from themselves, and there is for them no connection to work, community, nature, or God. Without the values and guiding principles of the past, which they have rejected, they are lost. For Tolkien, in contrast, alienation arises not from the inherent barrenness of the world but from human attempts to distort the meaning and purpose of it. This is in keeping with Tolkien's Christian beliefs, according to which, as Deborah Rogers writes in her essay, "Everyclod and Everyhero," "The rightful position of man is to be the ruling creature on this planet, to administer it in the best interests of all the local creatures, and God's viceroy … man now occupies only a parody of this position: he is the ruling creature here, but he kills his own kind and other creatures and damages and exploits the planet" (72). For Tolkien, we have a moral responsibility to engage with the world, both past and present. Therefore it is essential that we recognize the presence of a transcendent order within the cosmos as well as our own place within it, understand the values that endure across time and culture, make appropriate choices based on those values, and preserve the world against those forces that would make a wasteland of it. In this way, Tolkien's admirable characters are stewards. Whether or not they are initially aware of this, they come to understand it, largely through experience and a growing knowledge about their world and its history that moves them beyond their provincialism. This is particularly true of the hobbits, who come to fully understand their connection to each other, to the past, and to the wide world that lies beyond their beloved Shire.

In *The Lord of the Rings*, there are literal wastelands. What's more, the characters that represent evil are exactly those who would turn the whole of Middle-earth into a wasteland in order to achieve their ends, their wills to power and self-actualization. Indeed, the hope of Sauron is the despair of the world, for he would systematically strip the natural world down to bare rock through the devices of industrialization and war, in the process dominating and enslaving the free peoples who dwell there. The ultimate end of this process is the dehumanization of individuals and the loss of the beauty and diversity of the world. What is so compelling is the realization that the world over which Sauron would hold lordship, the world he envisions, looks very much like the modernist wasteland: a world where individuals are so thoroughly dehumanized that their agency, their actions within and upon the world, is negated and thus meaningless. What is left, apart from the will of Sauron, is not being but nothingness.

FOUR
Modernist Disaffection and Tolkienian Faith

"*Things fall apart; the center cannot hold.*" In 1919 the Irish poet William Butler Yeats composed his poem "The Second Coming," an emphatic articulation of the modernist sense that the Great War had fractured the story that was the history of Western civilization. The postwar world of Yeats' poem is chaotic and confusing. The poem opens *in media res* as the world spins violently out of control: "Turning and turning in the widening gyre / The falcon cannot hear the falconer" (Yeats 1–2). Within the whirlwind, the stable center of Western civilization—the old hegemonic forces of politics, religion, art, science, industry, and social convention—collapses on itself. In its place is a void that can neither sustain humanity nor point the way out of the confusion. The apocalyptic scene prompts the speaker to cry out, "Surely some revelation is at hand; / Surely the Second Coming is at hand" (Yeats 9–10). The poet, however, subverts the reader's expectations, for it is not Christ who appears, "come again in glory to judge the living and the dead," as expressed in Christianity's Nicene Creed (*The Holy See*). What appears instead is a grotesque mockery arisen from humanity itself, "*Spiritus Mundi*," soul of the material world (Yeats 12). This sphinx-like deity is no redeemer come to fulfill the promise of the Incarnation; rather, it looks upon humankind not with mercy or charity but with "a gaze blank and pitiless as the sun" (Yeats 15), shrouded in shadow, bringing not hope but despair. The advent of Christ was announced by the Holy Spirit, who came in the form of a dove. In Yeats' inversion of the Second Coming, the arrival of the sphinx-like monster is heralded by "indignant desert birds" (Yeats 17). At this point, the vision ends suddenly as "darkness drops again" (Yeats 18), and the speaker is left to reflect on what he has seen. In the Revelation of Yeats' "The Second Coming" human history has been a "rocking cradle" (20) that represents the tragedy of humanity in a fallen world, corrupt beyond salvation. In the world that Yeats imagines, two thousand years of civilization have brought not the kingdom of heaven on earth; instead, they've been a demonic and "nightmare" gestation that has begotten a "rough beast," no friend to humankind (20–21). Christian faith promises the return of Christ in glory. Tolkien had faith in this promise. Yeats' imagined future stands in striking contrast to Tolkien's, for the Second Coming of Yeats' poem is horrifying, bringing the monsters of Revelation but not the Redeemer of humanity.

First published in *The Dial*, Yeats' "The Second Coming" arrives on the literary scene in 1920 as the Western world begins in earnest to reflect on the horrors of World War I. As Daniel Hipp, author of *The Poetry of Shell Shock*, writes, "The war was the first wholly Modern military conflict, the first time Europe would be forced to reckon with such a slaughter of its populace effected by the technologies of 'total war' which were the by-products of the Victorian Age's forces of industrialization and its faith in progress" (191). The mass production of artillery helped to bring about the destruction of lives and landscapes on an unprecedented scale, and the use of chemical weapons brought new and even more horrifying images of death than any young soldier could have imagined before the summer of 1914. As the work of Wilfred Owen and other poets and novelists of the period demonstrates, these vivid memories haunted the dreams of many veterans.

In his biography of Tolkien, Humphrey Carpenter describes the nightmare images of the French battlefield, images that would stay with Tolkien throughout his life. The most horrifying of these were the remains of dead soldiers. Carpenter writes that "corpses lay in every corner, horribly torn by the shells. Those that still had faces stared with dreadful eyes. Beyond the trenches no-man's-land was littered with bloated and decaying bodies. All around was desolation. Grass and corn had vanished into a sea of mud. Trees, stripped of leaf and branch, stood as mere mutilated and blackened trunks" (*J.R.R. Tolkien: A Biography* 91). The carnage of the Somme had much to do with the advent of the machinegun and the use of poisonous gas, which could kill mass numbers of men simultaneously. These weapons, combined with the barren

Four. Modernist Disaffection and the Tolkienian Faith

landscape above and around the trenches, made the recovery of fallen soldiers extremely difficult. Consequently, their bodies lay heaped in and along the trenches or hung ensnared on barbed wire fences, caught there indefinitely, as their fellow soldiers could not safely retrieve them. Unrelenting barrages of artillery riddled the ground with craters oftentimes large enough to become mass graves into which rain would pool, thereby hastening the disfigurement and decomposition of the bodies within them. As a young soldier, Tolkien was an eye-witness to the brutality of front-line existence and the degradation that followed death on the battlefield of the Somme.

Tolkien would call up this imagery as he composed *The Lord of the Rings*, but he would combine it with elements of fairy-story. His tendency was not toward mimesis, that is, toward an imitation or mirror of reality; rather, as he wrote to his son Christopher in 1944, he chose "escapism" (Tolkien, *Letters* 85). For Tolkien this meant the creative expression of the human condition—the joy and sorrow of life and the inevitability of death in the world of time—in the context of his subcreated world of Middle-earth. The events of that Secondary world, like the Primary, or real, world are set against a backdrop of the struggle between cosmic forces for evil and good. On the one hand Tolkien gives us Morgoth, a figure of evil as ancient and tragic as Milton's Lucifer, and the corrupted beings who carry on his work in Middle-earth, Sauron and his legions of orcs and men. On the other hand, Tolkien gives us the Elves, his conception of humanity allowed to achieve its greatest potential for aesthetic beauty. Both writer and reader "escape" into the world of Middle-earth, but not in order to hide from it. In fact, the purpose is quite the opposite: Tolkien means for us to face the reality of life by encountering it afresh in the world of faery, where ordinary people find themselves rising to the most extraordinary challenges. Thus for Tolkien "escapism" entails a transformation of experience that allows us to better regard ourselves and our world by providing a measure of distance from it.

Part of the experience that Tolkien transformed was World War I. In a letter dated December 31, 1960, he explains that *The Lord of the Rings* was influenced more by the romances of William Morris than by either of the World Wars; nevertheless, he writes, "The Dead Marshes and the approaches to the Morannon owe something to Northern France after the Battle of the Somme" (Tolkien, *Letters* 303). Just as modern warfare turned the French countryside into a wasteland, the great Battle of the Dagorlad, in which the Last Alliance of Elves and Men fought against the Dark Lord Sauron, laid waste to the lands west of Mordor. Indeed, so scarred is that land that it can never again become verdant. Frodo and Sam find their passage across the marshes dispiriting. In this place there is nothing green except for "the scum of livid weed on the dark greasy surfaces of the sullen waters" (Tolkien, *The Two Towers* 632). What the hobbits see in the water of the Dead Marshes is hauntingly similar to the dead faces that must have looked up at the young Tolkien from the water-filled craters of no-man's-land. When Sam cries out in horror upon realizing that the water is full of dead bodies, Frodo's response is eerily calm as he describes what he saw in the water: "grim faces and evil, and noble faces and sad. Many faces proud and fair, and weeds in their silver hair. But all foul, all rotting, all dead" (Tolkien, *The Two Towers* 634). Like the Battle of the Somme, the battle before the Black Gates left thousands dead. In their mass graves, real or fictional, all soldiers are equal. In Tolkien's fantastical world, however, their images are more than memory, lingering in more than fireside tales. Even Gollum, once a hobbit-like child, has heard the tales. He tells Frodo and Sam of an epic battle from the deeps of time: "'Tall Men with long swords, and terrible Elves, and Orcses shrieking. They fought on the plain for days and months at the Black Gates" (Tolkien, *The Two Towers* 634). Like the thousands of soldiers in Flanders, Tolkien's soldiers "fought on the plain for days and months." In death, both the real and the fictional bodies remain dispossessed, homeless. Just as soldier-poets like Wilfred Owen would describe their vivid memories of death on the battlefield, Tolkien conveys, and even makes literal, those haunting images. In the world of Middle-earth, as in our world, evil is subdued at enormous cost, only to rise again to precipitate another global struggle.

    The cost of that struggle, the loss of so many young lives for a cause that in retrospect made many people wonder what they had fought for, brought with it a marked sense that somehow the foundation of the world had cracked. With that fracture came the rejection of the traditional notions of patriotism and heroism that had driven enlistment during the early days of the war. At the war's outset, a common belief among the British was the responsibility of all healthy young Englishmen

Four. Modernist Disaffection and the Tolkienian Faith

to enlist, and this imperative was closely tied to romantic notions of patriotic duty and the glory of battle. These notions were promulgated, as Paul Norgate explains in his essay, "Wilfred Owen and the Soldier Poets," in the propagandist poetry that was popular from 1914 to 1918. The work of the "Soldier Poets," he explains, was widely anthologized and served many purposes, including fundraising for the war effort, recruiting soldiers, memorializing the fallen, and boosting morale. Rarely, however, did it question "the essential 'rightness' of the war" (Norgate 516–17). Relentlessly confronted by the gruesome realities of war, the Soldier-poets consistently incorporated into their poems what Norgate refers to as "key 'motifs'—Courage, England, Home, God, Victory, Mother, etc." (518). Clearly, these poets, speaking with the authority of those who fought in the trenches, promoted notions of duty to one's country and one's home: they were fighting *pro patria* and *pro domo*. For example, the poem, "Without Shedding of Blood," by soldier poet Lt. G. Howard, expresses the popular rationale that preserving the beauty of England and the simple goodness of home was worth even the most terrible cost. Howard writes:

> Not till thousands have been slain
> Shall the green wood be green again,
> Not till men shall fall and bleed
> Can brown ale taste like ale indeed [quoted in Norgate 518].

Just as in the verses of his fellow Soldier-poets, Howard's poem implicitly urges England's young men to take up arms against the enemies of liberty, for no man of good conscience could enjoy even the simplest pleasures in life until all had done their part to defend them.

In the earliest days of the war, as David Roberts points out in his book *Out in the Dark: Poetry of the First World War*, public support for the war was very strong, and the number of men wanting to enlist was so great that "recruiting offices couldn't cope with the rush" (23). Britain's Prime Minister, Henry Asquith, called upon citizens to make the greatest sacrifice possible in the name of freedom. Asquith told the English people that never before had "any nation ever entered into a great conflict—and this is one of the greatest that history will ever know—with a clearer conscience or stronger conviction that it is fighting not for aggression, not for the maintenance of its own selfish ends, but in defence of principles, the maintenance of which is vital to the civilization of the world" (quoted in Roberts 23). In such an atmosphere of intense nationalism, it was not an easy decision for Tolkien to put off enlistment until he had finished the last year of his undergraduate studies (he was twenty-three at the time of his commission in the Lancashire Fusiliers). In a letter to his son Michael, himself an anti-aircraft gunner in World War Two, dated 6–8 March 1941, Tolkien recounts this period of his life, recalling how difficult it was to remain in school rather than enlist as most young men did. In fact, those healthy young men who remained in England were derided, sometimes even by their own families. Nevertheless, he wanted to finish his education before he was carried off by war. Once he had done that, he quickly joined up in July of 1915, married Edith Bratt in March of 1916, and in May of that year left England "for the carnage of the Somme" (Tolkien, *Letters* 53).

Tolkien was one of few exceptions among the mass of young men who enlisted before they had obtained their degrees. The dearth of undergraduates at Oxford during the war, its quiet lecture halls eerily juxtaposed against the military's bustling occupation of much of its buildings and grounds, gave poignant testimony to Secretary of State for War Horatio Kitchener's compelling call to service. In his book *Tolkien and the Great War*, John Garth describes the situation at Oxford in 1915. "The university" Garth writes, "was transformed into a citadel of refugees and war-readiness. The time-honored flow of undergraduates had hemorrhaged: a committee to process student recruits had dealt with 2,000 by September. Only seventy-five remained at Exeter College, and in the evenings unlit windows loomed over the silent quad" (48). In his autobiography, *Surprised by Joy*, Tolkien's friend C.S. Lewis wrote of wartime Oxford: "Half the College had been converted into a hospital and was in the hands of the R.A.M.C. In the remaining portion lived a tiny community of undergraduates" (187). Like so many other undergraduates, Lewis, an Irishman, had interrupted his studies to take part in the war. He writes, "I arrived in the front line trenches on my nineteenth birthday (November 1917)" and "returned to Oxford—'demobbed'—in January 1919" (Lewis, *Surprised by Joy* 188; 198). Lewis might be speaking for Tolkien as well when he explains that he "had the good luck to fall sick with what the troops called 'trench fever' and the doctors P.U.O (Pyrexia, unknown origin)" (*Surprised By Joy* 189). Tolkien and Lewis were among the lucky ones who lived to return to England.

Four. Modernist Disaffection and the Tolkienian Faith

Rather than face the "obloquy," as Tolkien called it (*Letters* 53), the hints that they were not doing their part for the war effort, virtually an entire generation of England's sons laid down their plows, abandoned the mines where their fathers and grandfathers had labored, turned away from their documents and ledgers, or set aside their volumes of Nietzsche, Darwin, Marx, and Freud. These young men left their homes to meet their deaths on the front lines of a muddy French battlefield. For the soldiers of World War I, idealistic patriotism and faith in the old traditions would also die on the battlefields of Europe.

Many of these men were, as Mrs. Bolton, the working-class nurse of D.H. Lawrence's *Lady Chatterley's Lover*, says, "some of the first lads as went off so blithe to the war and got killed right away" (172). Perhaps they enlisted blithely, to borrow Mrs. Bolton's word, because their knowledge of war did not prepare them for modern warfare. Once confronted with that reality, scores of soldiers sought to comprehend and articulate their experiences within the traditional form of lyric poetry. The work of these soldier-poets was disseminated regularly in the popular press and became a powerful form of pro-war propaganda. For example, "A Soldier's Cemetery," by Sgt. J.W. Streets, romanticizes the death of young soldiers by keeping death itself at the margins of the speaker's lament:

> Behind that long and lonely trenched line
> To which men come and go, where brave men die,
> There is a yet unmarked and unknown shrine,
> A broken plot, a soldier's cemetery.
> There lie the flower of youth, the men who scorned
> To live (so died) when languished Liberty;
> Across their graves flowerless and unadorned
> Still scream the shells of each artillery [quoted in Norgate 522].

These lines speak of death on the battlefield, but they do not paint a realistic picture of it. The speaker refers to the front line of battle as if it were as ordinary as a train station. There is a strange orderliness in the image of the men as they "come and go," as if one after another in turn, to bravely die. The melancholic tone of the poem helps to gloss over the horror of the battlefield and the brutality of death. In dying for a cause, "liberty," the soldiers have earned a kind of peacefulness that is not accessible to those who refuse to enter into the fight. Their graves become a "shrine," a testament to their honor and an example for others to quickly follow. The young soldiers to which Lawrence's Mrs. Bolton and the speaker of Streets' poem refer embraced what Wilfred Owen would come to call "the old lie."

If Yeats' "Second Coming" announced the death of Christian hope, Wilfred Owen's "Dulce et Decorum Est" announced the demise of blind devotion to political leaders and drove home that sense of disillusionment that so many war writers would express. Owen, who would lose his life in the "war to end all wars," vividly countered the romantic image of the soldier's final defeat by unforgivingly depicting the gruesome reality of death in battle. The poem takes aim at the romantic notion that it was "sweet and seemly to die for one's country." "Dulce et Decorum Est" provides a snapshot of the horrors of modern warfare, specifically the novel use of poisonous gas. The poem opens with the image of exhausted soldiers wearily moving toward safer ground and rest, the horrors of the battle receding behind them. The soldiers are sickened nearly to the point of unconsciousness, "deaf even to hoots / Of tired, outstripped Five-Nines that dropped behind" (Owen 7–8). In a moment of what should be respite as the young soldiers turn away from the battle, they find not the expected relief but fresh terror. When a gas shell explodes nearby, the soldiers must quickly put on their gas masks. One soldier, so battle-fatigued that he cannot get his mask on in time, blindly struggles in vain to do so. The poem's speaker, a fellow soldier, describes in graphic details the doomed soldier's death agony as he chokes on his own bodily fluids. Here the poem shifts from the past tense to the present, giving a sense of immediacy to the scene in which the men rush to put on their gas masks. The doomed soldier—like the others ostensibly "blind" and "drunk with fatigue," perhaps even more so—fails to get his gear on quickly enough (Owen 6,7). We hear him "yelling out" and see him struggling 'like a man in fire or lime" (Owen 12). The stanza then shifts to the speaker's individual perspective as he watches, horrified, through both his own mask and the palpable green of the gas: "As under a green sea, I saw him drowning" (Owen 14). This image will return to the speaker in vivid nightmares of the desperate soldier "guttering, choking, drowning" (Owen 16).

The speaker uses the conditional tense in the last stanza in order for the reader to stand in his stead, even if only in "smothering dreams" (Owen 17). Clearly, these are the speaker's own recurring dreams of the haunting images of the afflicted soldier, "flung" onto the wagon in a manner less befitting a human being and more fit for the "sacks" mentioned in the opening line of the poem (Owen 18, 1). Again, Owen dramatizes the moment in order to force the reader to see the soldier's "white eyes writhing," his "hanging face, like a devil's sick of sin" (Owen 19, 20). The reader is made to hear the sound of the soldier's blood as it comes "gargling from the froth-corrupted lungs" (Owen 22). Owen challenges traditional notions of patriotism, asserting that if his elders had to endure the hellish sight and subsequent memories of the soldier's death, they

> would not tell with such high zest
> To children ardent for some desperate glory,
> The old Lie: Dulce et decorum est
> Pro patria mori [Owen 25–28].

The "children" to whom this lie is told will become the soldiers of Owen's poem, soldiers he likens to "innocents," young men who have barely come of age. They have been subjected to a kind of indoctrination, the end result of which is the virtual annihilation of a generation of Englishmen in the flower of their youth. The "old lie," for Owen, is the romantic notion of patriotism and military glory. This sentiment is expressed by Major Sydney Oswald, one of the soldier-poets, in his poem, "Dulce et Decorum Est pro Patria Mori." Oswald writes, "Glory is theirs; the People's narrative / Of fame will tell their deeds of gallantry" (quoted in Norgate 521). For Wilfred Owen, the young men leave home not to become glorious heroes, forever remembered in song and story, but to become anonymous cannon fodder, their graves in foreign lands, their brief lives sunk into obscurity.

Tolkien himself referred to "trenchlife" as "animal horror" (*Letters* 72). In a letter to his third son, Christopher, who was stationed in Africa with the RAF during 1944, he writes of how overwhelming is the "utter stupid waste of war, not only material but moral and spiritual" (Tolkien, *Letters* 75). And he believed this was true in spite of "the poets" who romanticized war and "the propagandists" whose job it was to convince a generation to suffer immeasurable pain and loss willingly. Nevertheless, he felt that it always had been and would be "necessary to face it in an evil world" (Tolkien, *Letters* 75). Tolkien's remark echoes the invectives of Owen and his contemporaries, such as Siegfried Sassoon, against nineteenth-century romantic notions of war (promulgated in part by "the poets") and the overzealousness of statesmen ("the propagandists"). Like his contemporaries, Tolkien was well aware of the terrifying brutality of war. However, he maintained a belief that war must be waged, that we cannot avoid it if we hope to preserve the goodness of the world when it is threatened by all-consuming evil. Thus Faramir tells Frodo that while it is sometimes necessary to engage in war, he finds neither joy nor glory in it. Rather, he says, "'I love only that which they [the sword, arrow and warrior] defend'" (Tolkien, *The Two Towers* 678). Faramir is the character whom Tolkien said was most like himself (Tolkien, *Letters* 232), and he expresses here the author's attitude toward war: it is at times the only alternative for otherwise peace-loving men.

In discussing the nature of Tom Bombadil, Tolkien explains that *The Lord of the Rings* is concerned in part with the use and abuse of power on the sides of good as well as evil. Both sides, Tolkien writes, seek "a measure of control" (*Letters* 178). However, Tom Bombadil cares nothing for power (Tolkien, *Letters* 178). In this regard, according to Tolkien, Bombadil represents "a natural pacifist view" (*Letters* 179). However, without the willingness of the West to enter into war, Bombadil could not endure. Tolkien once described Tom Bombadil as "the spirit of the (vanishing) Oxford and Berkshire countryside" (*Letters* 26), the pastoral world of the author's youth. As such, Tom represents the very thing worth fighting for: one's home and the peace and beauty to be found there. More than this, though, Tom, who wants only knowledge of what is "other" than himself, is in some ways the antithesis of Sauron, who wants total control of all beings apart from himself. The people of Middle-earth want to maintain their freedom; therefore, they, too, want a degree of control. They understand that the only way to do so is to engage in war. The Council of Elrond recognizes that Bombadil's neutrality, his pacifism, will not save Middle-earth: his utter disregard for the "machinery" of domination, represented most completely by the Ring, would be his undoing. Paradoxically, it is only through war that the pacifist can survive the aggression of an enemy such as Sauron, whose goal is world domination. In Bombadil's case, only the victory of the West will ensure the safety of his Edenic world. Should he win, Sauron would turn all of Middle-earth into a wasteland. There would be no "others"—no willows, birds, plants, or running streams—to know.

Four. Modernist Disaffection and the Tolkienian Faith

In the world that Sauron would make, Tom Bombadil himself would be a slave or would simply be no more.

Clearly, Tolkien valued a peaceful, pastoral hobbit-like life; he valued life itself as well, even that of the soldiers on the "wrong" side. He believed that all men, as creations of God, have, or at least at some point had, goodness in them and are thus deserving of compassion. When Sam and Frodo are caught on the margins of a battle between Gondorian and Southron soldiers, this human sympathy is expressed in Sam's reflections upon seeing a fallen Southron soldier. The hobbit contemplates the man's identity, and he tries to imagine his circumstances and whether or not "he was really evil of heart, or what lies or threats had led him on the long march from his home; and if he would not really rather have stayed there in peace..." (Tolkien, *The Two Towers* 667). This sentiment is in some ways not so very far from that expressed by Wilfred Owen, who lamented the waste of humanity demanded by war. However, Sam's reflections do not convey the tone of anger and disaffection in the voice of the speaker of "Dulce et Decorum Est." Rather, Sam's tone is one of sadness and empathy, for he, too, has left his peaceful garden and the contentment of his home to play his part in a war not of his making but one that is necessary to defend the idyllic world of the Shire. This seems a marked difference between Tolkien and his contemporaries: where their work displays bitterness, disaffection, and even anger, *The Lord of the Rings* emphasizes pity, compassion, forgiveness, and what Clyde Manschrek calls "the old values of love, kindness, and humility" (87).

In his novel *Lady Chatterley's Lover*, first published in Italy in 1928, Lawrence takes up many modernist preoccupations, including the wastage of war, the disaffection and disillusionment of the returning soldiers, the ravages of industrialism to both the natural world and to the human community, the class distinctions that stand in the way of true human sympathy and kindness toward others ostensibly unlike ourselves, and the sense that the old world is slipping away and soon will be irretrievably lost. Perhaps most significantly, the novel underscores the sense that, in the aftermath of World War I, the world is empty, its people broken and dehumanized. Through the character of Clifford Chatterley, Lawrence portrays the split between the old beliefs and postwar disillusionment. Sir Clifford's experience of modern war turns out to be drastically different from the romantic images of the poetry of the past. He returned from Flanders, twenty-nine years old and paralyzed from the waist down, unfixable in body and spirit.

Connie Chatterley thinks, "The cataclysm has happened, we are among the ruins" (Lawrence, *Lady Chatterley's Lover* 3). Indeed, Lawrence's characters, particularly Clifford Chatterley, are themselves part of the ruins. Connie married Clifford late in 1917, and she was there to care for him when he was "shipped over to England again six months later, more or less in bits" (Lawrence, *Lady Chatterley's Lover* 3).

Connie Chatterley's words echo those of Owen when he writes of the dying soldier "flung" onto the wagon: in both cases the men are described more like objects than as human beings, just one more reminder of the dehumanization of once vital people. Like the world itself, Clifford, a former Cambridge student, emerges from the war in fragments, "shipped home smashed" (Lawrence, *Lady Chatterley's Lover* 11), physically, of course, but emotionally as well. The physical life he had known is essentially over, and his interior life is damaged beyond repair. Lawrence writes: "He had so very nearly lost his life, that what remained was wonderfully precious to him. It was obvious in the anxious brightness of his eyes, how proud he was, after the great shock, of being alive. But he had been so much hurt that something inside him had perished, some of his feelings had gone. There was a blank of insentience" (Lawrence, *Lady Chatterley's Lover* 4). To the casual observer, the impeccably dressed Clifford seems robust despite "the burden of his dead legs" (Lawrence, *Lady Chatterley's Lover* 51). But there is a more profound deadness inside him, a disaffection with the world and an insensibility to the humanity of others. This deadness, Lawrence writes, is a "blank of insentience," a void of *non*-feeling. Such an inability to feel the emotions that bind individuals to one another, and therefore nurture the human community, is a consequence of the extraordinary nature of modern warfare. In discussing Wilfred Owen's poem, "Insensibility," Daniel Hipp writes:

> The opposite of misery in the trenches is not conventional happiness but rather this state of insensibility where the soldier remains alive by casting away the emotional faculties, such as compassion, self-consciousness, imagination, fear, or sensitivity, which would make him aware of his own and others' suffering.... [this insensibility is] a protective measure which

Four. Modernist Disaffection and the Tolkienian Faith

characterizes the shell shocked soldier's shutting down of his senses by which the war experience could be understood [82].

Insofar as it privileges the instrumentality of individuals over any number of traditional values, such as kindness and compassion, war, like industrialism, strips individuals of their humanity and alienates them from one another, thereby depriving them of the fellowship that can help them to endure the most painful realities of human existence.

If Clifford Chatterley does feel anything it is a good deal of bitter disillusionment, and this alienates him from his fellow human beings. Community is precisely that from which Clifford shrinks. Brought up in a tradition of rigid class distinction, he is "a little bit frightened of middle and lower class humanity, and of foreigners not of his own class" (Lawrence, *Lady Chatterley's Lover* 9). However, at the same time, his utter disaffection with the ruling class also serves to isolate him. Clifford classifies as ridiculous all types of authority, from his own father to the government itself, "our own wait-and-see sort especially so." Clifford is convinced that "armies were ridiculous, and old buffers of generals altogether, the red-faced Kitchener supremely. Even the war was ridiculous, though it did kill rather a lot of people" (Lawrence, *Lady Chatterley's Lover* 9). Indeed, the Great War killed a vast number of people, on both sides. What is more, it decimated the Western world along with its Victorian self-assuredness and faith in an ever brighter future. Clifford's offhand thought, then, is so completely understated that it could only occur to a person so inured by war, so deadened inside by the horror of combat, that his best recourse seems to be to reject his own anguish over his losses. For Lawrence, human sympathy has also become a casualty of war.

Virginia Woolf dramatizes this phenomenon that Owen called "insensibility" through the character Septimus Smith in her 1925 novel, *Mrs. Dalloway*. The narrative encompasses one day in the life of Clarissa Dalloway, a socialite who is organizing a dinner party for that evening. Most of the novel explores the interiority of its main characters, Clarissa Dalloway and Septimus Smith, a young married man who has been profoundly psychologically damaged by his war experiences in France. Although the two characters never meet, their lives are connected, most notably when the death of Septimus is mentioned during Clarissa's dinner party. She is alarmed less by the death itself than by its ability to impinge on the perfectly ordered reality she has constructed amidst the chaos of the post-war world.

The anguish that leads Septimus to commit suicide results largely from his inability to reconcile his own insensibility, necessary to cope with the trauma of modern warfare, with his feelings of guilt over the death of his friend, Evans, who was killed in the war. Woolf writes:

> Septimus was one of the first to volunteer. He went to France to save an England which consisted almost entirely of Shakespeare's plays and Miss Isabel Pole in a green dress walking in a square. There in the trenches [...] he developed manliness; he was promoted; he drew the attention, indeed the affection of his officer, Evans by name ... when Evans was killed, just before the Armistice, in Italy, Septimus, far from showing any emotion or recognising that here was the end of a friendship, congratulated himself upon feeling very little and very reasonably. [...] he became engaged one evening when the panic was on him—that he could not feel [Woolf, *Mrs. Dalloway* 130–31].

Septimus began like the thousands of young men who were eager to enlist and fight to protect English culture and community, represented here by Shakespeare and small towns where young women like Isabel Pole live in safety. His war experiences, however, teach Septimus to abandon the emotions that would bind him to others. Like Clifford Chatterley, at the core of his being is "a blank of insentience." The alienation that Septimus feels indicates that the war had damaged humanity not only physically, but spiritually as well. In his book, *Literary Converts*, Joseph Pearce describes this profound and lasting impact of the war. "Not only did the war act as executioner of a whole generation" Pearce writes, "in the course of its four-year duration it often annihilated the spirit even when it failed to annihilate the body. It was the slaughter both of the innocents and of innocence itself" (*Literary Converts* 102). Many of those men who fought on the front lines of the war became wraith-like, their humanity somehow diminished by their inability to feel pain or disgust. Such insensibility was for many the only way to stave off the madness or psyche-crushing pain that resulted from modern warfare.

After the war, when Septimus sees a group of shell shocked men in London, he wonders if he, too, will go mad. He interprets the whole

Four. Modernist Disaffection and the Tolkienian Faith

episode as an act of mockery, as though the crippled "lunatics" are "displayed for the diversion of the populace (who laughed aloud)" (Woolf, *Mrs. Dalloway* 136). Septimus imagines that in the post-war world, civilians lack understanding and compassion for those who suffered on the front lines of battle. Permanently damaged by the process whereby he became an instrument for war, Septimus can no longer perceive of other people as anything but antagonistic. He is convinced that "human beings have neither kindness, nor faith, nor charity beyond what serves to increase the pleasure of the moment. They hunt in packs. Their packs scour the desert and vanish screaming into the wilderness. They desert the fallen" (Woolf, *Mrs. Dalloway* 136). Far from finding solace in connections with others, Septimus fears it. He imagines humanity as overwhelmingly animalistic and deliberately cruel. This is the hopeless conclusion at which Septimus Smith has arrived, and it leaves him unable to participate in the human community.

After the horrific experiences of the battlefield, Septimus can connect imaginatively only with the haunting memory of his dead friend Evans, killed in action during the war. In fact, so alienated is Septimus that he can no longer feel compassion towards his own wife, Rezia, another member of those whom Gertrude Stein famously referred to as the "Lost Generation." Saddened by the knowledge that she will never have children, for the first time in her married life Rezia cries. Septimus, however, is insensible: "Far away he heard her sobbing; he heard it accurately, he noticed it distinctly; he compared it to a piston thumping. But he felt nothing" (Woolf, *Mrs. Dalloway* 136). In comparing her crying to a machine, Septimus dehumanizes his wife, though the narrator gives no indication that he is aware that he is doing so. This inability to care about his wife's misery dehumanizes Septimus as well. Like the husband and wife in Robert Frost's poem "Home Burial," who cannot communicate to one another their pain over the loss of their child and thus cannot overcome their grief, Septimus is unable to articulate his repressed guilt and grief over the death of his friend Evans. He is therefore unable to relate to any living human being; rather, he sees quite clearly and even speaks to his dead friend. He chants to himself, "Communication is health; communication is happiness" (Woolf, *Mrs. Dalloway* 141), which is ironic precisely because he speaks these words not to his wife, but to the dead Evans, whom he believes is waiting for him outside his London home. On some level, Septimus understands that communication is crucial to the vitality of the individual and the community, but he is no longer able, in Forster's words, to "only connect" because he is trapped within his own consciousness, in an imaginary world of his own construction in which human connection is deadly, and the dead are more real to him than the living.

* * *

Tolkien's literary response to World War I was distinctly different from that of most of his contemporaries. In both wars Tolkien experienced personal losses and anguish. Two of his closest friends were killed at the Battle of the Somme, and two of his three sons fought in the Second World War. In a June 1944 letter to his publisher, Stanley Unwin, Tolkien wrote of his second son, Michael, who was sent home shell shocked from the war (*Letters* 86). Despite the pain caused by both of the World Wars, Tolkien's work does not depict the kind of disaffection and faithlessness that can be found in the greater part of modernist literature. In particular, he did not adopt the anti–Christian stance of the modernists; rather, one sees in Tolkien's letters an abiding faith in God and a constant belief that ultimately all things are in accordance with His will. He incorporated this faith into the entire legendarium, including *The Lord of the Rings*. The world of Middle-earth is monotheistic, and the hand of God is ever present, even if not explicitly identified. In one of his most poignant letters to Christopher, one can see Tolkien, the father, helping his son to stave off the disillusionment that so many others felt. In April of 1944 he wrote of his dismay over the widespread and intense suffering of the human community at that moment in history, including misery that is not directly related to war, such as "torture, pain, death, bereavement, injustice." He goes on to say, "If anguish were visible, almost the whole of this benighted planet would be enveloped in a dense dark vapour, shrouded from the amazed vision of the heavens!" (Tolkien, *Letters* 76). Tolkien continues by explaining that the events of the temporal world reveal only part of the story that is the history of the world and the human community that inhabits it as seen from a divine perspective. In the letter Tolkien goes on to say that the belief in a providential order invests all aspects of life with a worth that may not be immediately ascertainable; however, while we cannot in our

FOUR. *Modernist Disaffection and the Tolkienian Faith*

earthly lives understand the meaning of or reasons for circumstances and events, we can be certain that ultimately good will come of evil. He maintained a belief that even in the face of evil, humanity is under the care of a loving and merciful God. Tolkien writes, that "though we need all our natural human courage and guts (the vast sum of human courage and endurance is stupendous, isn't it?) and all our religious faith to face the evil that may befall us (as it befalls others, if God wills) still we may pray and hope" (*Letters* 76). Just as in *Out of the Silent Planet* C.S. Lewis depicts our world as enveloped in darkness, silent and cut off from heaven, Tolkien describes the world as being metaphorically wrapped in darkness. In Lewis' book, such a darkness results from Earth's fallen Oyarsa, "the Bent One," an angelic being who was once the brightest of his kind, but who sought to "spoil" other worlds beside his own and thus was bound its atmosphere (*Out of the Silent Planet* 120). Humanity's fallen state, in its turn, begets profound misery. Such is the state of the modern world, for evil never rests, and it can never be wholly overcome in the temporal world. Nevertheless, as all things ultimately work God's will, one must trust that even evil will be turned to good (a central theme in Lewis' book, *The Great Divorce*). Although from our perspective in the world of time we cannot perceive what that good will be, we must have faith in God. However, we must not rely solely on God's grace: we must do our part, and this takes courage as well as faith. In short, Tolkien is reminding his son that he must not despair, for even in our earthly lives we can pray for, and perhaps receive, God's grace.

Throughout both World Wars, Tolkien endured profound suffering and anxiety; however, at the center of his being there was an abiding faith that appears to have remained untouched. Tolkien was a man who studied and appreciated the lessons of the past, and this, along with his Christian faith, gave him a sense of perspective unlike that of most of his contemporaries. The modernists emerged from World War I and the events surrounding it in a state of great anxiety and alienation. Tolkien, on the other hand, seems to have maintained a sense of equanimity about the state of the post-war world. This is not to say, of course, that Tolkien was not deeply affected by both wars, but rather that he seems never to have abandoned the belief that there is a transcendent order into which our own brief lives are a part and which gives meaning to human existence. Such religious conviction was lost to the modernists, who ascribed to schools of thought that rejected the past, including Christianity, and who expressed a sense of the emptiness of their lives and of the world more generally.

To say that the devastating losses, on both the personal and national levels, of World Wars One and Two were overwhelming for most people would be an understatement. Tolkien confronted that suffering always in the context of his faith, and that included a faith in the goodness of human beings, despite the potential of some of them to commit acts of atrocity. In May of 1944 he wrote to Christopher that it was disheartening to consider "the everlasting mass and weight of human inequity," but one must not forget that "there is always good: much more hidden" (*Letters* 80). These assertions that point to the complex nature of human beings are typical of Tolkien's thinking: times change, but humanity does not. Human beings always have and always will have the potential to sink to their most base level and commit evil acts. Nevertheless, there is much more goodness in the world than we can perceive.

According to Tolkien's Catholic epistemology, ours is a fallen world; therefore, he writes, it "has been 'going to the bad' all down the ages" as we move ever farther away from the Edenic world that God created (*Letters* 48). This is akin to Galadriel's sense of Middle-earth's history as the "long defeat." Tolkien believed that Eden once did exist in our real world (*Letters* 110). In his book, *Tolkien: Man and Myth*, Joseph Pearce illustrates the centrality in Tolkien's writings of his Christian faith. In regard to Tolkien's remarks about a real Eden on Earth, Pearce writes, "Tolkien's longing for this lost Eden and his mystical glimpses of it, inspired and motivated by his sense of 'exile' from the fullness of truth, was the source of his creativity" (*Man and Myth* 87). In his conviction that there once was a place of uncorrupt nature and humanity in our real world, Tolkien seems to stand virtually alone against a wave of anti-religious sentiment, found even among practicing Christians. In January of 1945 he wrote about how belief in the Biblical account of Eden had been so deprecated by "the self-styled scientists" that even faithful Christians were embarrassed to admit to it when "modern taste began to sneer" (*Letters* 109). Tolkien makes reference here to the predominant sentiment among his contemporaries and its transmission into the larger culture. He refers to "some generations," which would bring us back to the nineteenth-century underpinnings of modernism, those schools of thought that

FOUR. *Modernist Disaffection and the Tolkienian Faith*

challenged Christianity and helped to give rise to a profound disaffection with it.

Tolkien, like his dear friend and fellow Inkling, C.S. Lewis, took issue with modernism's rejection of religion. In the same letter, Tolkien expresses his unequivocal belief that there once was a real Eden on Earth, and humanity still feels the loss of it (*Letters* 110). And while he recognized that free will allowed human beings to either ascend to heaven or sink to hell, he maintained a firm belief, as he describes it in a letter written in 1945, in "the prophesied thousand-year rule of the Saints, i.e. those who have for all their imperfections never fully bowed heart and will to the world or the evil spirit (in modern but not universal terms: mechanism, 'scientific' materialism, Socialism in either of its factions now at war)" (Tolkien, *Letters* 110). Tolkien's description of humanity's yearning for the unfallen world of the distant past and his faith in the eternal life through the Incarnation, calls to mind C.S. Lewis' autobiography, *Surprised by Joy*, in which Lewis describes his lifelong journey to understand an inexplicably gratifying sense of yearning. Through many stages of his life, Lewis was unable to identify the true object of his desire; however, he finally came to understand that such moments of joy as he had experienced since his childhood were fleeting apprehensions of the eternal love of God (*Surprised by Joy* 221). Since human beings are "appearances of the Absolute," Lewis argues, "we experience Joy: we yearn, rightly, for that unity which we can never reach except by ceasing to be the separate phenomenal beings called 'we'" (222). Tolkien, too, asserts that although we can at times apprehend this state of grace, our apprehensions are fleeting. As fallen beings, we are cut off from the possibility of pure peace in the temporal world. He believed that the state of fellowship that was lost with the Fall could never be regained; however, humanity might "recover something like it, but on a higher plane" (Tolkien, *Letters* 110). This recovery is dependent on both grace and free will, for, as Tolkien notes, all of humanity is free to commit unrepented sin and forsake redemption.

In his book, *The Road to Middle-earth*, Tom Shippey argues that Tolkien is among a group of writers whom he refers to as "traumatized authors." *The Lord of the Rings*, Shippey asserts, "is a war-book, also a post-war book, framed by and responding to the crisis of Western civilization, 1914–1945 (and beyond)" (*The Road to Middle-earth* 329).

According to Shippey, these "traumatized authors" used fantasy as a way to deal with the horror of modern warfare. He goes on to list a number of Tolkien's contemporaries who also chose "to communicate their thoughts and experience via fantasy," including C.S. Lewis, William Golding, T.H. White, George Orwell, and Kurt Vonnegut, among others. "All of these men," Shippey notes, "were writing obviously, or even self-declaredly, about the nature of evil, which they thought had changed in their time, or about which the human race had gained new knowledge" (*Road to Middle-earth* 329).

Tolkien, Lewis, and their contemporaries transformed old forms into new ones in order to express a new sensibility about war, much like the poets who transformed the conventional lyric poem into the trench lyric. Nils Clausson, in his essay, "The Origins of the Trench Lyric," argues that during the early years of World War I, no poetic form existed that was sufficient to describe the experience of modern warfare; therefore, soldier poets adapted the conventional lyric poem into the trench lyric. In their attempts to poetically render their war experience, the early soldier poets, according to Clausson, were constrained by the traditional forms available to them. These forms, "the patriotic sonnet and the Romantic lyric," he writes, were meant "neither to criticize war nor to represent it realistically" (107). According to Clausson, many of the soldier poets adapted the traditional form into the trench lyric, which allowed them to adequately express "what had only seemed alien and ungraspable" (107). In this respect, the soldier poets of World War I responded in much the same way as the "traumatized authors" that Shippey describes. Both groups were faced with the insufficiency of conventional modes of expression to relate the extraordinary events of modern war, so they adapted what did exist. That this response is so prevalent speaks to both the nature and the magnitude of the horror of World War I and the difficulty of comprehending how human beings could perpetrate such evil on one another.

Tolkien's work looks seriously at twentieth-century evil, in which war was wider in scope and more efficiently destructive than it had ever been. The War of the Ring is, after all, a global struggle. Tolkien's writing, however, also bears witness to his faith in God as well as to the beauty of the world and the goodness and courage to be found in humanity. In another of his many wartime letters to his youngest son, Tolkien com-

FOUR. *Modernist Disaffection and the Tolkienian Faith*

miserated with Christopher about the need to work out for oneself the meaning of one's experience and to find an outlet for one's emotions. He explains that for him, consideration of the nature of good and evil gave rise to his mythology, which extends as far back as the creation of the world and the introduction of evil into Creation itself. The earliest parts of this imaginative construction, Tolkien writes, were invented in the very midst of war (*Letters* 78). While Tolkien used the mode of fantasy to render evil, he maintained throughout his life a belief in the ultimate power of God and the promise that in the final reckoning, the forces for good would prevail over evil.

Tolkien was well aware of the world's evil, whether wrought by individuals, governments, or any number of agencies in between. As a Christian he believed that humanity had fallen from grace and that our world is corrupt. In "On Fairy-stories" he explains that even fantasy can be used, consciously or unconsciously, to promote evil.

"But of what human thing in this fallen world is that not true?" he asks (Tolkien, "On Fairy-stories" 75). Men have often worshipped what they themselves have invented, including, he writes, "their notions, their banners, their monies; even their sciences and their social and economic theories have demanded human sacrifice" (Tolkien, "On Fairy Stories" 75). Such corruption of our inherent ability to invent notwithstanding, the ability to sub-create can, and should, be put to positive uses. "Fantasy remains a human right," Tolkien writes, "we make in our measure and in our derivative mode, because we are made: and not only made, but made in the image and likeness of a Maker" ("On Fairy Stories" 75). Tolkien refers in the above passage to the evils of his time, and his list of "false gods" echoes the intellectual, social, and political underpinnings of the twentieth century. In regard to all of these, the cost of progress in our fallen world is our very humanity. Yet science, society, and government are not bad in and of themselves; rather, they are subject to corruption. Literature, specifically fantasy, is also subject to corruption, but this does not negate its essential value.

Tolkien had immediate contact with the evils of the world: he fought in one of the bloodiest, most destructive (to both humanity and nature) battles the world had seen. He knew how gruesome and wasteful war could be. He witnessed what he considered to be the most alarming effects of accelerated and dehumanizing industrialization: the mechanization of war, the advent of the tank and poison gas, the destruction of nature with the ever increasing use of automobiles, and urban sprawl. Born in 1892, Tolkien lived in the same world as Yeats, Eliot, Woolf, Lawrence and the other modernists; he was in no way oblivious to the events and changes that brought about their sense of being cast adrift in a world no longer anchored by the old beliefs. However, Tolkien, in contrast to many of his contemporaries, envisioned a world in which a providential order prevailed, despite human frailty and folly, a world from which the center had decidedly *not* dropped out.

Tolkien once described himself as a "Roman Catholic" (*Letters*, 255). Therefore he looked upon human history as "a 'long defeat'— though it contains ... some samples or glimpses of final victory" (Tolkien, *Letters* 255). Clearly, this indicates a sense of sadness, though not nihilism or despair, because through the Incarnation humanity can achieve redemption and regain the fellowship that existed before the Fall. And while Tolkien took much inspiration from Northern legends, his own legendarium offers, at least obliquely, what the Norse tales could not: the ultimate triumph of good over evil. In the Norse legends, at the time of Ragnarok, the final battle between good and evil, evil would triumph over good. In contrast, according to Christian belief, the advent of Christ, his birth, life, death and resurrection, offers hope beyond this world, as in the Catholic Creed which ends: "We look for the resurrection of the dead and the life of the world to come" (*The Holy See*).

The 'final victory' was won for humanity by Christ in what Tolkien described in "On Fairy-Stories" as "the greatest and most complete conceivable eucatastrophe," a term that Tolkien created to describe "the good catastrophe, the sudden joyous 'turn'" in the story, whether it be a fairy-story or the story that is human history. Some few sentences later, Tolkien goes on to explain that eucatastrophe "denies (in the face of much evidence, if you will) universal final defeat and in so far is evangelium, giving a fleeting glimpse of Joy, Joy beyond the walls of the world, poignant as grief" ("On Fairy-stories" 86). For Tolkien, it is wrong to despair, no matter how dire one's circumstances may be. After transcending both time and death, Gandalf resolutely tells the enthralled Théoden, "No counsel have I to give to those that despair," (Tolkien, *The Two Towers* 519). Apart from the damage to the individual psyche, despair is a dangerous state of mind. The conviction that one can do

Four. *Modernist Disaffection and the Tolkienian Faith*

nothing to impact the world, on any scale, is the enemy of action. Despair in a leader, who must inspire others to act, is especially dangerous because it has the potential to mire the whole community in inactivity. In his book, *Following Gandalf*, Matthew Dickerson links despair with the inability to engage in the continual process of choice that is required for individuals to follow the path that Providence has set before them. Dickerson writes, "Théoden is lost in darkness, unable to see the light. He is so hopeless that he is paralyzed; his inaction is a fundamental loss to his free will to act and is brought about by his despair. This is why Wormtongue encourages Théoden's feelings of hopelessness, so that he will remain inactive and continue to choose *not* to choose" (144). Théoden's passivity is extremely destructive, as it allows Saruman to embark upon the systematic destruction of the kingdom of Rohan.

Just as it is for Gandalf, for Tolkien action is informed by hope, which ultimately extends back to advent of Christ. "The Birth of Christ," Tolkien writes, "is the eucatastrophe of Man's History. The Resurrection is the eucatastrophe of the story of the Incarnation. This story begins and ends in joy" (Tolkien, "On Fairy-stories" 88–89). Of course, *The Lord of the Rings* also has its tragic turns, what Tolkien called "dyscatastrophe"; human beings must suffer and, indeed, die before "final victory" will be achieved. This is why choices are so important: in the face of loss and grief individuals must carry on, must continue to choose to follow the path set before them, as do, for example, Aragorn and Frodo, however dangerous and terrifying that path might be. In this manner, free will comes into contact with providential design.

Tolkien acknowledged the sadness of the world, a sadness wrought actively by the evil that fallen human beings inflict upon one another and passively by mortality and the passage of time to which nature, cultures, kingdoms, and, of course, human beings must all submit. Much of *The Lord of the Rings* belies a profound sense of loss. When the surviving members of the Fellowship first meet her, Galadriel says that for thousands of years, she and Celeborn, "have fought the long defeat" (Tolkien, *The Fellowship of the Ring* 359). Her words express a similar sentiment of Tolkien when he writes, "Wars are always lost, and The War always goes on; and it is no good growing faint!" (*Letters* 116). Galadriel is well aware that the destruction of the One Ring will bring an end to Lothlórien and Rivendell. It will bring an end to the life the Elves have known and loved in Middle-earth, though their own lives will go on long after Lothlórien fades beyond memory. Nevertheless, this knowledge does not prevent Galadriel from doing her part to defeat Sauron.

Like Gandalf, Aragorn, Frodo and so many others, as a true steward Galadriel will do her best to ensure that the world she leaves behind will not be the wasteland that Sauron would make of it should he regain the Ring. Nevertheless, evil will persist, even when Sauron is no more. As Gandalf tells his companions in Minas Tirith, "it is not our part to master all the tides of the world, but to do what is in us for the succour of those years wherein we are set, uprooting the evil in the field that we know, so that those who live after may have clean earth to till. What weather they shall have is not ours to rule" (Tolkien, *The Return of the King* 290). Just as Gandalf is an angelic messenger of Eru Ilúvatar, Tolkien's correlative for God, Sauron is a demonic messenger of Morgoth, the correlative for Satan in the world of Middle-earth. The wizard means to remind his friends that far older and more powerful forces are at work in the world and will be so until the world is no more. Gandalf's use of the phrase "clean earth" is a particularly Tolkienian metaphor which refers to nature both figuratively and literally. Gandalf would preserve a world free of the corruption of Sauron, and he would protect the world from the Dark Lord's "scorched earth policy" (Tolkien, *Letters* 179), for the world over which Sauron would hold dominion would be both a physical and a spiritual wasteland.

Five

The World as Wasteland
The Landscapes of Loss

"This late age of the world's experience had bred in them all, all men and women, a well of tears. Tears and sorrows; courage and endurance; perfectly upright and stoical bearing. Think, for example, of the woman she admired most, Lady Bexborough, opening the bazaar" (13). These are the thoughts of Clarissa Dalloway, from Virginia Woolf's 1925 novel, *Mrs. Dalloway*, as she stands before a shop window during the morning of the one day that encompasses the whole of the story's plot. Implicit in Clarissa's musing is the then commonplace notion that the social order of the time dictated that Lady Bexborough stand before the crowd and welcome everyone to the annual village fair, even though she held in her hand the telegram informing her of her cherished son's death in the Great War (Woolf, *Mrs. Dalloway* 5). Woolf juxtaposes the bazaar, an ordinary event, against the extraordinary anguish brought about by the First World War. Through the memory of Clarissa Dalloway, the author presents the image of the heartbroken woman holding the small piece of paper that delivers the most devastating news a parent can hear. The passage signifies that even after the war has ended, individuals experience grief and death in the very midst of life. Thus men and women in the post-war world carry within themselves "a well of tears."

The Great War had left so much in fragments: families, communities, even the foundations of Western civilization itself seemed by 1918 to have been blasted as thoroughly as the French countryside. Not surprisingly, then, themes of loneliness, loss, alienation, and fragmentation are the hallmarks of modernism, and they are to be found anywhere from the poetry of T.S. Eliot to the novels of Virginia Woolf, from the paintings of Picasso to the music of Stravinsky. All of these artists were looking for new modes of expression that broke free of the limitations of convention in order to come as close as possible to reality as they perceived it. We find this impulse toward new forms in, for example, the work of Picasso, whose paintings portray a subject from multiple perspectives simultaneously in contrast to traditional art which renders a subject from a single perspective. In poetry, T.S. Eliot, with the editorial input of Ezra Pound, broke away from conventional verse forms by drawing upon fragments of Western and non-Western cultural history and juxtaposing them against the present moment.

In his 1922 poem *The Waste Land*, Eliot brings together an array of literary, cultural, and religious allusions, truly bits and pieces, sometimes mixing them with scenes and dialogue from contemporary English life. In this way, the central speaker of the poem attempts to reintegrate atomized experience and thereby recover a sense of wholeness and unity. In other words, the speaker tries to construct what E.M. Forster in his 1910 novel, *Howards End*, refers to as "ramparts" against "panic and emptiness" or what Robert Frost described as "a momentary stay against confusion." Eliot articulates the modernist sensibility through the many voices of *The Waste Land*. Indeed, the poem's working title was "He do the Police in Different Voices," a line borrowed from Dickens' 1865 novel, *Our Mutual Friend*. The voices of *The Waste Land* spring from varied eras, regions, and social classes; they range from elevated to common, educated to ignorant, wistful to cynical, innocent to experienced. To the reader the voices and scenes seem disjointed and disconnected; indeed, the poem seems to be most unified by its distinct disunity, its lack of a stable center, whether that center be spiritual, intellectual, or even personal. This instability is meant to reflect the poet's perception of the modern world, echoing Yeats' declaration: "Things fall apart; the center cannot hold." Those "things" that were peeling off from an ostensibly once-stable core include the religious, intellectual, and political paradigms as well as societal norms that made up Victorian and Edwardian society. In the aftermath of World War I, the modernists found themselves crawling from the wreckage that once was the Western world.

In *The Waste Land*, Eliot engages with the past by recalling and incorporating significant moments of a past that reached back beyond the reigns of Edward and Victoria. The poem attempts to bring those disparate pieces together in a constructed whole, thereby moving beyond the peculiarly modern feelings of dislocation and fragmentation which the poem conveys. The opening section of the poem, entitled "The Burial of the Dead," describes a barren landscape. Eliot writes:

> What are the roots that clutch, what branches grow
> Out of this stony rubbish? Son of man,
> You cannot say, or guess, for you know only
> A heap of broken images, where the sun beats,
> And the dead tree gives no shelter, the cricket no
> > Relief,
> And the dry stone no sound of water [474].

Like the speaker, we are disoriented and lost in this wasteland world: we, too, are left with little more to guide us than a "heap of broken images," the ruins of Western civilization. The casting off of old standards that gave order and meaning to the world throws into question the stability of the individual. And so the individual, too, is in danger of losing his own sense of identity, his sense of his place and purpose in a world no longer perceived to be divinely arranged and attended to. This process of recalling the past is akin to Van Wyck Brooks' call to find or create a "useable past" that would enable individuals both to cope with contemporary post-war reality while at the same time move positively into the future. In the case of *The Waste Land*, the use of the past to restore a sense of wholeness and stability to the present enables the poem's central speaker to admit finally, "These fragments I have shored against my ruin."

Just as *The Waste Land* expresses fragmentation in its poetic structure, Virginia Woolf's 1927 novel *To the Lighthouse* demonstrates fragmentation in its narrative structure. The first section of the novel, "The Window," is an expansive description, emphasizing multiple perspectives, of one day in the life of its heroine, Mrs. Ramsay, and ending with a dinner party that represents the potential for meaning and harmony in human existence. In the final section, entitled "The Lighthouse," it appears that a main character, Lily Briscoe, is waking up the day after Mrs. Ramsay's dinner party, when, in fact, ten years have passed, during which World War I has begun and ended, and the novel's heroine as well as two of her children have died.

The middle section of the novel, entitled "Time Passes," describes the effects of time and nature on the Ramsay house, left uninhabited for a decade. The house has become a remnant of the past, and there hangs about it the pall of the wasteland. The only life there is a lesser wind, broken free and roaming about the house's interior. "Nothing stirred," the narrator tells us, "in the drawing-room or in the dining room or on the staircase. Only through the rusty hinges and swollen sea-moistened woodwork certain airs, detached from the body of the wind (the house was ramshackle after all) crept round corners and ventured indoors" (Woolf, *To the Lighthouse* 190). In the world of the novel, the Ramsay house has come to stand for the literal and figurative losses as well as feelings of emptiness brought about by World War I. On a literal level, the Ramsays have precipitously lost family members: Mrs. Ramsay and her children, Andrew, and Prue. This personal loss corresponds to the loss of loved ones in the real world of Woolf and her readers. On a figurative level, the disembodied "airs" that wander about the house correspond to the feelings of aimlessness and rootlessness that were part of the modernist sensibility. In other words, the desolate house can be viewed as an objective correlative for the modern wasteland and its inhabitants. If there is some kind of transcendent will for good that invests meaning in the everyday world of the novel, it reveals its secrets, the narrator suggests, only grudgingly.

In the "Time Passes" section of Woolf's novel, the narrator articulates the modernist sense that a unified vision of the world can be seen for only the most fleeting of moments. As compensation for post-war humanity's "toil and penitence," the narrator explains, one brief moment of clarity is afforded to us by "divine goodness." In this vision the ordinary becomes sublime: "the hare erect; the wave falling; the boat rocking, which, did we deserve them, should be ours always" (Woolf, *To the Lighthouse* 192–93). There is something eternal evident in the landscape surrounding the house, but its phantom-like quality makes it nearly impossible to apprehend. Amidst the engulfing darkness, there appears a unified vision that suggests the Eternal. Such a vision suggests that we are connected to something beyond ourselves, that we are not merely adrift in the world and in time, that time itself is more than a series of disjointed moments. This glimpse of the Eternal, however, is transitory,

FIVE. *The World as Wasteland*

for whatever transcendent power afforded the vision has a sudden change of heart:

> But alas, divine goodness, twitching the cord, draws the curtain; it does not please him; he covers his treasures in a drench of hail, and so breaks them, so confuses them that it seems impossible that their calm should ever return or that we should ever compose from their fragments a perfect whole or read in the littered pieces the clear words of truth. For our penitence deserves a glimpse only; our toil respite only [Woolf, *To the Lighthouse* 193].

The passage conveys a feeling of despair, a sense that however much we try to recover a sense of wholeness in ourselves or our world, we will fail. The tone is one of resignation rather than faith or hope. Inevitably, we will lose this vision which might give us a sense of well-being, a sense that we have a place in the world and we are not just floating around in a vast ocean of time and space. The passage also suggests that the individual's search for meaning in the post-war world is a search without end, since individuals experience that world as chaotic and fragmented, a jumble of "littered pieces." Even should the seeker perceive some eternal truth in discreet images, there will be no "divine promptitude" to create order, to make "the world reflect the compass of the soul" (Woolf, *To the Lighthouse* 193). Ultimately, each "soul" remains isolated, from other souls as well as from "divine goodness."

In an effort to reintegrate the jumbled pieces of modern reality, the mind seeks truth and hopes to capture it with artistic or intellectual effort. In *To the Lighthouse* Woolf puts forth several examples of such attempts: Mr. Carmichael's poetry, Mr. Ramsay's philosophy, Lily Briscoe's impressionistic painting, and Mrs. Ramsay's dinner party, which represents in part the attempt to create aesthetic beauty out of the everyday experiences of life. However, the novel's narrator returns again and again to the same conclusion: it is the work of the individual to impose order against the indifference and chaos of time and nature. For those who inhabit the post-war wasteland, Eternal Goodness and truth remain ever elusive.

Provided with only a brief glimpse, the inhabitants of Woolf's wasteland will once again find themselves surrounded by bits and pieces, fragments out of which the individual mind must make a unified whole. After a moment of hope, we are faced again with inevitable loss and a sense of despair because any vision of transcendence is so fleeting that it seems more like an illusion than a reality. The authorial voice that inserts itself into the narrative makes no promise that such an image of wholeness will ever again be accessible. Nevertheless, we must strive to apprehend that vision. "Through the open window," the narrator tells us, "the voice of the beauty of the world came murmuring," (Woolf, *To the Lighthouse* 213). Sadly, however, in the post-war world, the sleepers cannot wake from their shell-shocked sleep. They will not leave their beds and descend to the beach or even pull aside the window shade to see "the night flowing down in purple; his head crowned; his sceptre jewelled" (Woolf, *To the Lighthouse* 213). More than a century before Virginia Woolf published *To the Lighthouse*, William Wordsworth in his poem "The World is Too Much With Us," warned that human beings were losing their ability to see the transcendent in the world around them, to enchant nature and thus, the speaker says, "Have glimpses that would make me less forlorn" (12). The sleepers of Woolf's novel seem to have followed this trajectory of alienation from nature and the transcendent to which Wordsworth called attention in the early nineteenth century.

For Woolf, the inhabitants of the modern wasteland are cut off from transcendent truth, from sublime night and the eternal ebb and flow of the sea, cycles of nature that anchor us within the flow of time. The narrator describes the emptiness and desolation of the Ramsay's house: "The house was left; the house was deserted. It was left like a shell on a sandhill to fill with dry salt grains now that life had left it. The long night seemed to have set in; the trifling airs, nibbling, the clammy breaths, fumbling, seemed to have triumphed" (*To the Lighthouse* 206). Just as in a Robert Frost poem where the efforts of human beings to create order—to build a fence of stone or birch, to neatly stack firewood against the cold of winter—ultimately fail, Woolf portrays nature as a random force that will ultimately conquer humanity's attempts to impose order against the chaos of the universe.

The modernists try to achieve recovery in their literature by attempting to construct unified and coherent wholes. For them there is a fractured story that can be retrieved. For Tolkien, in contrast, humanity's story is continuous; the unified world already exists and thus does not need to be constructed in art, whose primary purpose for him is to

Five. The World as Wasteland

engage the reader while at the same time illuminate truth and glorify God's creation. Although Tolkien repeatedly asserted that *The Lord of the Rings* is not allegorical, he did believe that there is an element of allegory in any story. He wrote to W.H. Auden in 1955 explaining the difference between allegory *per se* and "the allegorical nature of any story that 'comes to life'" (Tolkien, *Letters* 212). For an example of the first type of allegory, one might point to Plato's *Allegory of the Cave*, in which ordinary people are depicted as prisoners in a cave; their limited understanding of reality is represented by their ability to perceive the material world merely as shadows on the opposite wall of the cave. In this case, the prisoners are meant to stand in for society, which relies on the philosopher's clarity of vision to explain the true nature of reality. In other words, simple allegory provides us with one-to-one correspondences between the abstract and the concrete.

It was not Tolkien's aim to tell a story that could be deconstructed with such methodical ease. As is often noted, Tolkien remarked quite emphatically in the book's foreword section that *The Lord of the Rings* is decidedly not allegorical (*The Fellowship of the Ring* xviii). As he explained to Auden, he believed that every individual is an allegory, "embodying in a particular tale and clothed in the garments of time and place, universal truth and everlasting life" (Tolkien, *Letters* 212). Each person's story has meaning because, for good or evil, it is part of the Whole Story that is God's plan; this was for him, absolute truth. Like the Beowulf poet, who looked sympathetically back across the centuries and endowed his pagan characters with Christian virtues, setting them in a world that Christ had redeemed, Tolkien set his apparently pagan characters in a world created and lovingly overseen by one God, Eru Ilúvatar. In this way he attempted to "rekindle an old light" in a world that he perceived to be suffering under a very dark cloud. To aid the wizard in his task, Círdan the Shipwright gave to Gandalf Narya, that one of the Three Rings of Power that contained the light of Ilúvatar's creation. He did so specifically to help Gandalf ignite the spark of courage in the hearts of the peoples of Middle-earth who would strive against Sauron. He tells Gandalf: "For this is the Ring of Fire, and herewith, maybe, thou shalt rekindle hearts to the valour of old in a world that grows chill" (Tolkien, *The Silmarillion* 313). This notion of rekindling the light of Truth, which in turn kindles the courage to face the world's evil in whatever guise one encounters it, is a theme that runs throughout Tolkien's letters and fiction.

In a 1954 letter draft to Peter Hastings, the owner of a Catholic bookshop in Oxford, Tolkien wrote that one aim of his work was to express truth and morality in the Primary world "by the ancient device of exemplifying them in unfamiliar embodiments" in his subcreated world (*Letters* 194). This is just what the *Beowulf* poet does, according to Tolkien in his essay, "*Beowulf*: The Monsters and Critics": "The author of *Beowulf* showed forth the permanent value of that *pietas* which treasures the memory of man's struggles in the dark past, man fallen and not yet saved, disgraced but not dethroned" (120). The Anglo-Saxon poet took up a story that greatly concerned itself with fellowship and nobility of spirit, and he invested his fifth-century fictional hero with eleventh-century Christian virtues, thereby helping his audience to see those virtues in a new and compelling light. Similarly, the author of *The Lord of the Rings* implicitly articulates that "universal truth" which for him simply inheres in the world: Tolkien was not attempting to put together broken pieces to construct a unified whole.

Many modernist writers use the wasteland image as an objective correlative for the modern world, but it is important to note that by the close of World War I much of Europe had become an actual wasteland. Along with the destruction of war, industrialism was rapidly consuming the old world to make way for the modern one, and this damaged physical reality had its counterpart in the individual psyche as well as in society more generally. It is therefore important to look at both aspects of the wasteland: the external and the internal. Wastelands can be figurative as well as literal, located within the individual as well as outside of the self. As such, they can represent the barrenness of a community or culture as well as alienation from others and, most distressingly, from God and oneself. In the perception of the modernists, the world is a literal and spiritual wasteland; thus their work reflects the feelings of randomness and rootlessness that cause their sense of alienation and despair. In Tolkien, on the other hand, we find order and meaning in the world, since for him any one life and any one moment in time are only small parts of what he called the "Whole Story," the author of which is God. For Tolkien, it is humanity that creates wastelands, and therefore it is humanity that must repair the damage it has caused. As Deborah Rogers

Five. The World as Wasteland

says of Christ: "He came, an actual person, in time and space, to repair for us the breach which Adam had made. Christ repairs the relationship between mankind and the extraterrestrial Creator. He does not repair the politics, economics, or ecology of the planet Earth. As He plainly said, 'My kingdom is not of this world'" (73).

In *The Lord of the Rings* the central characters are aware that theirs is part of a larger story, and this serves to anchor them and mitigate against the sense of dislocation that the modernists so often express. In Tolkien's subcreated world, individuals on the side of good are not caught in the cycle of despair that is the modernist reaction to the intellectual, social, and political climate of the first half of the twentieth century. Rather, they place their faith in each other, that is, in fellowship and community, aspects of life that writers from Herman Melville and William Morris in the nineteenth century to E.M. Forster and F. Scott Fitzgerald in the twentieth warned were quickly disappearing. Tolkien's characters, the many whom we admire, rise above their differences to create a widely diverse community of heroic individuals that share the same values of universal freedom and justice. In Tolkien's subcreated world, even the humblest person, the smallest of stature, can be heroic, for in this world heroism builds itself largely on faith. And though there is (deliberately, Tolkien said) no organized religion in Middle-earth, its inhabitants on the side of good have faith in the "Powers" that oversee Middle-earth, whether they recognize those powers as Ilúvatar and his regents in the West, the Valar, or simply as the eternal goodness represented by Gandalf and the powers he possesses.

In contrast to these faithful individuals, those of Tolkien's characters who despair are somehow already alienated from their communities as well as themselves. For example, Denethor, who has no hope of success against Sauron and will not consent to follow Gandalf's leadership, had forsaken his son Faramir long before the Fellowship arrived in Minas Tirith. In the ultimate break with community and the self, Denethor commits suicide, leaping onto the funeral pyre which he had built for Faramir. This is one of the most tragic moments of *The Lord of the Rings* because, as Charles Huttar writes in "Hell and the City: Tolkien and the Traditions of Western Literature": "A high and noble ideal, faithful stewardship for an absent lord, maintained for nearly a thousand years with little hope of the lord's return, collapses under the weight of pride and despair just as the hope is on the verge of being realized" (130). Unlike the small and humble Sam, the "high and noble" Denethor lacks the inner resources to overcome his disappointment and despair.

Saruman, also despairing of a victory against Sauron, severs his connection to the community of angelic beings of his own rank, the Maiar. He, too, destroys himself by abandoning the virtues of goodness and kindness that were meant to inform his guardianship of Middle-earth. Rather than acting in accordance with the charge put to him by the Valar that he care for and protect the world from the devouring evil of Sauron, Saruman creates an army that will help to lay waste to the world he was sent to protect. The most destructive outcome of alienation in *The Lord of the Rings* is the character of Sauron, once an angelic being of the same rank as Gandalf and Saruman, but by the time of the story long cut off from all humane society. The Dark Lord's alienation could not be more extreme, for he is consumed with hatred and wants only to dominate every living thing and thereby turn the whole of Middle-earth into a wasteland. The imminent death of the green world is foreshadowed early in *The Lord of the Rings* when the hobbits are through an evil enchantment trapped in an ancient burial mound. When Frodo comes back to his senses, he hears the Barrow-wight chant:

> *Cold be hand and heart and bone*
> *and cold be sleep under stone*
> *… till the Sun fails and the Moon is dead.*
> *In the black wind the stars shall die,*
> *and still on gold here let them lie,*
> *till the dark lord lifts his hand*
> *over dead sea and withered land* [Tolkien, *The Fellowship of the Ring* 141].

The nightmare world of which the Barrow-wight sings has the potential to become a reality in the real world of Middle-earth. Under his dominion, the Dark Lord would make a wasteland out of the world. In the end, however, the better part of Middle-earth is saved from the fate of the moderns, if only for a while. For Tolkien, the world is marred, as it has been since the Fall, and life involves struggle and pain, but his literature, essays, and letters consistently suggest that the world does indeed rest

FIVE. *The World as Wasteland*

on a solid foundation: the Primary world that God created remains unified, neither its history fractured nor its providential order fragmented.

* * *

In bringing together in *The Waste Land* fragments of literature from various cultures and eras, T.S. Eliot often inverts the images and themes which the original writers presented so as to merge earlier moments in Western and non–Western culture with the present time. It is via this creative act that Eliot engages with the past to restore to the present a kind of order, even if an imagined one. One example of this occurs early in the poem with the inversion of the opening lines of Geoffrey Chaucer's Middle English *Canterbury Tales*, a collection of stories framed within the larger tale of a pilgrimage of "sundry folk" who came by chance to form a "felaweshipe" on their way to Canterbury to visit the shrine of the "holy blissful martyr," Thomas Beckett, Archbishop of Canterbury, who was murdered in the cathedral there in 1170 by knights of King Henry II.

Chaucer's pilgrims begin their spiritual quest in spring, a season traditionally associated with rebirth. The tale begins with a celebration of this time of fecundity and hope:

> Whan that April with his showers soote
> The droughte of March hath perced to the roote,
> And bathed every vine in swich licour,
> Of which vertu engendered is the flowre;
> Whan Zephyrus eek with his sweete breeth
> Inspired hath in every holt and heath
> The tender croppes, and the yonge sonne
> Hath in the Ram his halve cours yronne,
> And smale fowles maken melodye
> That sleepen al the night with open ye—
> So pricketh hem Nature in hir corages—
> Thanne longen folk to goon on pilgrimages [General Prologue 1–12].

The world which Chaucer describes is one in which the cycles of nature are predictable and meaningful for humanity. The "sweet" showers of April "pierce to the root" the drought of March, bathing every plant, engendering flowers. The rain, the West Wind (Zephyrus), the "young" sun, and the singing of small birds combine to stir the hearts ("corages") of "folk," inspiring them to make the long pilgrimage to Canterbury. The scene appeals to the senses: refreshing rain, gentle wind, temperate sunshine, the songs of birds. Here there is light and music and activity in nature, which in turn stirs life in humanity; individuals are moved emotionally, and this prompts them to move physically, literally turning themselves toward hope and holiness in the form of the shrine of the Christian martyr.

In contrast to the opening lines of Chaucer's *Canterbury Tales*, which begins by describing April as the time when "a young man's fancy turns to love," Eliot's *The Waste Land* starts with the lines:

> April is the cruelest month, breeding
> Lilacs out of the dead land, mixing
> Memory and desire, stirring
> Dull roots with spring rain.
> Winter kept us warm, covering
> Earth in forgetful snow, feeding
> A little life with dried tubers [473].

Here, Eliot takes traditional images of fecund spring and rebirth and inverts them. April is not a joy but a torment; the landscape is not edenic but virtually barren. For the speaker, nature is not restorative but cruel, waking memories and feelings that he would rather bury under the "forgetful snow" of his consciousness. With this allusion to Chaucer, Eliot sets up expectations of hope; however, his subversion of those expectations startles the reader with the realization that traditional romantic notions of the courtly love which has its analogues in the awakening of nature have been lost to the post-war generation. The resulting disjoint therefore evokes feelings of loss and nostalgia in the reader.

In *To the Lighthouse*, Virginia Woolf subverts the reader's expectations in much the same way as Eliot does in *The Waste Land*. In the section "Time Passes," spring brings not comfort but false promise. Woolf writes, "The spring without a leaf to toss, bare and bright like a virgin fierce in her chastity, scornful in her purity, was laid out on fields wide-eyed and watchful and entirely careless of what was done or thought by the beholders. (Prue Ramsay, leaning on her father's arm, was given in marriage. What, people said, could have been more fitting? ...)" (Woolf, *To the Lighthouse* 198). In conventional terms, spring carries with it hope and the promise of birth, here signified by the correspondence between the words "virgin," "chastity," and "purity" and the young bride, Prue

Ramsay. This is the cycle of nature; however, in another aside we learn that "Prue Ramsay died that summer in some illness connected with childbirth, which was indeed a tragedy, people said, everything, they said, had promised so well," (Woolf, *To the Lighthouse* 199). The promise of spring is fertility and the renewal of life, and Prue's marriage and pregnancy mirror this cycle of fecundity and birth. However, in the wasteland world of the modernists, the promise fails. Woolf presents the devastating loss of mother and child as a parenthetical aside, as if merely incidental. The cycle of nature completes itself, but it is cruel in its indifference to the death of Prue Ramsay in childbirth. Once again, the hope of spring turns to despair, just as the inhabitants of the post-war world have come to expect. The narrator's tone is so matter-of-fact that it hardly seems ironic that the cycle of nature should collapse on itself as young Prue dies in the attempt of life to renew itself.

This inversion whereby spring exacerbates feelings of anguish rather than kindles hope is expressed as well in D.H. Lawrence's novel *Lady Chatterley's Lover*, in which Wragby Wood is associated with the restorative pastoral world. During one of Connie Chatterley's early walks there, she thinks, "Yet it was spring, and the bluebells were coming in the wood, and the leaf-buds on the hazels were opening like the spatter of green rain. How terrible it was that it should be spring, and everything cold-hearted, cold-hearted (Lawrence, *Lady Chatterley's Lover* 120). For the lost generation of the first quarter of the twentieth century, the old associations are gone, leaving in their place a profound emptiness. As with the speaker of *The Waste Land*, the rebirth that is taking place in nature does not revitalize Connie; rather, it primarily serves to remind her of the barrenness of her own life and of post-war society more generally. In both cases, the individual projects his or her subjective feelings of emptiness and alienation onto the landscape.

For Connie, Wragby Wood will ultimately become a place of freedom from the conventions of class as well as a place of genuine human sympathy and connection, as she finds meaning in her life with the working class gamekeeper, Mellors, who in part represents humanity in tune with the restorative pastoral world. Thus it truly does become for her a place of real hope and renewal. Connie's husband, Sir Clifford, on the other hand, idealizes Wragby Wood. Despite the ravages of war, for him the wood represents continuity with a romanticized past and with generations of tradition, including class distinction and privilege. His desire to preserve it is representative of modernist nostalgia for an imagined idyllic past and an impulse to overcome, or at least cope with, the effects of progress. As Clifford views it from his wheelchair, the narrator describes the landscape, once part of a much larger forest: "In the wood everything was motionless, the old leaves on the ground keeping the frost on their underside. A jay called harshly, many little birds fluttered. But there was no game; no pheasants. They had been killed off during the war, and the wood had been left unprotected, till now Clifford had got his gamekeeper again" (Lawrence, *Lady Chatterley's Lover* 44). In Clifford's mind, the wood is in fact a scrap of the Old England, with its wide expanse of forest where one might find "knights riding and ladies on palfreys" and Robin Hood riding with his band of men (*Lady Chatterley* 45). It is sadly ironic to see the war-wounded Clifford dreaming of feudal lords and their ladies riding on horses along a "greenish sweep" of land while he himself sits in his wheelchair, afraid to risk what for him would be a "very long and jolty down-slope" alongside a "ravel of dead bracken" (Lawrence, *Lady Chatterley's Lover* 45, 44). Just as Eliot juxtaposes past elements of Western culture against the present, through the nostalgic imaginings of Clifford Chatterley, Lawrence sets the pre-industrial against the post-war England.

The feudal England that Clifford envisions when he contemplates Wragby Wood represents for him a patriarchal world of deeply entrenched social distinctions. It is a world in which he feels comfortable, one in which his place, and therefore his identity, is stable and secure. The present diminished state of the wood is another example of the cost of war. Clifford's Edwardian father had felled the trees as England engaged in "total war," and in the process he capitalized on the wood. Like the industrialist Henry Wilcox in Forster's *Howards End*, Sir Geoffrey, Clifford's father, no doubt felt that such actions were necessary in the name of Progress. Henry tells Margaret, "As civilization moves forward, the shoe is bound to pinch in places, and it's absurd to think that anyone is personally responsible" (Forster 174). Henry's assertion is in regard to the poor, but it signifies his inability to make any connection between his actions and the consequences that they have for others. Similarly, the felling of so many of the trees of Wragby Wood may have been done to support the war effort, but Sir Geoffrey benefitted

Five. The World as Wasteland

financially. And unlike the "neighbors" in Morris' *News from Nowhere*, he took no thought to planting new trees to replace those taken. Notably, Clifford demonstrates the same nostalgia for the past that Morris had expressed over a quarter-century earlier. The world that Clifford Chatterley imagines is similar to the worlds that Morris creates in *The Wood Beyond the World* and *The Well at the World's End*. It represents what Henry Wilcox thought of as England's "dim, bucolic past" (Forster 185). There is no place for it in the England of the twentieth century.

As noted in the previous chapter, Clifford Chatterley appears mildly bothered by the fact that the war "had killed rather a lot of people," but he is absolutely livid at the increasing barrenness of the Midlands through the exigencies of industrialization and war. As he and Connie come to a part of forest that had been completely cleared "for trench timber," the narrator provides a glimpse of Clifford's sensibility:

> The whole knoll, which rose softly on the right of the riding, was denuded and strangely forlorn. On the crown of the knoll where the oaks stood, now was bareness; and from there you could look out over the trees to the colliery railway, and the new works at Stacks Gate.
> This denuded place always made Clifford curiously angry. He had been through the war, had seen what it meant. But he didn't get really angry till he saw this bare hill [Lawrence, *Lady Chatterley's Lover* 44].

As in the earlier passage, Lawrence juxtaposes the natural world of the past, represented here by the memory of the oak trees, against the industrialized modern world, represented by the railway and coal works. As he looks out over the place where "once there had been deer, and archers, and monks paddling along on asses," Clifford tells his wife, "'This is the Old England, the heart of it; and I intend to keep it in tact'" (Lawrence, *Lady Chatterley's Lover* 45). These words reflect Clifford's desire to return to the pre-war, pre-industrial world, yet even as he articulates this vain wish to halt progress, the "hooters at Stakes Gate colliery" sound the hour. Lost in his dream of the past, Clifford does not even hear them.

This preoccupation with the past and the longing to hold onto or recapture it in the face of ever increasing industrialization appears in the work of other modernist writers, including F. Scott Fitzgerald's 1925 novel, *The Great Gatsby*, in which we find a surrealistic wasteland situated in Queens, NY. Fitzgerald's objective correlative for the modern world is the "valley of ashes," a "desolate area of land" where the only thing that grows is a carpet of ash that obscures nature and humanity alike. For Fitzgerald, the pastoral world of his forefathers has been destroyed and replaced with a poor substitute indeed. At the end of *The Great Gatsby*, the story's narrator, Nick Carraway, imagines an edenic Long Island as

> a fresh, green breast of the new world. Its vanished trees, the trees that had made way for Gatsby's house, had once pandered in whispers to the last and greatest of all human dreams; for a transitory enchanted moment man must have held his breath in the presence of this continent, compelled into an aesthetic contemplation he neither understood nor desired, face to face for the last time in history with something commensurate to his capacity for wonder [Fitzgerald 189].

Apart from the "transitory enchanted moment," there is nothing eternal here. As Fitzgerald describes it, the modern world is stripped of enchantment, and even if there were a transcendent vision of the power and beauty of nature, that is, something far greater than a humanity that is hardly capable of apprehending it, the image is fleeting.

Like the vision on the night beach outside the Ramsay's house in Virginia Woolf's *To the Lighthouse*, it appears clearly only in the briefest flashes. When Nick Carraway engages with the past, the world that he imagines is not simply the pre-war world; it is the pre-industrial one that is irretrievably lost, despite the collective longing of a generation. Fitzgerald's words, "for the last time in history," underscore the notion that there has been a clean break with the past. This fracture in Western culture is the result not only of the war, but it was also brought about by the machines, rationalism, and secularization of the late nineteenth and early twentieth centuries. Like the trees of Wragby Wood, which Clifford's father felled for the war effort, the woods of Long Island have made way for the conspicuous consumption exemplified by Gatsby's house and Gatsby's parties. Nick's vision of the Long Island that emerged before the eyes of "Dutch sailors" is similar to the welcoming spring of Chaucer's pilgrims and the Robin Hood of Wragby Wood, all of them as ephemeral and illusory as the perfect past that Jay Gatsby in his quest to win back Daisy Buchanan hopes in vain to repeat and thus recover.

While modernist literature contains characters who look to an idealized past, Tolkien engages quite differently with the past. For example,

Five. The World as Wasteland

The Lord of the Rings depicts characters who feel deep nostalgia for a *real* edenic past, that is, Valinor, or Middle-earth itself in its earliest days. Tolkien's Elves—many of whom "awoke" during the First Age of the world and journeyed to the Blessed Realm to abide with the Valar, the divine regents of Middle Earth—remember the paradisal lands of the Uttermost West. In this way, Tolkienian nostalgia differs significantly from that of the modernists. Whereas the modernists look to the past to restore the present, Tolkien's Elves use enchantment to hold onto a moment in time in order to preserve the world of the First Age, before the breaking of the world (the sinking of the island kingdom of Númenor and the removal of the Undying Lands). In this way, they engaged in what Tolkien referred to figuratively as "embalming" (*Letters* 151). For example, Galadriel, exiled from Valinor for the sins of her people against the Valar, uses Nenya, one of the Three Rings of Power, to fashion Lothlórien. When the Fellowship stays there after the loss of Gandalf in Moria, they find that time passes much more slowly there than in the rest of Middle-earth. Frodo posits that in Lothlórien, "'maybe, we were in a time that has elsewhere long gone by'" (Tolkien, *The Fellowship of the Ring* 391). This nostalgia, combined with their efforts to preserve the past, however, paradoxically points to the great folly of the Elves, for as Tolkien explains, in their attempts to arrest time, the Elves act against God's design in which all things must succumb to time and change (*Letters* 236).

Tolkien conceived of the Elves as an aspect of human nature, as our imaginative and intellectual faculties exemplified. As such, he explained, they represent humanity's "artistic, aesthetic, and purely scientific" abilities to a level beyond our capabilities in the Primary world (Tolkien, *Letters* 236). Tolkien also explains that Elves are related to men in their physical aspect, but their spiritual existence is very different from that of human beings. Specifically, while men will die, and their fate after death is unknown even to the Valar, Elves are immortal in a special sense: though they can be killed or die of grief, they will continue to live as long as the world endures (Tolkien, *Letters* 236). Therefore, for the Elves, the passage of time and the ever changing nature of the world bring about a profound sadness. As noted in the previous chapter, Tolkien believed that human beings long for the unfallen world from which they have been exiled. This belief takes imaginative form in the Elves of Middle-earth, who represent the most refined aspects of humanity and who celebrate the beauty of Creation while at the same time lamenting what Galadriel calls "the long defeat."

As the Fellowship travels down the Anduin after their stay in Lothlórien, they reflect on the nature of time there. By Sam's reckoning, the phases of the moon do not match the number of days that the group abided there, and he wonders whether time itself is under the control of the Elves. As noted above, Frodo imagines Lothlórien as a vestige of the distant past. Sam and Frodo are correct in concluding that the nature of time itself has been affected by Elven magic, for Galadriel has maintained in Lothlórien a remnant of Middle-earth from its earliest ages, when the world was young. Elven enchantments, however, are not without their price. Only the Creator of time can change or stop it. He who created time also created the Elves and bound their lives to the world itself. The men of Númenor came to envy the Elves for their immortality because they did not understand that the death of the physical self is the gift of Ilúvatar to Men.

Legolas responds to Sam's and Frodo's postulations about Lothlórien by describing the burden that the Elves must bear. While time itself does not change, he explains, the Elves experience it differently from mortal beings in Middle-earth in that for them the flow of time is "both very swift and very slow. Swift, because they themselves change little, and all else fleets by: it is a grief to them. Slow, because they do not count the running years, not for themselves" (Tolkien, *The Fellowship of the Ring* 391). The Elves love the world created by Ilúvatar, who created and awoke them before all of the other races of Middle-earth. They therefore have, like Tom Bombadil, "a desire to understand it for its own sake" rather than as something to be exploited for their own benefit or as a means to achieve power (*Letters* 236). The Elves are immortal in the sense that even in the event of an unnatural death, their spirits do not leave the world: an Elf who is killed can either exist in disembodied form, or he or she can be born once more as a physical being. Bound to the world until its end, the Elves must witness and endure not only the inevitable effects of time, but "the malice and destruction" which is bound to occur in a fallen world (Tolkien, *Letters* 236). However, in the world of time, change must occur, and thus attempts to hold back the

FIVE. The World as Wasteland

forces of time are contrary the nature of the world as designed and created by God (Tolkien, *Letters* 236).

In the Elves' intense nostalgia for the ancient past of Middle-earth, Tolkien gives us one among several ways of engaging with the past. The truth that he imparts is that the attempt to arrest time is not the answer to our longing for an ideal past, whether real, as Eden in the Primary world, or, imagined, as Valinor in Tolkien's invented Secondary world. There cannot be a return to the past, either the feudal past that Clifford Chatterley imagines or the return to the future-past that William Morris imagines in *News from Nowhere*. Tolkien depicts this morbid clinging to the past in the character of Denethor, who is not trying to arrest time, as are the Elves, but who wants to turn back time, to go back to life as it was, for he will have it no other way.

Tolkien recognizes this longing for the past, and he sees its roots in the loss of Eden, the loss of pristine nature that sustained a human community that did not in any way seek to devour the world and turn it into a wasteland. Thus Tolkien explains that our whole nature is soaked in this sense of "sibb," that is, brotherhood (*Letters* 110). The Elves of Middle-earth are not trying to go back to the edenic world of the past; rather, they are trying to hold onto the last vestiges of it. Of course, this cannot be done with lasting success, because all things in the physical world must and will succumb to nature and time. Galadriel's ring, Nenya, gives her a power that neither Elves nor mortal men have. It is this power to preserve and protect that allows her to keep at bay the decay and degradation that time brings. The ruling ring, Sauron's One Ring, represents among other things the danger of machinery-as-magic that allows its owner to command a power or strength well beyond the individual's God-given ability. In contrast, the three rings made by Celembrimbor—Galadriel's Nenya, Gandalf's Narya, and Elrond's Vilya,—were made to preserve and protect the world. When the One Ring is destroyed, these three great rings lose their power; subsequently, Lothlórien, like all worldly creations, succumbs to the forces of nature and eventually fades away.

Driven by their longing for the idyllic world of the past, the Elves are vulnerable to the deceits of Sauron, who at the time of the making of the Three Rings of Power still retained a pleasing incarnate form. However, it is just those feelings of nostalgia that lead the Elves down a path that begins with good intentions but risks an inordinate desire for control, as in the case of Saruman. Thus it is only with the utmost forbearance that Galadriel is able to refuse the Ring when Frodo offers it freely to her. Galadriel knows that her ownership would begin with benevolent intentions, just as Gandalf had told Frodo that he would start with "the desire of strength to do good" (Tolkien, *The Fellowship of the Ring* 60). However, again like the wizard, Galadriel understands that the One Ring can work only evil, as its maker poured into it his desire to subjugate all wills to his own. She tells Frodo, "The evil that was devised long ago works on in many ways, whether Sauron himself stands or falls" (Tolkien, *The Fellowship of the Ring* 368).

In attempting to use the Ring, a kind of machine, to "actualize desire" with little effort and thereby more effectively continue what Tolkien called the "embalming" work of the Elves in Middle-earth, Galadriel herself would become a Dark Lord. She would be, she tells Frodo, as "beautiful and terrible as the Morning and the Night! Fair as the Sea and the Sun and the Snow upon the Mountain! Dreadful as the Storm and the Lightning! Stronger than the foundations of the earth. All shall love me and despair!" (Tolkien, *The Fellowship of the Ring* 368). In envisioning herself as the Lord of the Ring, Galadriel compares herself to powerful forces of nature, yet at the same time she would be stronger than those forces. As such, she would have corrupted her own nature far beyond the design of Ilúvatar, the All-father. This is, of course, the aim of the Ringmaker: to subvert the will and design of the Creator by usurping the power that belongs to Him alone.

Despite the great temptation to take the Ring even as a gift, Galadriel submits to ultimate Authority, accepting the reality that with the destruction of the Ring, "Lothlórien will fade, and the tides of Time will sweep it away" (Tolkien, *The Fellowship of the Ring* 368). In effect, she is at last accepting the natural order of the world, for all things must perish in time. For her selfless submission to God's will, Galadriel is forgiven the sins of her people during the time of the "kinslaying" in Valinor, and she is allowed to return to the Blessed realm, now only accessible by the Straight Road. Thus she tells Frodo, "I will diminish, and go into the West, and remain Galadriel" (Tolkien, *The Fellowship of the Ring* 368).

William Morris presents a similar theme of the temptation to use magic to subvert the laws of nature in his book, *The House of the Wolfings*, in which several Gothic tribes must come together under two leaders in order to protect their homeland against a massive and highly skilled Roman army. The leader of the house of the Wolfings, Thiodolf, accepts from his lover, Wood-Sun, an enchanted hauberk, a chain-mail shirt made by dwarves in ancient times. Wood-Sun, like Arwen Evenstar, is an immortal being in love with a mortal man. Through the gift of the hauberk, Wood-Sun hopes to protect Thiodolf from what seems to be inevitable death in battle. The armor does in fact protect the Wolfing war duke from death, but only at great cost to his honor as a warrior and to the men whom he commands. Three times during the fight against the Romans, just as his men look to him for leadership Thiodolf has a disturbing vision and subsequently faints. In each instance he is taken for dead by his men as well as the Romans, who are emboldened by the apparent demise of the Wolfing captain (Morris, *House of the Wolfings* 119,122). Thiodolf is ashamed to admit that he "blenched from the battle" (Morris, *House of the Wolfings* 121). He tells Wood-Sun of his shame after his third fall without an injury, when his mind finally clears after the evil enchantment of the hauberk. Thiodolf says, "'There then I sat ashamed among the men who had chosen me for their best man at the Holy Thing, and lo I was their worst!'" (Morris, *House of the Wolfings* 134). This is the first time in his life that Thiodolf felt ashamed of himself. In seeking to protect him from death, Wood-Sun is motivated by love for Thiodolf; however, her use of the magical hauberk represents an attempt to subvert the natural order of the world. In the process, the War-duke of the Wolfings becomes strange to himself: he is no longer a fearless leader. He abandons the values of his honor-bound society: courage in battle, self-sacrifice in the name of victory, and responsibility to his men and to his people, all of whom are fighting for nothing less than the survival of their homeland and their way of life. Thiodolf tells Wood-Sun: "And by then so evil was I grown that my very shame had fallen from me, and my will to die: nay, I longed to live, thou and I, and death seemed hateful to me, and deeds before death vain and foolish" (Morris, *House of the Wolfings* 135).

    The magical power of the hauberk, like the One Ring, seems to offer hope of victory to the wearer, who aims to use its power for good. However, like Sauron's Ring, the hauberk is evil, fashioned by the "dwarfs that hate mankind" (Morris, *House of the Wolfings* 134). When Thiodolf realizes that the hauberk is not beneficial but destructive, he casts it aside and thereby regains both his honor and his identity. He tells Wood-Sun, "'Therefore I will bear the Hauberk no more in battle; and belike my body but once more: so shall I have lived and death shall not have undone me'" (Morris, *House of the Wolfings* 135). In his refusal to use the enchanted hauberk, like the One Ring a kind of machine, Thiodolf overcomes the forces that would alienate him from his people and himself. Like Galadriel, he remains himself, and this ability to avoid the destabilization of one's identity has much to do with the ultimate victory achieved by both Morris' Wolfings and Tolkien's Alliance of the West.

Like the Wolfing Thiodolf, Galadriel, Gandalf, and Elrond, as keepers of the Three Rings, have made deliberate choices to restrain their power, especially in their refusal to take the Ring from Frodo, even for safekeeping. Since the One Ring embodies evil and the will to power, it will ultimately corrupt any who bear it. Apart from the prelapsarian Tom Bombadil, there are no unfallen beings in Middle-earth: it is, after all, as Tolkien explains, our world. "Malice," or evil, is part of the Whole Story of God's creation. In Middle-earth, it derives predominately from Sauron, whom Tolkien refers to as "Evil [in] a single dominant incarnate shape" (*Letters* 154), whose devastation of the land is part of the change that the Elves hold at bay. On their third day out of Lothlórien, the members of the Fellowship have their first sight of the wastelands of Middle-earth. The eastern banks of the Anduin have been damaged beyond repair: "brown and withered they looked, as if fire had passed over them, leaving no living blade of green: an unfriendly waste without even a broken tree or a bold stone to relieve the emptiness" (Tolkien, *The Fellowship of the Ring* 383). This landscape is antithetical to Lothlórien and Rivendell, and it demonstrates the danger of the Free Peoples of Middle-earth. If Sauron succeeds, the Elves will suffer more than feelings of loss and nostalgia: the whole of Middle-earth will be destroyed.

For all their piecing together of bits of the past, the modernists will return again and again to the grim belief that their world is a wasteland from which they can find no true escape. Rather, they must make the world over again. The currents of this world might carry us back into the past, as Fitzgerald suggests; as for tomorrow, however, as Connie Chatterley imagines it, "It is rather hard work: there is now no smooth

Five. The World as Wasteland

road into the future: but we go round, or scramble over the obstacles. We've got to live, no matter how many skies have fallen" (Lawrence, *Lady Chatterley's Lover* 3). Connie's metaphor of the "smooth road into the future" indicates the traditional belief that history progressed in a linear and progressive fashion. As noted, however, this belief was challenged by the intellectual atmosphere of the nineteenth and early twentieth centuries, and those ideas became operationalized largely by the First World War. Thus in the post-war world, one must "go round," in a recursive fashion, always, as Nick Carraway says, "borne back ceaselessly into the past" (Fitzgerald 189) in an effort to recover humanity's fractured story.

* * *

Readers of *The Lord of the Rings* are well aware that alongside its gardens, meadows, forests, and havens there are in Middle-earth many wasted landscapes. The once fertile gardens and stately monuments of North Ithilien have been defiled and desecrated by the Orcs of Mordor. Stinking vapors and fading sunlight loom over the watery cemetery that is the Dead Marshes, beyond which are the "arid moors" of the pathless Noman-lands, prelude to the utter waste of the Slag Mounds, the Morannon, and Mordor itself. Enclosed within the long arms of the Mountains of Shadow and the Ash Mountains are Udûn, literally hell on earth, and the Plateau of Gorgoroth, out of which protrude Barad-dûr, the Dark Tower, and Orodruin, Mount Doom. Across the great Anduin River, much of the primeval Fangorn forest has been hacked and hewn by Saruman's Orcs. So, too, have the pristine groves of Isengard been destroyed as the Wizard's Vale is converted into what is essentially a weapons factory.

Nan Curinir, the Wizard's Vale, was established by the Númenóreans (men who fought alongside the Elves against the Prime Dark Lord in the First Age and were therefore granted extraordinarily long life) long before Saruman came to occupy Orthanc, indeed, well before the Istari, or wizards, were sent to Middle-earth at the beginning of the Third Age. Before Saruman's time, the massive tower housed powerful and wise lords of Gondor, who kept watchful eyes on its Western borders. It was then a place of natural beauty: "Once it had been fair and green, and through it the Isen flowed … and all about it there had lain a pleasant, fertile land" (Tolkien, *The Two Towers* 558). By the time Gandalf returns with Théoden and their companies after the Battle at Helm's Deep, Isengard has been transformed into an industrial wasteland. Gone are the ordered "avenues" and the "groves of fruitful trees"; in their place "marched long lines of pillars, some of marble, some of copper and of iron, joined by heavy chains" (Tolkien, *The Two Towers* 559).

The hard stone and metal of the industrialized Isengard enclose a riotous disarray of invasive weeds and animals, punctuated by the remains of age-old trees. Although there are remnants of land still cultivated by the "slaves of Saruman," by the time of the War of the Ring, most of that lovely valley had been transformed into "a wilderness of weeds and thorns" (Tolkien, *The Two Towers* 558). Worst of all is the absence of trees, since many of the trees of Middle-earth are as alive and aware as any human being. The narrator explains that "among the rank grasses could still be seen the burned and axe-hewn stumps of ancient groves. It was a sad country, silent now but for the stony noise of quick waters" (Tolkien, *The Two Towers* 558). In a less dangerous past, plants and trees flourished under the care of the servants of Saruman; however, the time once given to the cultivation of plants is now devoted to the mass production of armor and weapons. Perhaps the most disturbing image in the passage recalls the violent burning and hacking of the "ancient groves" (Tolkien, *The Two Towers* 558). In Tolkien's Secondary world, such trees would have possessed a consciousness equivalent to that of human beings; to destroy them would be more than shameful: it would be murderous. This accounts for much of the feeling of pathos that the narrator inscribes on the landscape of industrial Isengard. What was once a self-contained community, with room for an agrarian lifestyle alongside the scholarly existence of the wizard in the tower, has become a microcosm of violent tyranny and enslavement. This indicates the depth of Saruman's fall, for though he began with good intentions, he succumbed to the danger of power: he came to desire power for its own sake, in the process destroying the land and enslaving others. The narrator points out in this passage that which Saruman, in his pride and self-delusion, cannot see: Isengard is "only a little copy, a child's model or slave's flattery" of Barad-dûr, the tower of Mordor, the most appalling wasteland of Middle-earth (Tolkien, *The Two Towers* 558).

The "smokes and steams" that hover about the barren circle of Isengard are evidence of the mass production of the weapons of war, as the wizard Saruman has forsaken his stewardship of all living things in Middle-earth in exchange for his Machiavellian allegiance to Mordor. In short, Saruman has paved paradise and put up a factory: "in the moonlight the Ring of Isengard looked like a graveyard of unquiet dead.... Iron wheels revolved there endlessly, and hammers thudded" (Tolkien, *The Two Towers* 559). Isengard has become a lurid place, Saruman a lord of darkness and machinery, who has created an underground world over which he holds dominion. However, this world does not possess the awesome beauty borne of magnificent craftsmanship that the Dwarves carved beneath the Misty Mountains. Rather, it recalls the suffocating underground world of "universal and constant darkness" which is the chosen home of the humanity-hating goblins of George MacDonald's *The Princess and the Goblin* (139). Of course, Saruman's underworld is far more sinister than that of the Goblin king in MacDonald's fairytale, but both point to the exploitation of the natural world and a hatred for the sunlit world of light and fellowship. The entrances to the underground factory of Saruman's war machine are capped in stone, and in the moonlight they appear to the viewer's eye as headstones. In this instance Tolkien, like many modernist writers, uses the image of the graveyard to underscore the passing of the pastoral world and the effects of industrialism and war on both humanity and nature.

In *The Lord of the Rings*, Tolkien speaks on behalf of nature in the face of such destruction, giving it a voice in characters such as Tom Bombadil, who embodies the spirit of the ever-diminishing rural landscape, and Treebeard the Ent, who is nearly as old as Middle-earth itself, and who curses Saruman for his treachery and murderous actions.

The trees that were destroyed under Saruman's direction were conscious beings, many of them well known to Treebeard, who, beneath his anger, is quite grief-stricken. He laments the loss of his friends as well as the loss of beauty when he says, "there are wastes of stump and bramble where once there were singing groves" (Tolkien, *The Two Towers* 472). In a letter to the *Daily Telegraph*, dated June 30, 1972, Tolkien objects to the phrase "Tolkien gloom" (quoted in *Letters* 420) used in the previous day's paper to describe the diminishing English countryside. He explains that in the world of the story, Fangorn Forest was ancient and sentient and therefore felt intense anger towards living beings such as men and wizards, especially since the latter, in the person of Saruman, was a menacing "machine-loving enemy" (Tolkien, *Letters* 420).

Similarly, Sauron, who is also the Necromancer of *The Hobbit*, feels only disdain and hatred for all living things. That the living things should strike back is a feature of fairy-story, in which trees can speak and walk and wage war against their enemies. Fantastic, yes, but true to the invented world of Middle-earth. In the author's subcreated world, Sauron, incarnate evil, is the Enemy, and the Ents, a Tolkienian invention whereby nature has self-awareness, are hostile to him as well as to Saruman. The mountain Caradhras, like Old Man Willow, on the other hand, is simply hostile to human beings and hobbits in general. As they attempt to cross the Misty Mountains, Aragorn tells his companions, "'There are many evil and unfriendly things in the world that have little love for those that go on two legs, and yet are not in league with Sauron'" (Tolkien, *The Fellowship of the Ring* 289). Aragorn's words echo Tolkien's implicit assertion that, were it possible, nature itself would be justifiably hostile toward humankind for its atrocities, including the making of wastelands. In the world of fairy-stories, nature is capable of such a response, and thus Old Man Willow ensnares the hobbits, Caradhras prevents the fellowship from crossing the pass, the Ents march on Isengard, and the huorns seemingly consume the entire surviving enemy army as it attempts to retreat from Helm's Deep. Were it not for age-old enchantments placed on the Tower of Orthanc, the Ents in their battle fury would have pulled it to pieces, thereby completely destroying Saruman's stronghold.

In his attempts to attain supremacy, Saruman deliberately and systematically stripped Isengard and converted it from an Edenic landscape to an industrialized stronghold. The destruction of Isengard, however, is child's play in comparison to the vast and irrevocable waste of Mordor, the work of ultimate evil on earth: Sauron. In the latter case the reader first sees the dead lands through the eyes of the Ringbearer. The land appears

> as if the mountains had vomited the filth of their entrails upon the lands about. High mounds of crushed and powdered rock, great cones of earth fire-blasted and poison-stained, stood like an obscene graveyard in endless rows, slowly revealed in the reluctant light.

Five. The World as Wasteland

> They had come to the desolation that lay before Mordor: the lasting monument to the dark labour of its slaves that should endure when all their purposes were made void: a land defiled, diseased beyond all healing—unless the Great Sea should enter in and wash it with oblivion. "I feel sick," said Sam. Frodo did not speak [Tolkien, *The Two Towers* 637].

In this passage Tolkien presents his version of the wasteland, a phenomenon especially endemic to the waning Third Age of Middle-earth as it gives way to the Fourth Age and the dominion of Men. So comprehensive is the destruction of the landscape that Sam's response is visceral, and Frodo seems unable or unwilling to articulate its impact on him. Like the modernists, Tolkien includes in his description images of sickness and death. Just as he likens Isengard to a graveyard, the narrator here describes the mounds of barren earth that call to mind a graveyard, an image often found in modernist depictions of the wasteland, particularly the valley of ashes of Fitzgerald's *The Great Gatsby*.

Despite these similarities, however, there is a profound difference between the wastelands of the modernists and those of Tolkien. For the former, wastelands are the result of the decimation of the Western world and western culture, in which, ostensibly, there is no spiritual center or foundation. In Tolkien's work, in contrast, God is always at the center of, though certainly not immediately present in, the world. Joseph Pearce explains that while the humane cultures of Middle-earth appear to be pagan, in a much more important sense they are Christian. Pearce argues that in the most significant sense for Tolkien, Middle-earth accords with Christian belief, even though the history of that world predates the advent of Christ and his teachings. Therefore, Pearce writes, "the God who is dimly discerned in Middle Earth is nonetheless the same God as the One worshipped by Tolkien himself. The God of Earth and the God of Middle Earth are One. This follows both logically and theologically from Tolkien's belief that his sub-created Secondary world was a reflection, or a glimpse, of the truth inherent in the Created Primary World" (*Man and Myth* 110).

Tolkien describes the desolation of Mordor as "the lasting monument to the dark labour of its slaves that should endure when all their purposes were made void." This is a typical example of the many subtle allusions to God in *The Lord of the Rings*: at the Great End of the Story, it is God who will make "void" all evil in the world. Tolkien kept such references obscure; nevertheless, as he explains, Middle-earth is meant to be "a monotheistic world of 'natural theology,'" although it lacks virtually all signs of organized religion (*Letters* 220). Another example occurs in the passage above when Tolkien writes that the land that lies before Mordor is "defiled, diseased beyond all healing—unless the Great Sea should enter in and wash it with oblivion." Again, this sentence in particular represents one of those places where Tolkien embedded his Christian beliefs in *The Lord of the Rings*, for it is only God who can refashion the world, submerging entire continents beneath the sea. Tolkien describes such events as "exceptions to all rules and ordinances which seem to crop up in the history of the Universe, and show the Finger of God," (*Letters* 204). In other words, in the invented world of Middle-earth, as in the real world, such miracles can and do occur.

Such an intervention by God takes place earlier in the history of Middle-earth when, in response to the Númenóreans' attempt to reach the Undying lands, the Valar lay down their authority and petition Eru Ilúvatar, the One All Father, to redress the breaking of the ban set upon Men. Tolkien explains that the Valar, as God's regents on earth and therefore lacking his power and authority, did not know how to address this astonishing act of "rebellion," so they asked God to intercede. Thus just as Ar-pharazôn, the king of Númenor, enters Valinor, he and his entire fleet are overwhelmed by a great wave, and Valinor itself is taken out of the world. Tolkien referred to this divine intervention as "a catastrophic 'change of plan'" (*Letters* 206), thereby confirming the notion that a providential order exists in the world of Middle-earth. The sinking of Númenor is a consequence of humanity's nature as fallen and their susceptibility to the guiles of Satanic evil, in this story represented by Sauron (Tolkien, *Letters* 154). Tolkien believed that any "story about Men" would have as one of its themes "a Ban, or Prohibition" (*Letters* 154). In his letters he often refers to Númenor as Atlantis and its downfall as an important precursor to the Third Age (Tolkien, *Letters* 213). The story derives in part from a recurring dream of the author of a great wave rising from the sea to submerge the land (Tolkien, *Letters* 361). Notably, Tolkien gave the dream to Faramir, the character with whom he most identified, and who descends from those Númenóreans faithful to Ilúvatar and the Valar. This group, under the leadership of Elendil, escaped in a manner similar to the Biblical Noah (Tolkien, *Letters* 206). Elendil and his sons

FIVE. *The World as Wasteland*

Anárion and Isildur went on to establish the kingdoms of Arnor in the North of Middle-earth and Gondor in the south.

The downfall of Númenor, as Tolkien notes, results from humanity's fallen nature. In their overweening pride and desire for ever more power and longevity of life, the Númenóreans believed the lies of Sauron. Specifically, Sauron convinced King Ar-pharazôn and his followers that they could acquire immortality by seizing the Blessed Realm from the Valar; however, according to the nature of Tolkien's imagined world, this is simply impossible. As Tolkien explains, Valinor is an earthly place that is blessed because angelic beings reside there; just abiding there would not transform a mortal being into an immortal one (*Letters* 205). Sauron, like Satan, the Father of Lies, uses deceit to convince King Ar-pharazôn and his followers to attempt to subvert the nature of their humanity by rebelling against divine authority. He convinces them that they can distort their nature, as he has distorted his own nature in his attempts to gain lordship over Middle-earth. It is a lordship that not even the Valar would claim, insofar as it would entail the subjugation of other free wills, for even Eru Ilúvatar himself does not subjugate wills to His own, but rather allows evil to exist.

This attempt to usurp the authority of God with the aim of dominating other free wills is the greatest sin of both Saruman and Sauron. Through their use of machinery, or dark magic, they would dehumanize and enslave others, in the process creating wastelands, to achieve power for themselves. Paul Kocher, in his book, *Master of Middle-earth: The Fiction of J.R.R. Tolkien,* addresses the damage caused by this will to power. "The people we master," Kocher writes, "become denatured of their humanity; and the process of enslaving them denatures us. In this way, as in others, evil is self-defeating. A Sauron who succeeded in making himself tyrant over all of Middle-earth would only be the slave of the slaves over whom he ruled" (66). Kocher's assertions point to the ultimate futility of enslavement, which represents the destabilization of identity and the ultimate instrumentality of individuals.

C.S. Lewis provides a similar example of such an extreme will to power in his book, *The Magician's Nephew*, the chronological first book of the Narnia series, and the story that explains the origins of the land of Narnia. Two children, Digory Kirke and Polly Plummer, are transported by magical rings created by Digory's uncle, the magician of the book's title, to "the wood between the worlds" (a concept itself that recalls William Morris' *The Wood Beyond the World*). This wood is a liminal place, a strange forest dotted with small pools that are revealed to be conduits to other worlds. With the recklessness of children, they jump into one of the pools and come out the other end to find themselves in an apparently deserted world. The children wander through a maze of lonely courtyards, which, the narrator explains, were once "magnificent places" (Lewis, *Magician's Nephew* 33). In one of these they find a great fountain in the shape of a winged monster. Lewis writes:

> Under it was a wide stone basin to hold the water; but it was as dry as a bone. In other places there were dry sticks of some sort of climbing plant which had wound itself round the pillars and helped to pull some of them down. But it had died long ago. And there were no ants or spiders or any of the other living things you expect to see in a ruin; and where the dry earth showed between the broken flagstones there was no grass or moss [*Magician's Nephew* 33].

This is the wasteland world of Charn, and its images are strikingly familiar: the emphasis on stoniness, specifically in relation to the absence of water, the transformation of cultivated nature into a wilderness of climbing plants that undo human attempts to create order and beauty, and the pronounced lack of any living thing, either plant or animal.

When they escape from the crumbling Hall of Images, Jadis, the White Witch of *The Lion, The Witch and the Wardrobe*, and the children emerge into the profound emptiness of a "vast city" (Lewis, *Magician's Nephew* 40). In the stillness of this once great metropolis, the children can see that "all the temples, towers, palaces, pyramids and bridges cast long, disastrous-looking shadows in the light that withered in the sun. Once a great river had flowed through the city, but the water had long since vanished, and there was now only a wide ditch of grey dust" (Lewis, *Magician's Nephew* 40). The postwar world of Charn is a literal wasteland, and it corresponds to the postwar wasteland which the modernists so often describe. Lewis' description of the ruins of Charn includes a catalog of the underpinnings of Western culture: religion, science, government, and monuments to the achievements of a society. A great people lived and flourished here once, but now in place of vitality and community the children find "disastrous-looking shadows" which make their surroundings seem ghostly and ominous. The desolation that was

FIVE. *The World as Wasteland*

once the vibrant world of Charn was created by its inhabitants in their inability to sustain a community of fellowship and their failed attempts at mastery over one another. In Lewis' novel, as in Tolkien's legendarium, the wasteland is often the result of an individual's will to power, in this case Jadis, and her use of dark magic, an analogue for machinery, which accelerates the process whereby power is achieved.

In *The Magician's Nephew*, Jadis uses the Deplorable World, just as Sauron uses the One Ring, in her attempts to dominate and enslave all other living beings. In her pride and supreme arrogance, Jadis literally destroys her home world, Charn. So myopic is her vision that she can perceive nothing but her own ambitious ends, which drive her to speak the "Deplorable Word." She tells Digory and Polly that the leaders of her race knew of the word and of the dark magic that "would destroy all living things except the one who spoke it. But the ancient kings were weak and soft-hearted and bound themselves and all who should come after them with great oaths never even to seek after the knowledge of that word" (Lewis, *Magician's Nephew* 60). Jadis scorns the "ancient kings" who understood that they were stewards of the world. They were morally bound to protect and preserve the world for future generations, and therefore they swore not to use the Deplorable Word. The word itself can be linked to Tolkien's conception of machinery as magic insofar as it endows its user with abilities far beyond the scope of her nature. In addition, as Tolkien explained, such magic could reduce labor nearly to the vanishing point.

By using the magical word, Jadis reduces the "work" of battle to no more than an utterance. She claims to have used such ancient and perilous magic as the last resort to win a war against her own sister. This is, of course, an absurdity, at the very least a paradox: in order to achieve supreme authority—for Lewis and Tolkien a way of taking a role reserved for God—human beings cause supreme destruction. What is left to Jadis but to escape to another world where she can exercise supreme authority? And in Narnia she accomplishes just that by once again arresting time, making it always winter, and by using her wand to transform creatures into stone. Moreover, by creating endless winter in Narnia, the White Witch has disrupted the cycles of nature and humanity's celebrations of those cycles which in turn are the cycles of life. In Narnia it is "always winter but never Christmas," and the long-ago woodland dances of the nymphs and fauns recalled by Mr. Tumnus are no more than the nostalgic longings of an enslaved people. In Middle Earth, Sauron would conduct his own sort of "freezing" of the world in time by leveling all of humanity in a state of slavery and further disrupting the cycles of nature by torturing the land itself.

Insofar as they prohibit growth and suspend the world and its inhabitants in a moment in time, wastelands represent disruptions in the life of the natural and the human world. They splinter the story that unfolds itself in the cycles of nature such as the emergence of flowers, the leafing out of trees, the swelling of rivers, the rains that fuel the growth of all living things. None of these things can happen in a wasteland world. Wastelands are also antithetical to identity- and life-affirming activities such as celebrations of marriage and birth, events which reinforce our shared humanity and the sense that our lives are connected to one another as well as to a time, a place, or a tradition. Without these rituals, it becomes more difficult to invest meaning in life, to feel that human beings are more than soft machines moving through space at a certain moment in time, a moment that exists on its own and will be forgotten as soon as it has passed. Wastelands, whether inventions of the modernists or of Oxford Christians such as Tolkien and Lewis, have this in common: they preclude the possibility for human connection through the process of renewal and celebration. Thus there is a fractured story in nature, just as there is a fractured story in culture and history. The world of nature and the world of humanity can never be completely divorced from one another: any wasteland signifies the degradation of both.

* * *

In Tolkien's world there will always be wastelands—the grass won't grow where the fell beast died (in contrast to Snowmane's grave, upon which flowers grow), and nothing will ever grow in the heart of Mordor. The wastelands we find in Tolkien and Lewis are cautionary tales about the effects of overweening pride and the uncontrolled will to power to which fallen humanity is so very susceptible. For the modernists, however, the wasteland *is* the world, not merely an aspect of it, and this leads them into a despair out of which they can never fully emerge. Tolkien depicts that despair, but he offers the reader hope as well. He addresses

FIVE. The World as Wasteland

this perhaps most explicitly through Sam as he steps away for a moment from the sleeping Frodo during the final stage of their tortuous journey. From the heart of Mordor's darkness, Sam looks at the night sky:

> There, peeping among the cloud-wrack above a dark tor high up in the mountains, Sam saw a white star twinkle for a while. The beauty of it smote his heart, as he looked up out of the forsaken land, and hope returned to him. For like a shaft, clear and cold, the thought pierced him that in the end the Shadow was only a small and passing thing: there was light and high beauty for ever beyond its reach. Now, for a moment, his own fate, and even his master's, ceased to trouble him [Tolkien, *The Return of the King* 932].

In the midst of the most dire circumstances that the hobbits have faced, Sam is blessed with an epiphany that confers on him an extraordinary sense of peace and calm, for he suddenly gains a new understanding of the relationship between good and evil.

Isolated from virtually all humane fellowship in the heart of a land ruined by evil, Sam realizes that the wasteland world of Sauron will not be the end, but rather just a part of the Whole Story. Ultimately, Sauron will fail because the power of Good is far greater than any other force in the universe. This is an extraordinarily long view, especially for a hobbit, and it helps to demonstrate the ennoblement of Tolkien's "everyman," Samwise Gamgee. Sam is graced with this vision because his has been a life of selfless service, immediately to Frodo, but by extension to all of Middle-earth. He has known intuitively all along what for Tolkien is absolute truth: the life of any individual, no matter his stature, is a small but profoundly significant part in the long story of human history. Sam achieves the "recovery" that Tolkien describes in "On-Fairy Stories." He is blessed with a transcendent vision that has a permanence that cannot be achieved in the world of Woolf's *To the Lighthouse* or Fitzgerald's *The Great Gatsby*, that is, the world of the modernists. Sam's vision endows him with an understanding of his place in the world as well as a proper perspective of the nature of evil. Any particular evil is transient: the great Story begun before Creation, the story of which the events of *The Lord of the Rings* are only a small part, will continue. For Tolkien, even in the heart of the wasteland, there is hope.

In the work of the modernists as well as that of Tolkien, one effect of industrialization is the transformation of the pastoral world into a wasteland. In the modernist wasteland individuals are barren on the inside; they can't recover, can't repair the world or themselves. In Tolkien's world, however, individuals do not demonstrate the sense that the world is fragmented. Rather, it is in great danger from machines and the individuals who use them to gain power over others and to achieve a kind of lordship to which they have no God-given right. Modernist writers offer little hope for recovery from the despair that haunts them. But in Tolkien there is more than the hope or the possibility of healing: there is real healing. It is no accident that Aragorn, the rightful king of Gondor, is a healer, nor that his Elvish name is Estel, "hope." Through him not only will individuals such as Éowyn and Faramir will be healed: it will be hope that restores humane community in Middle-earth.

Six

The Wasteland Within
Alienation in Tolkien and the Modernists

We have lingered in the chambers of the sea / By sea-girls wreathed with seaweed red and brown / Till human voices wake us, and we drown. In the closing lines from his 1915 poem "The Love Song of J. Alfred Prufrock" T.S. Eliot underscores an important modernist theme: individuals have become isolated, each person trapped within his own bubble of consciousness, his own perception of the world, so much so that connection with others—and therefore community—is impossible. In the world of the modernists, individuals are alienated from themselves and one another, and the wasteland that is modern society has its correlative in the interior self as well. Throughout the poem we see Prufrock's mind in conflict between the desire to connect with others and a paralyzing fear of connection.

T.S. Eliot's "Prufrock" was written just as the First World War fractured the history of Western culture, and it demonstrates the alienation and disaffection expressed by the modernists in general. Prufrock's world is already a kind of wasteland—the streets he imagines are lonely and sordid places where one finds only dirty restaurants and flophouses in which human connection is not life-affirming but debased:

> Let us go through certain half-deserted streets,
> The muttering retreats
> Of restless nights in one-night cheap hotels
> And sawdust restaurants with oyster-shells
> Streets that follow like a tedious argument
> Of insidious intent
> To lead you to an overwhelming question
>
> —[Eliot, "The Love Song of J. Alfred Prufrock" 130].

The speaker's analogy of the streets as "tedious arguments" suggests the failure of communication and foreshadows a central theme of the poem: the inability of the mind to move beyond itself to a place of genuine reciprocity with others. The streets of this emotionally bankrupt world seem to lead to an "overwhelming question," overwhelming because it implies engagement with the outside world. The question, however, is never posed; rather, the "tedious argument" leads only to a mundane remark: "Let us go and make our visit" (130). For Prufrock, something as simple as asking a question would disturb the universe because it would involve contact with other minds.

Eliot portrays Prufrock as being paralyzed with self-consciousness and worries about what other people must think of him. The better part of his concerns are superficial and insubstantial: he frets over his thinning hair, wonders if his appearance is refined yet not ostentatious, seems uncomfortable with his own body. As in much modernist literature, attempts at communication are frustrated, and genuine human sympathy is out of reach. Prufrock is constrained by the sense that, even at his most forthcoming, no one would understand, not even his lover. He imagines that even if he could project his essential being for the outside world to see, those other minds would not comprehend because, like Prufrock, they are sequestered within the prisons of their own perceptions.

Virginia Woolf's Clarissa Dalloway echoes this sentiment when she poses the rhetorical question, "Are we not all prisoners?" (Woolf, *Mrs. Dalloway* 293). Although she engages in a good deal of social activity, as does Eliot's Prufrock, her relationships remain as cursory and unfulfilling as his. Despite her efforts to connect with others, Clarissa lacks faith in the possibility of genuine human community. Woolf writes, "[d]espairing of human relationships (people were so difficult), she often went into her garden and got from her flowers a peace which men and women never gave her" (Woolf, *Mrs. Dalloway* 293–94). John Gardner's postmodern Grendel suffers from the same sense of alienation, the feeling that there is nothing that connects individuals. In Grendel's case, he imagines that the "creatures" in his cave are perhaps his own relatives, though they are "separate, isolated," each one existing in "his private, inviolable gloom" (Gardner 21). Both a literal and figurative outlander, Gardner's Grendel is unable to find fellowship, though he seeks it throughout his life.

"The Love Song of J. Alfred Prufrock" suggests that the inhabitants of the modern wasteland are disconnected, lonely, and suffering from feelings of restlessness and emptiness, despite their cocktail parties and their sophisticated conversation. Their comments are perfunctory: twice in the poem an anonymous speaker announces "In the room the women come and go / Talking of Michelangelo" (Eliot, "The Love Song of J. Alfred Prufrock" 130, 131). Clearly, one cannot maintain a conversation of any substance if one is busy wandering from one room to another in an effort to mingle aggressively. Prufrock laments:

> For I have known them all already, known them all—
> Have known the evenings, mornings, afternoons,
> I have measured out my life with coffee spoons
>
> —[Eliot, "The Love Song of J. Alfred Prufrock" 132].

Prufrock suffers from ennui, the refined boredom of his circle of cosmopolitan acquaintances. All of his attempts at human connection produce not enjoyment but hopeless fatigue. He recalls social visits that follow a prescribed social pattern in which people behave seemingly by rote, demonstrating neither genuine feeling nor originality of thought. As in much modernist literature, life as the speaker describes it is episodic, each moment followed by another but not connected to it in a coherent way. Individuals drink coffee, listen to music, talk absently of art, but they fail to make real connections with one another and the circumstances that surround them, the worth of which connections E.M. Forster portrays through the sensibility of Margaret Schlegel in *Howards End*. These parties and social calls are the scope of Prufrock's world, and as such they demonstrate his sense of hopelessness about human interaction, for all his own attempts at it are frustrated by his painful self-consciousness and fear.

So self-conscious is Prufrock, in fact, that his sensibility has split: he cannot help but view himself always from both the internal and the external perspectives, and the effort paralyzes him. Eliot portrays feelings of alienation and self-consciousness in Prufrock's preoccupation with small matters: his hair, his clothes, a piece of fruit. He moves from these banal thoughts to a romantic vision of mermaids on the tide of a windswept sea; however, in another jarring turn, the vision ends in despair. Prufrock's own image of himself is that of the claws of a crab moving about at the bottom of the ocean: "I should have been a pair of ragged claws / scuttling across the floors of silent seas" (Eliot, "The Love

Song of J. Alfred Prufrock" 133). Eliot's use of metonymy suggests that so fragmented is his psyche that Prufrock envisions himself as only the claws of the crab; indeed, in using the image of the claws, what Prufrock denies himself is nothing less than his own humanity. By his own reckoning, he is better fit to crawl along the ocean floor than even to exchange trivial comments with other socialites in a fashionable London flat.

Prufrock's is a world of barren social occasions which he describes as a series of fragmented and mundane images such as "the cups, the marmalade, the tea" and "the novels," "the teacups," and "the skirts that trail along the floor." Prufrock has known "[a]rms that are braceleted and white and bare" and again we see the use of metonymy: the women are shown only as "arms" and are thus, like Prufrock himself, fragmented and dehumanized. There is a weariness here as he repeatedly echoes phrases such as "I have known them all already" (Eliot, "The Love Song of J. Alfred Prufrock" 134, 132), as though he has seen everything that there is worth seeing until there is nothing left to see or know or talk about. Prufrock's emphatic loneliness and isolation are symptomatic of a much more profound anxiety and self-consciousness that is expressed in much of the literature of the early twentieth century.

Overall, "The Love Song of J. Alfred Prufrock" exhibits a sense of despair about the potential for genuine fellowship and community: any attempt to connect with another person, in Prufrock's case through a proposal of marriage, risks a rejection so profound that identity itself becomes unstable. At best we remain locked inside the prison of our own consciousness; at worst, we are overcome by a wave alienation and anxiety, as "human voices wake us, and we drown" (Eliot, "The Love Song of J. Alfred Prufrock" 135). The image of the drowned man recalls Phlebas, the Phoenician sailor from Eliot's poem, *The Waste Land*. It is also an image that Woolf's Septimus Smith invokes repeatedly, as he imagines himself as "a drowned sailor, on the shore of the world" (Woolf, *Mrs. Dalloway* 140). Convinced he has been "deserted," he transforms his alienation into something transcendent: "there was a luxury in it, an isolation full of sublimity; a freedom the attached can never know" (Woolf, *Mrs. Dalloway* 140). His sense of alienation in post-war society is so complete that he considers himself to be an "outcast" who exists "on the edge of the world" (Woolf, *Mrs. Dalloway* 140). Septimus, unable to form attachments after the extraordinary losses of his war experience,

Six. The Wasteland Within

retreats to the community of the dead, that is, to the liminal place inhabited by the ghosts of his dead comrades. Despite his pleasure in the natural world, Septimus will commit suicide in order to escape from the human community. The narrator explains that Septimus "did not want to die. Life was good. The sun hot. Only human beings—what did *they* want?" (Woolf, *Mrs. Dalloway* 226). Just as in Prufrock's world, connection with others is more than frightening: it is deadly.

In the world as wasteland, individuals find themselves isolated on several levels, often simultaneously. Modernist writers portray individuals who are alienated from their loved ones and, more generally, their communities. Tolkien, on the other hand, while depicting alienation, at the same time provides many examples of the fellowship and community that is so central to his faith. Of course, in *The Lord of the Rings* Tolkien gives the reader a literal and perhaps more striking portrayal of this internal alienation in the split personality of Sméagol/Gollum. However, it also appears, to lesser degrees, in characters such as Théoden, Boromir, and Denethor. In contrast to the modernists, whose characters tend to be more determined and fixed, for Tolkien's characters, the fragmentation and damage of the self or psyche is not irreparable. In his final moments, Denethor at least acknowledges his love for Faramir and the folly of his behavior towards his younger son. For Théoden and Boromir, recovery of the whole self, and thus healing, is achieved through service to others, ultimately by way of literal self-sacrifice. In Tolkien's world, redemption is possible. Even Gollum, who seems to be the most hopeless case, comes very close to a re-integration of his split psyche. Were it not for Sam's contempt at the very moment of his wavering, Gollum might have moved even nearer to the recovery of his own humanity. For Tolkien, then, alienation is a real danger: the outcome of pride, possessiveness, ambition, or despair; however, according to Tolkien's Christian epistemology, no individual, no matter how wretched, is beyond the reach of God's grace. In *The Lord of the Rings* "human voices," insofar as they represent fellowship and community, and individuals who act as "God's instruments" within His providential design, not only awaken but restore the world of Middle-earth.

* * *

While the modernist wasteland can be literal, depicted as a precise location such as Fitzgerald's valley of ashes or the desolate remnants of

Lawrence's Wragby Wood, it is always at the same time an abstraction insofar as the images work as a metaphor for society as a whole, as in the case of Eliot's *The Waste Land*. Nevertheless, whether portrayed as literal or figurative, concrete or abstract, for the modernists the wasteland always influences identity. Indeed, in some cases the wasteland is located not only outside of the self but within it as well. Modernist literature contains many examples of individuals who express feelings of alienation and loneliness, whether they are in a crowd, a gathering of acquaintances, or even in an intimate setting with those closest to them. Fitzgerald portrays this in *The Great Gatsby* in the character of Nick Carraway, who does not so much take part in life as watch it go by in what appears to him to be a lonely and meaningless manner. Nick, a Midwesterner is drawn to the mechanized feel of the city, "the constant flicker of men and women and machines." He confesses that at times he would construct a narrative about certain young women whom he had picked out of the crowd. In his mind he "followed them to their apartments on the corners of hidden streets, and they turned and smiled back" at him. Nick says, "At the enchanted metropolitan twilight I felt a haunting loneliness sometimes, and felt it in others—poor young clerks who loitered in front of windows waiting until it was time for a solitary restaurant dinner—young clerks in the dusk, wasting the most poignant moments of night and life (Fitzgerald 61–62). The vision that Fitzgerald presents through Nick's perception is bleak: the men and women are grouped with the machines, arguably because they themselves have become like machines, unaware of life's potential for beauty and meaning. The mood of the passage is at best wistful; there is nothing life affirming in it.

In *The Great Gatsby*, Fitzgerald in some ways responds to *The Waste Land*. In the passage above in particular Fitzgerald's words echo Eliot's depiction of human beings as isolated and robotic, cut off from their own humanity. The speaker of *The Waste Land* says:

> At the violet hour, when the eyes and back
> Turn upward from the desk, when the human engine
>   Waits
> Like a taxi throbbing waiting [Eliot 479].

Through his use of metonymy, Eliot underscores the dehumanization of individuals: the clerks are represented as "eyes and back"; human beings are referred to figuratively as "the human engine." In this manner,

Six. The Wasteland Within

the poem suggests that the mechanization of the twentieth century that helped to make a wasteland of the world encompasses individuals as well. The implicit suggestion of the instrumentality of the office workers follows the trajectory of Melville's warning against the loss of humane fellowship in "Bartleby the Scrivener."

Like the speakers of many of Robert Frost's poems, Fitzgerald's Nick Carraway projects his sense of rootlessness and isolation onto the landscape, in this case Manhattan at the end of the workday. As he wanders the streets of the crowded city, Nick observes others but does not take part in the human community there. Of course, it is Nick who wastes "the most poignant moments" of life, but he lacks the self-awareness to see how truly isolated he is. He is voyeuristic, watching others from a safe distance and merely imagining engagement with them. Nick, like Prufrock, is solipsistic, caught in the bubble of his own consciousness, never truly connecting with another human being; it is safer to remain isolated. Thus he breaks off his relationship with Jordan Baker, for whom he feels only an emotionally impoverished "sort of tender curiosity" (Fitzgerald 58). Nick's is a wasteland world characterized by sadness, separation, missed opportunity, and failed chances.

Virginia Woolf presents a very similar episode in her novel, *Mrs. Dalloway*, in which Peter Walsh follows an unknown woman throughout the heart of London. She seems to Peter "to shed veil after veil, until she became the very young woman he had always had in mind; young, but stately; merry, but discreet; black, but enchanting" (Woolf, *Mrs. Dalloway* 78–19). He imagines approaching her and receiving a positive greeting, and he narrates her thoughts and moods as he follows behind her along many streets. However, although Peter engages imaginatively with the anonymous young woman, he refrains from making any real connection. After the woman disappears into her home, Peter understands that the entire episode is nothing more than his own construct: "it was half made up, as he knew very well; invented, this escapade with the girl; made up, as one makes up the better part of life, he thought—making oneself up; making her up; creating an exquisite amusement, and something more. But odd it was, and quite true; all this one could never share—it smashed to atoms" (Woolf, *Mrs. Dalloway* 80–81). As does Nick Carraway, Peter builds a narrative around an image, and for him this takes the place of participation in any real human community. Unlike Nick, however, Peter is fully aware of the distinction between his invention and the real world in which the young woman exists, more than likely as a very ordinary person. While Peter purports to engage imaginatively with reality as a form of "exquisite amusement," like Nick and Prufrock, he is in danger of living in isolation within the fiction he himself has created. The real human community intrudes only momentarily with the memory of Clarissa's voice reminding him of her upcoming dinner party.

Like Nick and Prufrock, Peter is trapped within his own mental projections, which he can neither sustain nor bring to any sort of fruition: he cannot connect with the young woman, and he cannot share the experience with anyone else. The vision he invents, the story of himself meeting and interacting with the young woman, is ephemeral. His fiction has no substance in itself that can be carried forward into the world to enhance the human community; rather, this reality must be made up, moment by moment. So fragile is this invented reality that to share it would be to break it into fragments. In this way, the coherent vision that Peter has constructed becomes once again part of the chaotic experience that is the modern world. For the novel's reader, the young woman does not exist as a reality apart from his imagination. In inscribing his own meaning on the image of the anonymous girl, Peter erases her own identity, her agency. He has substituted his invention for the reality of the young woman, and in so doing has dehumanized her. However, this inscribing of reality via an act of imagination is Peter's way of coping in the post-war world. Like so many modernist characters, he lacks the ability to make a connection, so he protects his own fragile consciousness by keeping an emotional distance and constructing a private, unified reality that exists only within his own mind.

For the modernists, individuals have lost their humanity, the world lacks meaning, and there is no comfort to be found in community. Moments are strung together, lacking the coherence that would lend significance to personal experience. Lawrence portrays this sensibility in Connie Chatterley when he writes, "For Connie had adopted the standard of the young: what there was in the moment was everything. And moments followed one another without necessarily belonging to one another" (Lawrence, *Lady Chatterley's Lover* 17). So desolate has Connie's life become after the return of her wounded husband that she fixates on the idea of the "nothingness" of life. Early in the story the narrator describes her despair: "Nothingness! To accept the great nothingness of life seemed to be the one end of living. All the many busy and important little things that make up the grand sum-total of nothingness!" (Lawrence, *Lady Chatterley's Lover* 58). Lawrence's words recall Prufrock's sense of life as a series of banalities: the trappings of afternoon tea, books, women's clothing.

Much of modernist literature itself is paratactic, that is, episodes are set side by side without the rhetorical connections that would help the reader to make sense of the story of the novel or poem. In this way, writers attempted to mirror life as they knew it, as fragmented and incoherent. In Connie Chatterley Lawrence gives us the articulation of this feeling that Western culture has gone to bits, and it cannot be put back together again in any truly sufficient way. Connie's sense of disaffection is quite representative of the modernist sensibility. Lawrence writes, "All the great words, it seemed to Connie, were cancelled for her generation: love, joy, happiness, home, mother, father, husband, all these great dynamic words were half dead now, and dying from day to day.... It was as if the very material you were made of was cheap stuff, and was fraying out to nothing" (Lawrence, *Lady Chatterley's Lover* 66).

Connie speaks here not only for herself, but for the lost generation of post-war Europe and America. Her thoughts reflect the disenchantment that so many modernist writers express in their work. She is profoundly disappointed in everyday life, for none of her social or even familial relationships bring her any sense of fulfillment or satisfaction. Her husband, Clifford, scorns fathers, generals, and governments as being "ridiculous" because he has become disaffected with the patriarchal traditions of the past, though not with the ideal of patriarchy. For Lord and Lady Chatterley, the social and political systems of the past are useless. In their place is a "nothingness" so encompassing that identity itself becomes insubstantial, and individuals become wraith-like.

Fitzgerald's characters express this same feeling that the modern world and its inhabitants have nothing of substance to offer. When Nick Carraway first visits his cousin Daisy Buchanan in her opulent home on the North Shore of Long Island, he finds her in the company of the seemingly emotionless Jordan Baker. Insofar as their talk is superficial and without conviction, they are like Eliot's cocktail party women who talk in a perfunctory manner about great art. Among his recollections of his first dinner party at his cousin's home is the meaningless talk of Daisy and Jordan, which is marked by "a bantering inconsequence that was never quite chatter, that was as cool as their white dresses and their impersonal eyes in the absence of all desire" (Fitzgerald 16–17). Like Prufrock, the women are stylishly dressed, but their dress, like his, merely covers over an inner emptiness.

In Fitzgerald's post-war world, there is no comfort in community. Daisy and Jordan seem merely to be passing time; their conversation, like their lives, is aimless, random. Nick is at first captivated by his attractive and sophisticated cousin, but as she continues he soon realizes that her words are without meaning: "The instant her voice broke off, ceasing to compel my attention, my belief, I felt the basic insincerity of what she had said. It made me uneasy, as though the whole evening had been a trick of some sort to exact a contributory emotion from me" (Fitzgerald 22). Daisy says what is fashionable, not what she really believes in—if indeed she really believes in anything apart from her wealth and status. Lacking emotion herself, for her own amusement she hopes to evoke it in Nick. Like Prufrock, Daisy conveys the sense that she has done everything, seen everything, and there's nothing left in the world worth doing or seeing or learning. Physically, spiritually, and emotionally, the modern world is empty and meaningless.

In *The Great Gatsby*, Fitzgerald represents the modern world as a "valley of ashes," a shadow land in which nothing grows and men themselves appear to fade into indistinct ghostliness. The landscape helps to underscore the book's emphasis on modernist themes of loss, dislocation, and alienation. As the central characters of the story make their way through Queens to Manhattan, they must travel through a "desolate area of land." The narrator describes this monotonously grey and surrealistic world as

> a fantastic farm where ashes grow like wheat into ridges and hills and grotesque gardens, where ashes take the forms of houses and chimneys and rising smoke and finally, with a transcendent effort, of men who move dimly and already crumbling through the powdery air. Occasionally a line of grey cars crawls along an invisible track, gives out a ghastly creak and comes to rest, and immediately the ash-grey men swarm up with leaden spades and stir up an impenetrable cloud which screens their obscure operations from your sight [Fitzgerald 27].

Here, in a perverted fecundity, barren ash grows in a "grotesque" mockery of what is natural, alive, fertile, and life-sustaining. In this passage,

Six. The Wasteland Within

"fantastic" is an important word insofar as it suggests the surreal quality of the landscape in which the human connection and comfort of "houses and chimneys and rising smoke" is obscured and thus nullified under a blanket of ash. The track is "invisible"; the trains are real, but their motion is odd: they "crawl," slowing with a "ghastly creak" like ghosts in a graveyard. This is the world as the author sees it, for unlike Middle-earth, which, as noted, Tolkien meant to be our world in a distant and imaginary past, Fitzgerald's world is contemporary: it is not only the world of the novel, but the world of the author and his readers.

In depicting the valley of ashes, Fitzgerald takes the ordinary—trains, houses, people—and makes it extraordinary. He does this in order for the reader to see the world as he, the author, sees it, and the author ostensibly sees it as it is in truth: a wasteland. In his essay "On Fairy-stories," Tolkien argues that fairy stories help us to recover an understanding of the world and our place within it (77). In the valley of ashes passage of *The Great Gatsby*, Fitzgerald, arguably, is using what Tolkien called "creative fantasy" (the valley of ashes is a "fantastic farm") to express a truth underpinning the reality of his story: the modern wasteland is insubstantial, and its inhabitants are alienated and dehumanized.

Devoid of identity, the "ash-grey men" are devoid of will. They have become enslaved by twentieth-century mechanisms of progress. Their actions seem not of their own, and their movements are slow and mechanical, without meaning or purpose. In fact, they are not exactly men: they are insect-like, they "swarm," but their motions are heavy, laborious, as they work with "leaden spades." Both men and work are veiled behind "an impenetrable cloud" as the "crumbling" men labor at what appear to be meaningless and "obscure operations" which, Fitzgerald writes, are hidden from "your" view. By addressing the reader directly, Fitzgerald closes the rhetorical distance, thereby bringing the reader immediately into this fantastic world. Nowhere in this passage is there a sense of will or agency, neither in the men nor behind their surroundings. The depiction is of a literal shadowland distinct in its randomness. With "transcendent effort" the ashes become men, but the source of this transcendence is not identifiable, for there is no higher power here, either for good or evil.

The ash-grey men are shadowy, insubstantial, something twisted, and turned not toward the divine, but into something less than human, all the worse, all the sadder, because once human. This transformation is one of the costs of industrialization, itself driven by Victorian ideals of progress and the belief that machines would only improve society. As both Tolkien and William Morris before him note, however, the machines that human beings create to save themselves time and effort not only increase their labor but debase it as well, as people become more and more alienated from the objects that they take part in producing. The ash-grey men are one of the end results of "progress." Their devotion to machinery and their subsequent enslavement to it have stripped them of their humanity until, finally, they become little more than shadowy figures in the ash. They are, in fact, wraith-like.

In his book, *J.R.R. Tolkien: Author of the Century*, Tom Shippey describes the process whereby human beings become wraiths. He argues that people can become wraiths "as a result of a force from the outside" (*Author of the Century* 125). However, this loss of humanity usually starts from within the individual. According to Shippey, Tolkien's Ringwraiths were once men who may well have begun with good intentions when they took the gifts that Sauron offered them. In time, however, the means that they use to achieve those ends become less and less ethical. They begin, Shippey writes,

> to cut corners, to eliminate opponents, to believe in some "cause" which justifies everything they do. In the end the "cause," or the habits they have acquired while working for the "cause," destroys any moral sense and even any remaining humanity. The spectacle of the person "eaten up inside" by devotion to some abstraction has been so familiar throughout the twentieth century as to make the idea of the wraith, and the wraithing-process, horribly recognizable, in a way non-fantastic [*Author of the Century* 125].

The gifts that Sauron bestows are, of course, the Rings of Power that he used against the lords of Men in order to corrupt them and to subjugate their wills to his own. Each of these men, no matter what his original intentions, eventually came to value his own power above all else. Like the One Ring, each of the lesser rings is a kind of machine, for, as Tolkien explains in regard to magia, or magic, their purpose is in part to reduce to nearly nothing the space between thought and action (*Letters* 200). In taking the rings, the kings of Men hoped to achieve more power than possible with their own abilities, or, as Tolkien writes, their own "inner

Six. The Wasteland Within

powers or talents" (*Letters* 145). The machines of the twentieth century often serve this same purpose, much to the detriment of humanity.

Even the few examples provided here, including Eliot's Prufrock, Woolf's Septimus Smith, Lawrence's Connie Chatterley, Fitzgerald's Nick Carraway and the ash-grey men, underscore Shippey's assertion that twentieth-century literature is rife with wraiths. As they near Mordor, Gollum tells Frodo and Sam that if Sauron gets the Ring, "'He'll eat us all, if He gets it, eat all the world'" (Tolkien, *The Two Towers* 644). Here, Gollum astutely articulates the nature of evil as devouring, and the wretched creature does not mean simply that the Dark Lord will kill people. For even Gollum, or perhaps *especially* Gollum, whose identity has been devoured by the power of the Ring, knows that Sauron would torture the humanity out of every living being in Middle-earth.

Through the wraithing process, individuals become not only alienated, but so severely distorted that they appear to themselves or to others as something not only non-human but ugly as well. Both Eliot and Lawrence use the image of the crab to signify this damage to identity. Recall that Prufrock identifies himself with the claws of a crab crawling around the ocean floor. D.H. Lawrence uses this same image to express Clifford Chatterley's loss of humanity. When her husband settles into his role as an industrialist, Connie Chatterley realizes that since Clifford has undergone this appalling transformation of his nature from a man into a kind of "creature, with a hard, efficient shell of an exterior and a pulpy interior, one of the amazing crabs and lobsters of the modern, industrial and financial world, invertebrates of the crustacean order, with shells of steel, like machines, and inner bodies of soft pulp, Connie herself was really completely stranded" (Lawrence, *Lady Chatterley's Lover* 116). This metamorphosis is a kind of ruination, like the ruination of Western culture and the natural world, all for the sake of politics and progress, and the "machines" greatly facilitate the process.

In the course of becoming a creature, or wraith, Clifford alienates the person closest to him, leaving his wife "stranded." He wants her physically near, but he keeps her emotionally distant, such that Connie, too, becomes enslaved by the wraithing process that is stripping Clifford of his humanity. Lawrence writes, "The curious pulpy part of him, the emotional and humanly-individual part, depended on [Connie] with terror, like a child, almost like an idiot" (Lawrence, *Lady Chatterley's Lover* 117).

In Clifford Chatterley, Lawrence exemplifies the notion of the self as split through the effects of war, industrialization, greed, possessiveness, and the need to gain a measure of control in a rapidly changing world. Tolkien addresses this theme, making it fantastical in a way that is true to his fairy-story. However, the meaning is the same for both Tolkien and the modernists: the Sarumans, or planners, of the world are damaging it. Either under the banner of their egotism or the State or progress or business, their so-called improvements are destructive to both the human community and the natural world.

For the modernists, war and industrialism are in large part responsible for so distorting individuals that they are no longer whole human beings. As noted, D.H. Lawrence takes up at great length the notion that through industrialization not only is the land destroyed, but people are dehumanized as well. Sir Clifford hopes to restore the idealized England of the past with its entrenched class system of avuncular feudal lords and happily ignorant peasants. The narrative of England's past that he constructs lends dignity to human beings within a distinct patriarchal structure. The past that Connie imagines is just as idealized: "Merrie England! Shakespeare's England!" (Lawrence, Lady Chatterley's Lover 162). Connie, however, unlike her husband, sees clearly the ravages of industrialism. She reflects on post-war England and its working class and comes to the frightening conclusion that humanity has been fundamentally changed for the worse by industrialization. To Connie's mind, human beings in the twentieth century have become "half-corpses," and this is a condition that cannot foster community. Connie asks:

> How shall we understand the reactions in half-corpses? When Connie saw the great lorries full of steel-workers from Sheffield, weird, distorted, smallish beings like men, off for an excursion to Matlock, her bowels fainted and she thought: Ah, God, what has man done to man? What have the leaders of men been doing to their fellow-men? They have reduced them to less than humanness; and now there can be no fellowship any more! It is just a nightmare [Lawrence, *Lady Chatterley's Lover* 162].

Connie Chatterley's words echo the ubiquitous image of human beings as creatures or things: Owen's poisoned soldier, monstrous in his death agony; Eliot's Prufrock and Lawrence's own Sir Clifford, hard-shelled crustaceans; Fitzgerald's ash-grey men, insubstantial automatons;

Six. The Wasteland Within

and Woolf's Septimus Smith, caught in a liminal world where ghosts are more real than the living. These images are profoundly sad, and it is not surprising that they leave the reader, like Connie Chatterley, with a sense of hopelessness. The damage is widespread and seemingly beyond repair. More disturbing than the damage itself, however, is the source of the damage, for, as Connie laments, "Ah, God, what has man done to man?" The leaders of men have destroyed their followers, stripped them of their humanity and individuality so that they are, as Connie describes them, "half-corpses," neither dead nor alive but rather some monstrous combination of the two. Connie's shocking revelation comes full circle from Melville's narrator's poignant lament over the body of Bartleby, "Ah humanity!"

For the modernists as well as Tolkien, the effects of war and industrialization are devastating. The leaders of men, whom Tolkien referred to as planners, initiated and perpetuate this misery, distorting humanity in the name of nationalism and progress. The process amounts to a kind of domination in the name of good, in the guise of social, scientific, economic, or political advancement. Notably, Connie equates this new, postwar England as an "underworld," a hellish place. In Tolkien's Middle-earth we find the industrial and martial underworlds of Isengard and Mordor, inhabited by orcs, Uruk-hai, and Ringwraiths, all of them twisted, corrupted beings, all of them slaves of so-called leaders of men who would remake the world as they see fit. In their efforts to achieve power and control beyond their nature, however, these leaders, or improvers, run the risk of becoming slaves to their own desires and ambitions, in the process alienating themselves from both humane fellowship and divine grace.

To Tolkien's mind, virtually all human beings were *not* meant to exercise power over their fellows. Even the Valar self-limit their power so as not to exercise force against the free wills of others. This was, of course, Sauron's prime motive for making the Ring: to subjugate other wills to his own. Divine in origin, he could do far greater harm with the Ring than any mortal being could have done. Thus Gandalf, a divine being of the same stature as Sauron, refuses to take the Ring from Frodo, even to safeguard it. The wizard explains that because he himself is a powerful being, the Ring would have tremendous power and thus potential to do the greatest harm. It is clear that Gandalf has all along been keeping very careful control of his angelic powers, but the Ring would make it virtually impossible to continue such self-control. He is genuinely fearful of the loss of this ability when he tells Frodo, "Do not tempt me! For I do not wish to become like the Dark Lord himself. Yet the way of the Ring to my heart is by pity, pity for weakness and the desire of strength to do good. Do not tempt me!" (Tolkien, *The Fellowship of the Ring* 60–61). Even though he is an angelic being, Gandalf, like all the peoples of Middle-earth, is subject to temptation and corruption. He may even to fall to darkness, as does Saruman.

It is notable that the wizard twice warns Frodo not to tempt him by offering him the Ring. Quite possibly he is warning not only Frodo, but himself, against the potential danger of a wizard's possession of the Ring. Gandalf understands the limitations of his power, and he knows exactly where his vulnerability lies: in pity and compassion. In Tolkien's subcreated world of Middle-earth, the ability to inform one's choices and actions with feelings of pity and compassion is among the highest virtues. However, so evil is Sauron's Ring that it has the power to contort virtue to such an extreme extent that even the goodness of a kind wizard would be turned to evil. Gandalf knows that his kind intentions of helping the most vulnerable inhabitants of Middle-earth, the hobbits, would ultimately end in his mastery over them. Such would be the nature of Gandalf's fall: to dominate and enslave those whom he was charged by the Valar to protect.

Gandalf will not fall, but Saruman will. Blinded by his pride, Saruman cannot see that the Ring would turn him into another dark lord. He would become something foreign to himself, alienated from the self he once was: a messenger sent from the Valar, God's Regents of Middle-earth, to assist its free people in their struggle against the evil brought into the world by Morgoth, whose work was taken up by Sauron. The process whereby the Ring transforms goodness into evil is a dehumanizing one. Gandalf knows this. He knows that through the power of the Ring he would become a monster, a corruption of himself. In a most profound and shocking transformation, the Ring would cause Gandalf to lose his identity, to lose his connection to all that is good, and to the "human" communities of Middle-earth. This is the terrifying disease of the One Ring: it robs its wearer of his very self. As his actions in Moria prove, Gandalf is willing to sacrifice himself for the greater good, but

Six. The Wasteland Within

he does not want to contort his essential nature into evil; rather, he will use the power that divine Authority conferred upon him and nothing more. The One Ring represents a form of dark magic that would reduce the wizard's labor and his risk to almost nil; however, the cost of such an expedited achievement is the soul of the individual who wears the Ring. Gandalf is keenly aware that the Ring would corrupt his nature so thoroughly that he, like Sauron and Saruman, would eventually become completely alienated from all that is good, in the end becoming unrecognizable even to himself.

In one of his many wartime letters to his son Christopher, Tolkien explains that no person was meant to dominate others, since our natures were not designed for it. He notes that those most fit to lead are often those who do not seek leadership positions (Tolkien, *Letters* 64). In other words, the best leaders are those who do not seek leadership for its own sake. Thus Aragorn first appears as Strider, a dignified but humble leader who places the welfare of others above his own needs and desires. Tolkien's conception of power stems from his sense of the world as literally created and overseen by God, who is author of "the Story" that is both human history and, more generally, the history of all of Creation. Rightful power over human beings belongs only to God; any power that human beings possess, including the power to create, is derivative from Him. For Tolkien, understanding this larger perspective makes sense of our place within the great Story that begins and ends with God. In *The Lord of the Rings* characters who lack this understanding fall subject to their less noble impulses and thereby abuse the derivative power they possess. Even wizards are prone to this folly. In Saruman, most notably, Tolkien demonstrates the devastating effects of power on individuals and communities.

Saruman begins with good intentions but is ultimately overcome by his own pride and sense of importance. He distorts his nature as a Maiar, an angelic spirit of a lesser order than the Valar yet on a par with Gandalf and Sauron (himself a Maiar in origin). Saruman has become alienated from the Valar, from the good folk of Middle-earth, and, most sadly, from the benevolent being he once was. He has become, as Treebeard implies, a machine. The Ent is well aware, perhaps more than anyone else, that Saruman has transformed himself into one of the monsters of Middle-earth. He tells Gandalf, "He is plotting to become a Power.

He has a mind of metal and wheels; and he does not care for growing things, except as far as they serve him for the moment" (Tolkien, *The Two Towers* 476). Treebeard's account of Saruman's behavior suggests that although the wizard appeared friendly and solicitous towards the Ents, he had the ulterior motive of learning information that would be useful to him in his schemes to gain mastery. The desire to dominate others is immoral in itself; that Saruman dissembles, pretending to care for the caretakers of the trees as a way of discovering their mysteries in order to harm them later, adds yet another layer of evil to his nature. Saruman's lack of reciprocity in gathering information from Treebeard but offering none of his own in return signifies his disdain for others. He has no interest in community building, nor does he seek to cultivate relationships with others that would extend beyond his own use of those individuals as instruments by which he can accomplish his own goals. His refusal to take part in the "human" community of Middle-earth is one aspect of Saruman's transformation into a robot, or machine, and Treebeard's words hit the mark when he says that the wizard "has a mind of metal and wheels."

Saruman the Wise succumbs to folly when he forgets the task which the Valar appointed to him—to aid in the struggle against Sauron—and seeks to increase his own power. In essence, he seeks to achieve a degree of control that far exceeds the authority granted to him by the Powers that oversee Middle-earth. When Gandalf seeks his counsel regarding the Ring, Saruman tries to convince him that the Black writing of Mordor is on the wall, and there is no use in trying to blot it out. Rather, they two wizards should appear to join Sauron so that they may someday overthrow him. In his overweening pride, Saruman cannot recognize the absurdity of his argument. He tells Gandalf that going over to Sauron's side, which he believes to be the winning side, would be "wise" and in fact is their only hope.

Even though Sauron is supremely evil, Saruman believes he can have a measure of control over the power of the Ring and in time overcome the Dark Lord himself. He tells Gandalf that as "the Wise," the two great wizards "can keep our thoughts in our hearts, deploring maybe evils done by the way, but approving the high and ultimate purpose.... There need not be, there would not be, any real change in our designs, only in our means" (Tolkien, *The Fellowship of the Ring* 260). In the pas-

Six. The Wasteland Within

sage, Saruman repeatedly uses the word "wise," as though he knows and understands the present circumstances of Middle-earth better than others and is thus better fit to rule, to guide the course of the future. Improvers and planners begin this way: convinced that they are superior in knowledge and wisdom, they feel justified in claiming a measure of authority and control beyond that which they could achieve through their own talents and abilities. Saruman's promise to Gandalf that one day they may "control" the growing power of Sauron underscores this point. Thus in this regard as well Treebeard is exactly correct: Saruman is plotting to become a power.

Saruman's manner of speaking and the import of his words are Machiavellian in the worst sense: while he purports to have the good of Middle-earth in mind, it is obvious that Saruman above all seeks power and control. This is perhaps his greatest sin, for, as Tolkien explains, in regard to the stories of Middle-earth, "'power' is an ominous and sinister word" unless it is associated with the Valar (*Letters* 152). Thus Gandalf chides Saruman for speaking in the manner of "'emissaries sent from Mordor'" (Tolkien, *The Fellowship of the Ring* 260). Gandalf's words are particularly apt, since the Istari, or wizards, were sent as emissaries from Valinor, home of the divine regents of Middle-earth, to aid in the struggle against Sauron. Implicitly, Gandalf thus indicates how deeply alienated Saruman has become, particularly insofar as he has chosen a path similar to Sauron's.

In his pride, Saruman has lost sight of his original purpose in becoming incarnate, a purpose antithetical to the coercion or control of other wills. He presumes to vie with Sauron and promises to share the power of the Ring with Gandalf, though, as the latter tells him, only one individual can wield the Ring. Clearly, Saruman, a master rhetorician, is distorting the truth. Perhaps, alternatively, he has so perverted his own nature, so alienated himself from the community of the benevolent Valar and the good peoples of Middle-earth, that he actually believes his own rhetorical constructions. Gandalf, however, is wise enough to understand the true meaning of Saruman's words, which gloss over the terrible details of waging war, in the process enslaving or killing other sentient beings and irreparably damaging the world.

In a 1956 letter, Tolkien defines "wizard" as "an angelos or messenger from the Valar or Rulers" (*Letters* 237). He goes on to explain that

Gandalf's purpose in Middle-earth, like that of the four other wizards, is to help its people in their struggle against Sauron. In his subcreated cosmos, Tolkien explains, any power exercised over others without their freely given consent is evil. Therefore, the wizards, who are essentially spiritual beings, took on the physical attributes of humankind and subsequently were subject to all the same potential physical and emotional frailties. This means that they, like all others, were capable of committing sins, even of "falling." Tolkien goes on to explain that this would most likely occur through the corruption of genuine care for others, as their method of helping would be transformed from encouragement to coercion. In the end, they would use any means, even unethical ones, to accomplish the ends they sought. This was the weakness that Saruman could not rise above, though Gandalf, through obedience to the will of God, was able to overcome such temptation. However, even though Gandalf's choices were consistently good, Saruman's folly brought about far greater challenges and hardships, including the temporary loss of Gandalf, for the Fellowship than if the great wizard had applied wisdom rather than pride in coping with the growing power of Sauron (*Letters* 237).

This is precisely Saruman's problem: his greatest desire is control, and this folly he compounds through his proud refusal to accept compassion from those whom he considers inferior. When Gandalf offers him the chance to leave behind "folly and evil" and be of service in the fight against Sauron, Saruman becomes livid, accusing Gandalf of wanting the very things that he himself has long sought to gain: the power of the kings of men and of all the wizards combined (*The Two Towers* 587). Gandalf understands that Saruman cannot abide taking direction from another and that he will settle for nothing less than a position of authority. Gandalf, in contrast, has no desire to control others. When Pippin asks him what he will do with the broken Saruman, Gandalf replies, "'I will do nothing to him. *I do not wish for mastery*'" (Tolkien, *The Two Towers* 588, emphasis added). Gandalf wishes only to do what he and the other wizards were sent to Middle-earth to accomplish: to fight Sauron by inspiring and encouraging others to strive against the Enemy, and fighting Sauron means saving all that lives and grows peacefully within its own sphere and in its own time.

In contrast to Saruman, who regards himself as wiser and thus more

Six. The Wasteland Within

fit to rule than any other being in Middle-earth, Gandalf maintains his humility and follows his appointed path even to the point of his own physical destruction. As an exemplary leader, Gandalf at all times puts the welfare of his community, the community of the free folk of Middle-earth, above his own. Like Saruman, Gandalf is capable of falling into any degree of temptation, including what Tolkien described as the "absolute Satanic rebellion" of Morgoth and Sauron (*Letters* 202). However, Gandalf's selflessness and devotion to the greater good prevents this. Tolkien explains that only Gandalf succeeds in avoiding this temptation, especially because he sacrifices himself to save the Fellowship at the Bridge of Khazâd-dûm, since he did not know what would become of himself if his body should perish in the struggle against the Balrog, itself a fallen spirit once of the same rank as the wizards. Gandalf's sacrifice is especially great: although he was far more powerful than his companions, his self-sacrifice called for a more profound surrender, which Tolkien described as a "humbling and abnegation of himself in conformity to 'the Rules'" (*Letters* 202–03). Tolkien explains that Gandalf's fall at the Bridge of Khazâd-dûm is providential, and it is in accordance with providential design because the messengers of the Valar, the wizards, could not overcome Sauron nor even stay his power (*Letters* 202–03).

Just as the rebellion of the Númenóreans was too great for even the power of the Valar, the menace of Sauron was too great for their emissaries. In the case of the breaking of the Ban that prohibited the men of Westernessee from setting foot on the Blessed Land, the Valar lay down their power and looked to God. Similarly, in the deadly confrontation with the demonic Balrog, Gandalf, in an act of supreme faith and selflessness, puts himself in God's hands. Indeed, when he stands face to face with the Balrog, who embodies hellfire, "flame of Udûn," Gandalf invokes the divine light that brought Creation itself to life. Armed with the power of the Imperishable Flame, he challenges the demon, crying, "'I am a servant of the Secret Fire'" (Tolkien, *The Fellowship of the Ring* 331). In both cases, God, or "Authority" intercedes in the world he has created. In short, Gandalf's return is a miracle. In a deliberate contrast to Saruman, Tolkien writes, "Gandalf sacrificed himself, was accepted, and enhanced, and returned" (*Letters* 202–03). Tolkien goes on to explain that the plan to send the Istari to Middle-earth was devised by the Valar, but at the precise moment when that plan fails with the fall of Gandalf in Moria, a miracle occurs whereby death itself is turned back. Gandalf tells his companions that he was sent back, but the question every reader asks is, *by whom*? Tolkien answers this question in the draft of a letter written in 1954 by explaining that it was "Authority" who interceded, not the Valar, "whose business is only with this embodied world and its time; for [Gandalf] passed 'out of thought and time'" (*Letters* 203).

In the letter draft, Tolkien is very clear in pointing out that Gandalf is one of God's instruments for the benefit of humankind. Eight years later, in the summer of 1962 Tolkien told the historian and writer Edmund Fuller that the wizard is indeed an angel. Fuller, in his essay, "The Lord of the Hobbits," writes that Tolkien explained to him that Gandalf "had voluntarily accepted incarnation to wage the battle against Sauron. Gandalf the Grey does indeed die in the mortal flesh in the encounter with the Balrog in the Mines of Moria. Gandalf the White, who returns, is the angel in the incorruptible body of resurrection" (Fuller 29). According to Fuller, Tolkien emphasized Gandalf's self-abnegation: by protecting the Fellowship from the Balrog, a demon from the dark past of Middle-earth, the wizard puts himself into God's hands. In doing so, Gandalf demonstrates a profound faith and a complete submission to the will of God, whom Tolkien refers to as "Authority."

As Tolkien notes, wizards, like men, can be tempted, and both Saruman and Gandalf are tested. Saruman is tempted by the vision of absolute power and control, and he falls. Thus when his physical being is destroyed, his spirit looks to the West, to the home of the Valar. The divine regents of Middle-earth, however, reject this silent plea, and the long process of Saruman's alienation is complete. When he can no longer abide the degradations of servitude, Gríma Wormtongue, himself dehumanized and instrumentalized by Saruman, murders his master. After which Frodo and the others stand by in amazement as "about the body of Saruman a grey mist gathered, and rising slowly to a great height like smoke from a fire, as a pale shrouded figure it loomed over the Hill. For a moment it wavered, looking to the West; but out of the West came a cold wind, and it bent away, and with a sigh dissolved into nothing" (Tolkien, *The Return of the King* 1032). The death of Saruman is significant largely for what it lacks: dignity, nobility, and honor. To Boromir and Théoden Tolkien gave the most honorable death of the pagan war-

Six. The Wasteland Within

rior on the field of battle. To Gandalf he gave a Christ-like journey of sacrificial death, the harrowing of the underworld, and a glorified resurrection. After his struggle with the Balrog, Gandalf is taken up by "Authority" and given even greater power before being sent back into the world of time to more effectively fight against Sauron.

Saruman's death is a striking contrast to all of these: he is grabbed from behind to have his throat slit by a "worm," the literary analogue for the snake and the dragon, both traditionally associated with evil. Saruman's alienation is thorough and complete: by the end of his earthly existence he has isolated himself from the other wizards, from the Ents, whom he had once befriended, from the people of Middle-earth, from spiritual beings of his own kind, the Maiar and the Valar, from even the servant closest to him, Gríma Wormtongue. In what might be a moment of regret and contrition, the remnant of goodness left of his spirit looks to Valinor. However, having rejected all of Gandalf's attempts to bring him back into the humane community of Middle-earth, he is beyond redemption. Finally, with a cold wind from the West, the shadow of Saruman's being dissolves into nothingness.

Tolkien explained that in contrast to Saruman, Gandalf "fully passes the tests," (*Letters* 202–03), and thus he is sent back to join the community of Middle-earth with greater power and authority, though he sought neither. He sought only to follow to the best of his ability the path that Authority had placed before him. In other words, he accepted his place within the Great Story that is God's providence. Gandalf's angelic nature is especially evident in his regard for Gollum, whose identity has been completely destabilized by the One Ring. He is also an extreme example of the damage of instrumentality, since the Ring, insofar as it has an agency of its own via Sauron's will, uses Gollum as a vehicle by which it can return to the Dark Lord.

Gandalf lives by the principle that nothing is bad in the beginning, and individuals must strive for redemption, for themselves or for others. They must do this for the sake of that remnant of goodness that remains in an individual, since all were created by Ilúvatar. For nothing that God created can be evil; rather it becomes evil, just as the orcs were once elves whose nature became corrupted through the influence or torture of the Prime Dark Lord. Gandalf believes in the possibility of redemption for Gollum, and in his typical nondirective way, he helps Frodo to have compassion for others, even if they appear to be monstrous, as Gollum certainly does. In reference to Bilbo's encounter with Gollum and their playing the riddle game, the wizard tells Frodo: "'Even Gollum was not wholly ruined. He had proved tougher than even one of the Wise might have guessed—as a hobbit might. There was a little corner of his mind that was still his own, and light came through it, as through a chink in the dark: light out of the past" (Tolkien, *The Fellowship of the Ring* 54). Among other things, this passage signifies Tolkien's belief in the possibility of redemption. Gandalf believes that there is still some good left in Gollum, as he is, like all beings in Middle-earth, part of God's Creation. Despite the almost complete corruption of his nature by the Ring, there exists a remnant of his past self that long ago abided in a world where kindness and the simple joys of nature were valued. Tolkien represents this goodness and innocence as light, and the evil and corruption of the world as darkness.

Gollum is alienated in the most extreme sense from the community that once nurtured him, a community insulated and silently protected from the corruption and evil, or "darkness," of the world by the Rangers of the North, descendants of the great and long-lived men of Númenor. That darkness is analogous to the "outer darkness" that surrounds the mead hall in Bede's story of the brief flight of the sparrow: it represents those forces that are hostile to and threaten the human community. For Tolkien, the light is more powerful. It is the light that shines through and around the Elf lord Glorfindel at the Ford of Bruinen. It is the light that Gandalf wields against the Balrog on the Bridge of Khazâd-dûm, the Flame Imperishable that kindled Creation into life, which is also the light of the White Wizard's ring, Narya, so powerful that it repels the Nazgul above the Pellenor field before the gates of Minas Tirith. It is the light of Galadriel's phial that guides Frodo in the infernal darkness of Mordor. Whether that light comes from a ring or water that has captured the light of a star that was once a Silmaril, or, indeed, from another plane of existence shining through an Elf warrior, it is the light of Divine Love, and nothing in Middle-earth is more powerful.

In connecting Gollum to the light, as tenuous as that connection may be, Gandalf holds out the possibility for redemption, even for Gollum, whose psyche has been so profoundly damaged by the One Ring. Far from seeing Gollum as merely an instrument for delivering the Ring

Six. The Wasteland Within

into the hands of the Good, Gandalf looks upon Gollum the creature and at the same time is able to see Sméagol the hobbit. He hopes that the evil part of Gollum can be overcome, that Sméagol can be healed. What could bring about the cure? In the world of Middle-earth, the answer is compassion, kindness, mercy, and also fellowship. In the little community made up of Frodo, Sam, and himself, and even in spite of Sam's mistrust of and dislike of him, Gollum finds the beginning of the antidote to his loneliness, alienation, and misery. Gollum has truly suffered, not only from the corrupting power of the Ring, but far more from his enslavement by "the Precious." The Ring has tremendous power to dominate its wearer to the point where he no longer has free will. This is a crucial aspect of Gollum's misery: he no longer "owns" himself. He has become de-humanized, perhaps more precisely, de-hobbitized, to the point where he is no longer even recognizable as a hobbit. Like the Grendel of the Anglo-Saxon poem, he is cut off from all humane fellowship. Like John Gardner's twentieth-century Grendel, there is a measure of humanity in the monster, some part of him that longs for companionship, some part of him to which others can relate. Gollum, unlike both the poetic and the novelistic Grendel, is able to communicate with others. This enables Frodo, Sam, and him to establish a community based on a shared past, however remote in time.

Gollum achieved what both versions of Grendel could not: he found companionship, however briefly and however clouded by suspicion and evil circumstances. In addition to his own ability to communicate, Gollum's brief possibility for redemption derives largely from Frodo's ability to feel compassion for and kinship with him, which in turn enables Frodo to feel pity for and therefore show mercy to Gollum. Frodo is able to "only connect." He makes the connection between himself and Sméagol/Gollum as part of the hobbit (and therefore humane) community. Memory is at work here as well. Gollum is able to remember a time of innocence and happiness, and Frodo is able to make the imaginative connection from Gollum back to Sméagol. In other words, there is a humane shared past which informs his understanding of Gollum. Sam, who is not graced with the perceptive acuity of Frodo, is unable to make the imaginative connection that would see Gollum as anything but a monster.

In the process of his journey, Frodo has gained the wisdom to understand that as part of God's creation, Gollum could not have been evil in origin. Frodo finally comes to truly understand what Gandalf told him long ago as they first talked of the Ring amidst the comfort of Bagend: Gollum's story is part of the Whole Story, and no one can know what that is except for the Author of that story. The hobbit's part, therefore, was to follow his appointed path and strive to make all of his choices on the basis of kindness, compassion, and a sense of fellowship towards others.

Between Gollum and Frodo there is a flicker of something that only begins to approach friendship, for there is an affinity between the two. This is partly because they are both hobbits, and partly because they both possessed the Ring for a time. As Gandalf well knows, no one but Sauron can truly possess the Ring; rather, the Ring possesses the wearer. Nevertheless, Frodo has compassion for Gollum because Frodo is a compassionate person to begin with, especially once he sees Gollum and how wretched he is. Perhaps more importantly, Frodo must at some level realize that there but for the grace of God goes he. In her book, "Splintered Light: Logos and Language in Tolkien's World," Verlyn Flieger interprets Gollum as the darker aspect of Frodo's psyche. Flieger argues that Frodo's physical journey is at the same time a psychological one which forces him to confront the monster of his own subconscious mind. For Frodo, Gollum is "that Grendel-like prowler in the wilderness of the psyche that Jung called the Shadow ... the emblem of Frodo's growing division from himself, a division that we do not see in its entirety until the final moment at the Cracks of Doom" (Flieger 151).

It is, as Tolkien says, only by grace—not blind chance—that Gollum attacks Frodo at the very moment when Frodo's resolve finally and completely crumbles. Tolkien once wrote that he was very interested in that part of the Lord's Prayer that says "lead us not into temptation, but deliver us from evil" (*Letters* 233). Frodo's path in life did lead him to temptation, and it was more than he could overcome; however, in the manner in which events unfold, God, or "Authority," delivered the tortured hobbit from evil. Gollum acts as God's instrument when he bites off Frodo's finger and falls with the evil Ring into the fires of Mount Doom. Gandalf apprehends the possibility of such moments of grace happening in the temporal world, which is why very early on he tells Frodo not to act as Gollum's judge, jury, and executioner.

Six. The Wasteland Within

For his part, Gollum has followed to the bitter end the trajectory of possession of the Ring. First, he slowly lost his free will as the power of the One Ring enslaved him to the point where he cared about nothing else but possessing it. Next, he slowly lost his sanity as his consciousness divided itself into two distinct beings: Sméagol, who once lived in the world of light and humane community, and Gollum, who hated all of nature's lights: sunlight, moonlight, and starlight. He hated them so much, in fact, that they caused him physical pain. Finally, he lost his identity as the Gollum-creature part of his psyche finally won out over the Sméagol-hobbit part. In other words, the murderous, treacherous part won out over the part that still retained a scrap of goodness, the part that still followed an ethical code: don't cheat at the riddle game, don't break a vow (in this case to obey the Master of the Precious), and don't commit an act of cruelty against a person who has been kind to you (again, Frodo). Even very close to the end of his life, the Sméagol part of Gollum is capable of making moral choices and abiding by those choices. In the end, like Frodo, he fails on a personal level. However, the events at Mount Doom ultimately work for the benefit of the Good in the providential world of Middle-earth.

Seven

Postmodern Monsters and Providential Plans

"The world is all pointless accident." These words are spoken by the main character of John Gardner's postmodern novel, *Grendel*, which tells the Beowulf story from the monster's point of view. Throughout the story, the monster struggles to make sense of his world, to find some kind of order within the universe, but his efforts are repeatedly undermined by his own cynicism. As Barry Fawcett and Elizabeth Jones argue in "The Twelve Traps in John Gardner's *Grendel*," throughout the novel the monster suffers from this internal conflict between "reason and faith" (634) as he confronts the central values of Western culture, specifically: life itself, nurturing love, the artistic ideal, society, knowledge, heroism, self-sacrificial love, loyalty, organized religion, hope, and, finally, fellowship. These ideals suggest a stable center of Western Culture, and many of them extend back to its beginnings. Taken together or individually, such values provide human beings with a sense of purpose and place in the universe, and each shows humanity's ability to make imaginative connections. They are in fact the traditional beliefs that much modernist literature rejects. Notably, each one signifies generosity towards others in some way; each involves the individual consciousness reaching beyond itself to make a connection with others. As Fawcett and Jones write, Grendel "insists that he is caught up in a meaningless cycle of life and death, yet he longs for meaning" (636). Therefore the monster tries out, so to speak, all of these values only to reject each one of them in its turn.

Gardner's Grendel is incapable of adopting any of the Western ideals that he confronts because the world that he inhabits is a wasteland, like the modernist wasteland, in which spring brings with it pain rather

SEVEN. Postmodern Monsters and Providential Plans

than the promise of new life. The reader sees this world from the monster's perspective: Grendel says, "The sun spins mindlessly overhead, the shadows lengthen and shorten as if by plan. Small birds, with a high-pitched yelp, lay eggs. The tender grasses peek up, innocent yellow, through the ground: the children of the dead" (Gardner 7). The imagery that Grendel uses is profoundly disturbing. The birds lay eggs, which suggests rebirth, renewal, and the cycles of life, but the monster emphasizes pain: the birds "yelp." Grendel perceives spring's earliest blooms as menacing: "startling tiny jaws of crocuses snap at the late winter sun like the heads of baby watersnakes" (Gardner 7). In this way, he classifies the flowers with the creatures that inhabit the watery darkness that surrounds the subterranean cave where he lives with his mother, another monster of the outer darkness. For Grendel the cycles of nature are "mindless," happening only "*as if* by plan," thereby signifying his belief that nature is chaotic and indifferent to humanity (emphasis added). The young grass is fed by the mulch where he once murdered people, where blood sank into the ground to feed vegetation on gruesomeness.

The memory of the murderous acts that he committed in this place reminds Grendel of his constant sense of self-loathing and despair. Like that of Eliot's Prufrock, his sensibility has splintered such that he sees himself simultaneously as both the viewer and the viewed. However, Grendel's response to the vision of himself is even more destabilizing to his identity than Prufrock's insecurity and alienation. This is because Grendel's sense of his own identity is in a constant state of flux. At this moment, in the context of April, which the speaker of T.S. Eliot's *The Waste Land* described as "the cruelest month," Grendel characterizes his own identity as absurd, and the universe as marked by randomness. He views himself as a "pointless, ridiculous monster crouched in the shadows, stinking of dead men, murdered children, martyred cows" (Gardner 6). Grendel can find no reference point by which he can define himself and his actions. Although he makes several attempts to do so throughout the novel, he can neither rise above his own cynicism and faithlessness nor make sense of the universe and his place within it. When he looks to the night sky, he is unable to find transcendence; rather, he perceives only "the cold mechanics of the stars" (Gardner 9).

Gardner's postmodern Grendel has inherited the post-war wasteland world of Yeats, Eliot, Woolf, Lawrence, and Fitzgerald, among others. The intensity of his own existential crisis, arguably, surpasses that of any of the anguished characters of modern literature, even Eliot's Prufrock. Moreover, Grendel cannot apprehend even for a fleeting moment a glimpse of transcendence, as is described, for example, in Woolf's *To the Lighthouse*. Though he makes several attempts to communicate with others, including Hrothgar's thanes, these efforts always end in failure. While he does manage to get his point across to Unferth, the brother-killer, the monster's fragmented exchange with the dishonored warrior serves only to mock and abuse the thane. Grendel refuses to be defined as the enemy who gave Unferth the opportunity to win back his honor: he will not give Unferth the glorious death in battle that the shamed man seeks. The postmodern Grendel rejects the ancient warrior code by which Boromir recovered his identity after it had been destabilized by the One Ring. John Gardner's postmodern Beowulf confronts the monster with this very same set of beliefs, but Grendel again rejects these values. Persistent in his belief that the Geat warrior is insane, Grendel refuses to accept his role as the monster of the outer darkness. In all of these instances, Grendel is unable to follow E.M. Forster's imperative to "only connect." For Gardner's Grendel, there is only the isolation of the self in a universe of chance.

Rather than finding any inherent order in the universe, Grendel regards himself as the reference point from which he constructs order moment by moment. He thinks, "Space hurls outward, falconswift, mounting like an irreversible injustice, a final disease. The cold night air is reality at last: indifferent to me as a stone face carved on a high cliff wall to show that the world is abandoned" (Gardner 9). The first image that Grendel uses in this statement recalls Yeats' "Second Coming," which opens with the image of an outward-moving spiral, emphasizing the phenomenon of objects moving away from a once-stable center. Gardner's use of the word "falconswift" recalls Yeats' image of the falcon unable to hear his master, thereby suggesting a breakdown in communication and order.

In Grendel's perception of it, reality, or, the universe, is marked most significantly by indifference to individuals: little flowers grow where murders have taken place, the sun appears to robotically rise and set day after day, and the stars are merely mechanical. In Grendel's universe, there is no God to tell the sun to rise each day, nor is there any-

SEVEN. *Postmodern Monsters and Providential Plans*

thing significant or romantic about the stars. They represent nothing beyond themselves, either in terms of their creation or any ancient stories about them or shapes one might see within them, such as the signs of the zodiac. They do not even suggest the half-life image that Prufrock projects on them when the night sky appears to him as "a patient etherized upon a table" (Eliot 130). Grendel's assertion that the world has been "abandoned" signifies that at one time he believed, or perhaps hoped, that there was some kind of supernatural power behind the world. This is a belief, however, that the monster is unable to sustain.

In his youth, Grendel understood the world in the most fundamental manner: objects were either "mother" or "not-mother." Without her, the world around him was simply chaos; upon her appearance, all objects would "snap into position around her, sane again, well organized" (Gardner 19). However, in her absence, anything could potentially become the focal point of his self-made reality. In one instance, a threatening bull suddenly becomes the center of the universe, as "the world snapped into position around him" (Gardner 19). Grendel manages to outsmart and thus survive the bull's repeated attacks. This confrontation with the bull gives rise to Grendel's epiphany that any apparent order in the universe is nothing more than a construct. Grendel expresses this more profound awareness when he tells the reader that he understands that the world is nothing more than "a mechanical chaos of casual, brute enmity on which we stupidly impose our hopes and fears. I understood that, finally and absolutely, I alone exist. All the rest, I saw, is merely what pushes me, or what I push against, blindly—as blindly as all that is not myself pushes back. I create the whole universe, blink by blink.—An ugly god pitifully dying in a tree!" (Gardner 21–22). In the world that Grendel inhabits, the center of the universe is constantly shifting, from himself to his mother to a bull, for example. Such instability contributes to the monster's sense of dislocation and alienation. To Grendel's mind, the universe is indifferent at best and hostile at worst. As the Dragon's nihilistic reasoning makes clear, there is no divine plan, no God who orders the universe and all that happens within it; there is only "God as the history of Chance" (Gardner 65, 74).

The question as to whether or not there is a transcendent power that supports human existence is one that is endemic to twentieth-century literature, but it is a question that Tolkien's literature never poses, since for him there absolutely was order within the universe. Providence is at work throughout *The Lord of the Rings*, but its presence is so subtle that we might miss it on a first reading. In a letter written in 1954, Tolkien explains that he carefully omitted explicit references to the divine elements of the legendarium that figure in the story of *The Lord of The Rings*. However, there are in the story many oblique references to Tolkien's correlatives for God and angels. For example, the Valar and Valinor are referenced by several characters, including Gandalf when he tells Frodo that there was a force at work when Bilbo found the Ring, as well as, Tolkien writes, "Faramir's Númenorean grace" in Ithilien (*Letters* 201). Another reference to Valinor occurs when Galadriel overcomes the temptation to accept the Ring when Frodo offers it to her in Lothlórien. In doing so, she redeems herself from the sin of her people who committed kinslaying as they left Valinor ages before. She says, more to herself than to Frodo and Sam that she will become less powerful and then "go into the West" (Tolkien, *The Fellowship of the Ring* 368). In another example, after the scouring of the Shire when Saruman is murdered by his servant, Gríma Wormtongue, the wizard's spirit is rejected by the divine Valar. Finally, and obviously, Gandalf's return from death is a powerful indicator that the hand of God is at work in Middle-earth.

Early on in *The Lord of the Rings*, it is clear that beyond the everyday world there is a power that has a hand in bringing about specific events. These events might at first seem insignificant, but taken together they represent a substantial chain of causal links that all lead up to the story's climax at Mount Doom. Indeed, at that moment several causal chains converge on Frodo. The first link, of course, as far as hobbits are concerned, occurs sixty years prior to the start of the tale when Bilbo lays his hand on the One Ring in the deeps of the Misty Mountains. This circumstance is, as Gandalf tells Frodo, "the strangest event in the whole history of the Ring so far: Bilbo's arrival at just that time, and putting his hand on it, blindly, in the dark" (Tolkien, *The Fellowship of the Ring* 55). Of course, if we trace the chain back to its beginning, we would find ourselves at the moment of Creation, ages before Sauron forged the One Ring, before the Valar descended into the world, indeed before time itself when the disharmonic music of Melko, the brightest of Ilúvatar's angels, brought evil into the world, before Eru Ilúvatar gave reality to

SEVEN. *Postmodern Monsters and Providential Plans*

the vision elaborated in the music of the Ainur, the highest ranking angels of Tolkien's cosmology (Tolkien, *The Silmarillion* 4, 6–8).

When recounting the story of Bilbo's acquisition of the Ring, the narrator refers three times to the hobbit's "luck," but, after all, it only appears to be luck. Bilbo's finding the Ring "*seemed* then like *mere luck*"; he wins the riddle game "*more by luck (as it seemed)* than by wits (Tolkien, *The Fellowship of the Ring* 11, emphasis added). When Bilbo realizes that Gollum means to kill him, the narrator tells us that Bilbo flees in the nick of time and is again, "*saved by his luck*" (Tolkien, *The Fellowship of the Ring* 12, emphasis added). Although the narrator's final use of the word "luck" is not qualified as it is in the first two instances, the point is clear: the events surrounding the transfer of the One Ring from Gollum to Bilbo are not happenstance. "Mere luck" signifies a lack of purpose or design behind events, just chance if even against tremendous odds. In retrospect, it is clear that some agency beyond that of the Ring itself, which can expand and contract and thereby release itself from its temporary "owner," is at work. Decades later, after Gandalf explains to him the nature of the Ring, Frodo asks the crucial question as to how such an object of power, so greatly coveted by the one who made it, should come to such a person as himself Gandalf responds without doubt, even if a bit cryptically: "There was more than one power at work, Frodo ... beyond any design of the Ring-maker.... Bilbo was *meant* to find the Ring, and not by its maker. In which case you also were *meant* to have it" (Tolkien, *The Fellowship of the Ring* 55, emphasis added).

Though Gandalf never speaks explicitly about Divine Authority or his relationship to it, he clearly puts his in faith in a benevolent providence. His remarks help to demonstrate that there is in Middle-earth a transcendent force that sustains life and gives meaning to existence. Paul Kocher explains that, although some characters in *The Lord of the Rings*, such as Gandalf and Aragorn, may have premonitions about forthcoming outcomes and events, they can never know with any certainty what the future will bring. Kocher notes that only God, "the One who plans it," can possess such knowledge; however, this does not mean that the actions of human beings are not of their own choosing. This is evident, for example, in Bilbo's deliberate choice not to kill Gollum, a choice which, Kocher points out, "is genuinely free, and only after it has been made is it woven into the guiding scheme. Tolkien leaves it at that. Human (or hobbitic or elvish or dwarfish or entish) free will coexists with a providential order and promotes this order, not frustrates it" (Kocher 36). To Gandalf's mind, there is intentionality behind Bilbo's acquisition of the Ring, quite apart from its attempts to make its way back to Sauron. The Ring, which has agency insofar as it magically embodies the will of its maker, fails in its attempts to return to Mordor. This is one indication that for Tolkien, in both the real Primary and his own invented Secondary world, there is no question that there is a design of goodness and light, and it is more powerful than any design of darkness. The world that is Middle-earth is decidedly not, as Gardner's Grendel asserts, "pointless accident" (32).

* * *

In much modernist and postmodernist writing, there is a sense that human beings are adrift in a world of random forces, that there is no divine or transcendent order within the universe that supports and makes sense of human existence. Therefore, many modernist writers sought to impose an order of their own construction on what they perceived to be a fragmented and chaotic world. Wallace Stevens, for example, makes such an attempt in his poem "Anecdote of the Jar," in which the speaker simply sets a jar on a nameless hill in Tennessee. The result of this simple human act is a temporary triumph over chaotic nature, as the landscape organizes itself in reference to the jar, which has a distinct shape of its own. The effect of the speaker's placing the homely object amid "the slovenly wilderness" (Stevens 3) is to create a kind of order and control over nature, whereby the jar, a human-made artifact, becomes the focal point of the landscape. Modernist literature often portrays nature as undoing human attempts to order and thereby make sense of it. Frost describes this impulse and its inevitable failure in his poem "The Woodpile," in which we find the speaker wandering through a swamp frozen over by winter's cold.

Modernist writers often place individuals in various social settings so as to highlight personal alienation within the larger scope of society. The worlds of J. Alfred Prufrock, Septimus Smith, and Nick Carraway, for example, show the individual's feelings of dislocation and disorientation in the cosmopolitan post-war world. The poet Robert Frost, on

Seven. Postmodern Monsters and Providential Plans

the other hand, tends to set his speakers against natural landscapes and thereby cast nature as "other," something distinctly outside of the self which, like community in the wasteland, brings little or no comfort to the individual. In Frost's poetry, as in Eliot and Lawrence, for example, traditional notions of nature as restorative are undercut, and nature itself comes to represent the indifference of the universe to the lives of human beings. In Frost's poems, individuals seek comfort in nature, but they are rather more likely to see there reflected back at them their own sense of the randomness of the universe and are thereby affirmed in their loneliness and isolation. Frost gives us, then, the private wasteland: the emptiness within.

On the surface, the landscapes of Frost's poetry generally appear to be peaceful and serene—at least they seem traditionally pastoral, but on a deeper level those comforting images of nature are often only a facade. While his speakers inhabit pastoral settings, what they often see there is a projection of their own loneliness and despair. What they tell us is not that they are in union with nature but that they are cut off from it, as well as from their families, their communities, even themselves, just as are the husband and wife in "Home Burial." As one often finds in Frost's poetry, the speaker in "The Wood-Pile" is attracted to the wilderness. He finds himself in the midst of a snowy wasteland; however, rather than turning back toward home, the speaker decides, on second thought, to continue. Once there he feels alone, and there is barely a human element in this part of the woods. As in Eliot's *The Waste Land*, nature is inhospitable: the snow in some places caves in beneath his feet, and the denuded trees growing in lines around him demonstrate a disorienting sameness that leaves him with a feeling of dislocation. While there seems to be a natural order in the swamp—the trees grow in rows—this order is of no comfort to the speaker because the vastness and sameness of the scene overwhelm him. The swamp is a kind of no-man's land, and the speaker becomes part of the vast nothingness that surrounds him.

Someone has been in this desolate place, however, and has left behind a testament to human attempts to control nature and create order in the form of a long abandoned woodpile. The woodpile helps the speaker to feel for a moment less isolated, somehow connected to humanity through the efforts of the anonymous laborer. Another person has inserted himself, however remotely, into the landscape. In addition, there is a sense of imposed order in the carefully arranged and measured stack of firewood, though no home will ever be warmed and no family comforted by it. His initial sense of order humanizes the experience for the speaker, yet the order created by human beings is tenuous: it will eventually break down completely through the overriding forces of time and decay. In this way the poem conveys a sense of the futility of man's efforts to order or control nature. The clematis vine and tree are taking over, while the manmade supports are crumbling. Frost's poem therefore implies that the power and effect of human beings seems but slight in comparison to the slow but constant, often destructive, workings of nature.

In "The Wood-pile," Frost suggests that humanity's attempts to control nature will ultimately fail; moreover, there is no appeal to a force beyond nature, that is, God, to make sense of the wilderness. Humanity exists only in the moment, which is evident because the creator of the woodpile for some reason simply left it there to rot. The speaker tries to make sense of what appears to him to be a great waste of energy and care. He reasons that only

> Someone who lived in turning to fresh tasks
> Could so forget his handiwork on which
> He spent himself, the labour of his axe,
> And leave it there far from a useful fireplace
> To warm the frozen swamp as best it could
> With the slow smokeless burning of decay" [Frost 134–35].

Despite the speaker's imaginative connection with his predecessor in the frozen swamp both the poem's speaker and the person he imagines as having built the woodpile exist in isolation. Someone labored in this place and left behind a trace of himself, but the message he leaves behind is one of the futility of human effort. Nowhere in the poem is there an indication that these two moments in time, the past of the builder and the present of the wanderer, are part of a transcendent or providential order that could demonstrate any sort of cause and effect between them. Frost's poem, then, provides another example of the impulse in modernist literature to construct reality moment by moment without necessarily linking those moments together. As Woolf writes, the experience becomes atomized. It does not fit into any larger, coherent pattern.

For the lost generation, the citizens of the wasteland, individuals

SEVEN. *Postmodern Monsters and Providential Plans*

are subject to random forces with no design or meaning behind them. Though they may look for order, they are more likely to suffer from disillusionment or confusion. For example, in Virginia Woolf's novel, *Mrs. Dalloway*, Septimus Smith, trapped in the prison of his shell-shocked psyche and unable to differentiate the real from the imaginary, confuses skywriting over London with a transcendent message. His ineffectual doctor had told Rezia, Septimus' wife, to encourage her husband to "take an interest in things outside himself" (Woolf, *Mrs. Dalloway* 31), so she and Septimus visit The Regent's Park. While they sit side by side on a park bench, a plane flies by overhead, slowly making letter shapes. Various people visiting the park try to decipher the letters, and Rezia, desperate to bring Septimus out of his disturbing interior world, calls to her husband to look at the writing in the sky.

Lost in the world of the past that is ever-present in his mind, Septimus interprets the whole episode as pertaining quite specifically to himself. He thinks that he is being sent a message by some transcendent power, or powers. The language is unreadable, but he reasons that this is because it is mystical. Despite its unreadability, Septimus understands the sublimity of the message. The transcendence that he perceives in it affects him in a way that nothing in the world any longer can. Septimus is enraptured by the ethereal letters

> melting in the sky and bestowing upon him in the inexhaustible charity and laughing goodness one shape after another of unimaginable beauty and signalling their intention to provide him, for nothing, for ever, for looking merely, with beauty, more beauty! Tears ran down his cheeks.
> It was toffee; they were advertising toffee nursemaid told Rezia. Together they began to spell t ... o ... f ... [Woolf, *Mrs. Dalloway* 31].

Who is signaling to Septimus? Whom does he mean by "they?" In his search for evidence of a providential order that would give meaning to his wartime experiences and suffering, Septimus ascribes transcendent meaning to the vapor-letters in the sky. For him the letters are the gift of divine benevolence, a sublime vision of "unimaginable beauty" which he has done nothing to earn. His interpretation of the letters as a gift is significant because most of the time Septimus feels unworthy. He suffers from, among other things, terrible survivor's guilt, especially in regard to the death of his friend and captain, Evans, whom he could not save.

In his profound alienation from civilian society, Septimus projects onto the skywriting the acceptance and sense of peace that has been driven out of his mind by his horrific experiences on the front lines of battle in France. From the mystical letters, his sublime vision spreads to include all of the everyday details around him: the trees, the leaves, the birds, the bench on which he sits, and even his own body. All of these things become in his consciousness part of a unified whole. For Septimus, the entire scene becomes something deliberately and serenely organized. He thinks, "Sounds made harmonies with premeditation; the spaces between them were as significant as sounds. A child cried. Rightly far away a horn sounded. All taken together meant the birth of a new religion" (Woolf, *Mrs. Dalloway* 33). Unable after this war experiences to move forward in the real world, Septimus constructs a reality that connects even minor physical details of nature, seen and unseen, with the world of humanity. Significantly, his invented world encompasses Septimus so completely that his vision becomes metaphysical, investing meaning in the "spaces between" and creating an order so effective that sounds may be judged as "rightly" and therefore following some kind of fixed and determined rules.

Taken together, these elements work in harmony with one another to become a "new religion," something to live by when all else has failed him. This is Septimus' attempt to heal himself, since clearly modern medicine in the persons of Dr. Holmes and Dr. Bradshaw of Harley Street, is failing him on every level. In fact, Septimus comes to equate them with inhumanity. Tragically, Septimus' physicians fail to recognize that there is anything legitimately wrong with him. He soon comes to identify them as the enemy. Woolf writes, "Dr. Holmes seemed to stand for something horrible to [Septimus]. 'Human nature,' he called him" (Woolf, *Mrs. Dalloway* 213). Trapped within the psychological trauma of his battlefield experiences, Septimus feels he must escape from the cruelty of men like Dr. Holmes, and he is convinced that the only way he can finally do so is to let himself fall out of the window as the doctor angrily approaches him.

Septimus Smith's fear and suspicion of other people, like his strange interpretation of the skywriting over The Regent's Park, provide an example of the modernist sensibility that in the post-war world, our vision, or perception of and therefore engagement with, the world has become alarmingly distorted. Fitzgerald expresses this notion in *The*

SEVEN. *Postmodern Monsters and Providential Plans*

Great Gatsby in the character of George Wilson, the husband of Tom Buchanan's mistress. After his wife, Myrtle, is killed by Daisy Buchanan's recklessness while driving Gatsby's car, Wilson is inconsolable. He confesses to Michaelis that he told his wife that "she couldn't fool God." As he looks out over the valley of ashes, he recalls his words to Myrtle:

> "—and I said 'God knows what you've been doing, everything you've been doing. You may fool me but you can't fool God!'"
> Standing behind him Michaelis saw with a shock that he was looking at the eyes of Doctor T.J. Eckleburg which had just emerged pale and enormous from the dissolving night.
> "God sees everything," repeated Wilson.
> "That's an advertisement," Michaelis assured him [Fitzgerald 167].

In his depiction of the world as wasteland, Fitzgerald expresses the loss of faith in part as a kind of confusion. So distorted has his vision become that Wilson, in his despair over his wife's infidelity and death, has come to believe that the image on the billboard rising up from the barren landscape is God. In this respect, Wilson is similar to Septimus Smith: in their trauma each man interprets an advertisement to be a transcendent message. Each man attempts to inscribe order on the world around him, though both men are no longer able to engage in the reality of a post-war world. In what appears to be an indictment of the ubiquity of capitalism's ethos of profit and loss, both Fitzgerald and Woolf portray characters who conflate the presence of divinity, or even the sublime, with advertisements.

In reality, presiding over the nothingness that is the valley of ashes are the emotionless eyes of what passes for God in the wasteland world of *The Great Gatsby*. In the place of God there is a faded image, and it is passive, indifferent, and ineffectual. Fitzgerald writes:

> The eyes of Doctor T.J. Eckleburg are blue and gigantic—their retinas are one yard high. They look out of no face but, instead, from a pair of enormous yellow spectacles which pass over a nonexistent nose. Evidently some wild wag of an oculist set them there to fatten his practice in the borough of Queens and then sank down himself into eternal blindness or forgot [them] and moved away. But his eyes, dimmed a little by many paintless days under sun and rain, brood on over the solemn dumping ground [27–28].

In Fitzgerald's landscape of dead ash, the dust drifts "endlessly," and this gives us a sense of "eternally," yet there is no Eternal presence. Within this barren world, the absence of the divine, the transcendent, is brought home to the reader: we—because Fitzgerald writes "you perceive"—find here not God but just the huge, disembodied eyes covered over in sickly yellow, thereby signifying the disease inherent in the landscape itself. Arguably, the valley of ashes is diseased precisely because there is no healing Christ, nor God, no Creator behind the world that Fitzgerald is describing.

In Fitzgerald's fictional world there is, nevertheless, a "maker." Again, as noted, the inhabitants of Fitzgerald's wasteland confuse the maker with the Creator. In the case of Dr. T.J. Eckleburg, the "maker" is the mocking artifact of a faithless world, a "wild wag of an oculist," ostensibly (and ironically in a world of indistinct shapes) one who improves sight. One who himself has "sunk down" into blindness, into obscurity and indifference. Eckleburg has sunk down yet not been cast down, and there is no drama here. One finds in the modernist wasteland no great battles, such as that of the Dagorlad, where Sauron, who would usurp the place of God, is struck down by the forces within and beyond the world, leaving him disembodied but certainly not without agency or will. Sauron, once an angelic being of the same rank as Gandalf, falls, but he does not sink into meaningless obscurity. In the modernist wasteland there are no epic heroes or villains, only shadows, only pale imitations without substance or agency. In the absence of God, the benevolent power behind the world, there is in Fitzgerald's world a corresponding absence of Satan, or the will to power and evil embodied in a physical form. At best there is meaninglessness, at worst the pride and recklessness that arises from faithlessness.

Unlike Fitzgerald's world, where decay is a mere outcome of random forces, the most significant desolation of Middle-earth is the work of a demonic being, Sauron, whose very existence points to its binary opposite: Eru Ilúvatar, the One All Father, Tolkien's correlative for God. Unlike the lifeless eyes of Eckleburg, the Eye of Sauron pierces far beyond his barren lands, watching over his legions, ever searching for the One Ring. The burden of the Ring bears down on Frodo; on the slopes of Orodruin it will literally pull him down finally to his knees. However, as they draw closer to the Black Gate it is the lidless Eye that impales the Halfling. Frodo perceives the Eye of Sauron as "a hostile will that strove with great power to pierce all shadows of cloud, and earth, and flesh, and to see you: to pin you under its deadly gaze, naked, immovable" (Tolkien, *The Two Towers* 636). Under the gaze of the Great Eye, Frodo feels vulnerable and excruciatingly self-conscious. In this he is like Eliot's Prufrock, who imagines himself pinned like an insect for others to see, still alive and struggling helplessly to break free. Both individuals experience alienation and the destabilization of their identities. However, whereas Frodo is trapped by the horrible gaze of Evil Incarnate, Prufrock, in striking contrast, is metaphorically pinned by a pack of tea-drinking socialites.

Prufrock's anxiety points to the emptiness of his life and the failure of community in the modern wasteland, a world which lacks any kind of meaningful design. Frodo's anguish, on the other hand, is the result of an epic struggle between forces, both supernatural and earthly, of good and evil. The hobbit is literally weighed down by the Ring as these forces intersect. Goodness pushes him toward Mt. Doom and the destruction of the Ring. Evil bears down on him, holding him back, working in opposition to his free will which continually pushes him closer to his goal in the heart of the infernal wasteland. This is the third power at work here: Frodo's free will, his ability to choose, over and over again, to persevere along the path that has been appointed to him. He maintains this power nearly until the end of his quest, when he breaks down finally under the burden of the One Ring.

Frodo's failure to voluntarily cast the Ring into the fire is the outcome of the long process of torture which the hobbit has undergone through the power of Sauron's Ring. Again, it is clear that the Ring causes an ultimate kind of alienation: by its powerful corrupting force Frodo is slowly stripped of his free will. In a letter written during the winter of 1956, Tolkien explains that the plan to carry the One Ring into the heart of Mordor in order to destroy it was doomed to fail, and in fact it did. However, he differentiates between the outcome for Frodo on a personal level and the outcome for the whole of Middle-earth. In much larger terms, Frodo is successful. The quest culminates in Frodo's final surrender to temptation and Gollum's final treachery in forsaking his promise to his master. In regard to this moment, Tolkien explains that despite the failure of the plan, the "salvation" of both Frodo and Middle-earth rests on Frodo's compassionate treatment of Gollum, despite the creature's treachery. The success of the plan is an outcome of Frodo's kindness, for, as Tolkien writes, "by a 'grace,' that last betrayal was at a precise juncture when the final evil deed was the most beneficial thing any one cd. have done for Frodo!" (*Letters* 233). "Authority," as Tolkien calls it, placed Frodo in a "sacrificial situation" in which the hobbit's own welfare had to be subordinated to the welfare of the world and its inhabitants (*Letters* 233). Such a circumstance, Tolkien explains, would demand more "suffering and endurance" than an individual could bear, and therefore Frodo was in an impossible situation: someone much stronger could not have held out as long as Frodo did, but someone of such humble stature would not be able to overcome the resistance to destroy the Ring when the moment finally came to do so (*Letters* 233).

As noted earlier, Frodo did in fact fail in terms of the temporal world and his own life within it: in the final moment he is quite incapable of casting the Ring into the fire. Similarly, Gollum, in accordance with his nature after so many years of possessing the Ring, could never prevent himself from attempting to take it from Frodo. Thus the best laid plans of the Council of Rivendell were doomed to fail. However, the success of the plan depended largely on the Christian values of compassion and mercy as well as what Clyde Manschrek refers to as "the old values of love, kindness, and humility" (87). In that same letter, Tolkien writes that Frodo's choice to spare Gollum's life represents "a mystical belief in the ultimate value-in-itself of pity and generosity even if disastrous in the world of time" (*Letters* 233). Within the providential world of Middle-earth, it is not mere coincidence that Gollum turns on Frodo at the exact moment when the hobbit fails in his resolve to destroy the One Ring. In this way, Gollum's evil deed is turned to good, and Frodo's act of Christian charity, his kindness and compassion toward Gollum, saves the world.

In the passage above, Tolkien refers implicitly to Frodo's capacity for charity, the most divine-like of C.S. Lewis' Four Loves. Frodo's willingness and ability to forgive a seemingly unforgiveable individual, his pity and forbearance in not destroying the ruined hobbit, Sméagol, makes possible the "grace" which in the end achieves victory for the West through the destruction of the One Ring. Just as Gandalf's self-sacrifice at Khazâd-dûm and the loss of his leadership might well have ruined all chance of success for the Fellowship, Frodo's choice not to kill

SEVEN. Postmodern Monsters and Providential Plans

Gollum might have been disastrous to the Quest. However, both Gandalf and Frodo submit to a will far greater than their own, the will of God, or "Authority," largely because they understand their places within the cosmos. In his essay, "Tolkien: Archetype and Word," Patrick Grant argues that in *The Lord of the Rings* Tolkien puts forth the "principles of Christian epic" as "embodied themes" (164). These themes, as Grant describes them, are "first, and most important, that true heroism is spiritual; also that love is obedience and involves freedom; that faith and hope are based on charity; that Providence directs the affairs of the world" (164). Frodo and Gandalf submit to the will of God because they have faith in a power greater than themselves. In accordance with that providential design, the actions of the hobbit and the wizard lead ultimately to the triumph of good over evil.

In December of 1965, Tolkien wrote to his publisher, Rayner Unwin, in regard to *The Hobbit* and the copy that would be used to market the book. In his comments about the character of hobbits, Tolkien makes clear that their role in the war against Sauron and the quest to destroy his Ring was not accidental. He points out that although they are a small and relatively docile race, they possess many admirable qualities, including "a strong 'spark' yet unkindled" (Tolkien, *Letters* 365). He also states quite plainly that *The Hobbit* and *The Lord of the Rings* are concerned with the deeds of "ordained individuals, inspired and guided by an Emissary to ends beyond their individual education and enlargement" (Tolkien, *Letters* 365). It is Bilbo and Frodo who were meant to be Ring-bearers, and it is Gandalf who is the messenger who helps them along their appointed paths. Of course, the hobbits have free will and thus can choose not to follow those paths, but loyalty is another quality that hobbits possess. Frodo accepts the heavier burden, but he does not do so blithely.

Frodo at first wonders how such an important and powerful artifact as the Ring came to him. Tolkien does not address Frodo's question directly, but the answer can be found in the legendarium. When characters in *The Lord of the Rings* refer to "the West," this is often metonymic for the Valar, the "Powers" who took part in the creation of the world and so loved it that they withdrew from the presence of Ilúvatar to become its stewards. Indeed, they are bound to the world, like the Elves, until its end. The West also refers to the land of Valinor, the land to which the Elves are returning throughout *The Lord of the Rings*, which is, after all, the end of the story of the time of the Elves in Middle-earth. The Valar sometimes intercede in the affairs of the world, and this is why characters sometimes pray to them, even if they are speaking a language only dimly known to them. As Paul Kocher points out, "The direct need for every sort of providential aid and the most direct and unequivocal answers to it come during Frodo and Sam's long ordeal in the dark in Mordor. What finally routs Shelob is a prayer to Elbereth in the elfin tongue, which springs into Sam's mind though he does not know the language" (47). While the Valar are among those Ainur who took part in the creation of the world (notably, their vision is only made real upon the word of Ilúvatar, "Ea!"—Let it be!), and while as stewards they may intercede in its history, providence itself can only be attributed to Ilúvatar. Thus when Gandalf tells Frodo that he and Bilbo were "meant" to find the Ring, it is likely that he means they were meant by Ilúvatar, as part of a divine plan.

It is very clear that Frodo was chosen to be a Ringbearer, though the story's narrator is not so forthcoming, again, regarding who did the choosing. After learning from Gandalf the history of the One Ring and the many dangers of having it in his possession, Frodo is very sensibly afraid. He is reluctant to accept what Gandalf has been telling him about his part in the story and the deliberateness of the Ring's coming to him. He wishes that he had never been given the Ring, that Bilbo had never found and kept it. Ingenuously, he asks the wizard why he did not direct Frodo to give up the Ring long ago. Gandalf replies with some astonishment, "Let you? Make you?" (Tolkien, *The Fellowship of the Ring* 59). Of course Gandalf would not have taken the Ring by force from Frodo: the wizard was not chosen for the task of bringing the One Ring into Mordor. Rather, according to Tolkien in his letters, Gandalf was sent by the Valar to assist and encourage others, not to overpower them or do their work for them.

Gandalf invites Frodo to destroy the Ring, yet when Frodo attempts to throw it into the fire he finds himself putting the Ring in his pocket instead. The narrator explains that the Ring was to Frodo "an admirable thing and altogether precious" (Tolkien, *The Fellowship of the Ring* 59). The narrator's use of the word "precious" to describe Frodo's spellbound devotion to the Ring foreshadows Gollum's self-destructive connection

SEVEN. *Postmodern Monsters and Providential Plans*

to it. At one time the hobbit-like Sméagol, Gollum serves as a foil for Frodo, who is also in danger of losing his identity and free will to the power of the Ring. With Gandalf's help, Frodo begins to understand that he cannot change the past, he cannot hide or destroy the Ring, and, most distressing of all, he cannot easily part from the Ring, even for a moment. Rather desperately, then, he asks Gandalf the inevitable question: "Why me?" Frodo does not question the notion that a greater power is at work, but the meaning of that providence is beyond not only Frodo's knowledge and understanding but beyond even that of the wizard, who admits that there is no definitive answer to that question, at least not an answer that is ascertainable to finite minds. Gandalf tells Frodo that it certainly is not because he has qualities that others lack. However, he says, "*you have been chosen*, and you must therefore use such strength and heart and wits as you have" (Tolkien, *The Fellowship of the Ring* 59, emphasis added). Frodo's response underscores one of the characteristics that will help him succeed in his quest: humility. The hobbit exclaims, "But I have so little of any of those things!" (Tolkien, *The Fellowship of the Ring* 60).

Frodo begins to demonstrate his courage early on in the story, most fundamentally by agreeing to take the Ring out of the Shire, but soon after by rallying himself against the barrow wight when he and the others are caught in a deadly trap after their brief stay with Tom Bombadil. When he finds himself trapped in the barrow and his companions laid out there as in death, Frodo determines to fight rather than succumb to the dark enchantment of the wight. The narrator explains that this terrible circumstance combined with the love for his friends, ignites the "seed of courage" that rests dormant within each and every hobbit (Tolkien, *The Fellowship of the Ring* 140). By the end of the story Frodo will have demonstrated plenty of "strength, heart, and wits." At this point, however, he is not aware of the deep well of his own inner resources. And this is good, for had Frodo been self-assured, he would have betrayed the pride that provides the Ring with an inroad to the wearer's heart, thereby making it easy to corrupt and dominate that individual. The humility, strength, and loyalty of the hobbits are largely responsible for the success of the quest, but faith, too, plays a role. The faith of all the members of the Fellowship guides them: their trust in and respect for one another as well as their belief that a greater power for good is at work in the world help them to maintain hope in the face of great loss and suffering.

* * *

Tolkien believed in a divine, providential order, in values that do not change across generations and time. Aragorn says as much to Éomer when they first meet on the plains of Rohan. According to the laws of Rohan, Éomer is compelled to bring "strangers" before the king, but he is not unsympathetic to Aragorn's cause. Thus Éomer is caught between duty and compassion. He is also somewhat disoriented, as his remarks to Aragorn make clear: "'Elf and Dwarf in company walk in our daily fields; and folk speak with the Lady of the Wood and yet live; and the Sword comes back that was broken in the long ages ere the fathers of our fathers rode into the Mark! How shall a man judge what to do in such times?'" (Tolkien, *The Two Towers* 440). In response to Éomer's confusion, Aragorn states plainly that good and evil transcend time and place, and thus can be recognized by any man of good judgment. Nevertheless, he tells Éomer, "'It is a man's part to discern them, as much in the Golden Wood as in his own house'" (Tolkien, *The Two Towers* 440–41).

For Éomer, the experience of meeting a man of Númenorean descent, an elf prince of Mirkwood, and a dwarf, whose folk are known to have a legendary and mutual antipathy for Elves, would be astonishing in its own right. To meet them in company, however, traveling across lands that to him contain the commonplaces of his world is so extraordinary as to be virtually unbelievable. Indeed, so jarred is his sensibility by this confrontation, that even though he is a captain of men, and perforce a decision-maker, he has difficulty determining what action he should take. In this moment, Éomer's vision is acute. Should he help a man whom he deems honorable, or should he adhere to the laws of his king? Aragorn's urgent demand that Éomer assist him, let him pass, or prepare to fight spurs the latter to a decision. More than this, though, Éomer is influenced by Aragorn's wisdom and clear thinking, which provides for the Riders a much wider perspective.

Aragorn's holistic vision brings into the present wisdom from a past that extends far beyond the founder of Rohan. Perhaps most importantly, however, is Éomer's liberty and ability to make his own judgment,

SEVEN. Postmodern Monsters and Providential Plans

according to his own reason and perception, which now has been enlarged by this extraordinary experience. Éomer will allow the companions to pass and will aid them by the loan of two horses whose owners have fallen. He binds Aragorn to the promise of returning the horses, thereby vouchsafing his judgment, saying, "'In this I place myself, and maybe my very life, in the keeping of your good faith'" (Tolkien, *The Two Towers* 441). The abrupt appearance of the legendary-made-real in his everyday world widens the scope of Éomer's knowledge and wisdom, and his judgment is proven sound by the terrible events that will follow as well as the heroic actions of the three companions, especially at the Battle of Helm's Deep. This seemingly minor incident on the plains of Rohan exemplifies a major theme in *The Lord of the Rings*.

Through the appropriate perspective, which is a holistic sense of history and one's place in the temporal and eternal worlds, individuals are able to make sound judgments.

Because there is in Middle-earth a divine order, a power behind the universe, Providence provides the framework within which people act and events occur. It is providential that Aragorn and his companions meet Éomer on the plains of Rohan at just that time, and there is room to believe that grace works through Aragorn, whose enlightening words and noble manner move Éomer's will to act according to what he deems morally right as opposed to blindly adhering to the edicts of his king.

In Tolkien's subcreated world, individuals are in the care, ultimately, of a benevolent and forgiving Eternal power. In this world, though they may not consciously recognize "Authority" as the Supreme Power, those mortal characters on the side of good strive to make choices informed by kindness, compassion, and a devotion to the wellbeing of the world and those who inhabit it. This provides for them the possibility to escape from the soul-crushing isolation, loneliness, and despair experienced by so many characters in modern literature. Even the most noble of Tolkien's characters, however, are complex, neither purely good nor purely evil, and like individuals in the real Primary world, they are subject to temptation and fall.

In The Lord of the Rings, Tolkien shows us both the fall and the recovery from grave sin. In the example of Boromir the author depicts both the frailty and honor of fallen humanity. Despite his sin of pride, of believing that with the One Ring he would be a great captain who would lead Gondor to victory against the Dark Lord, Boromir recovers his true nature and is redeemed. In the final moments of his life, he chooses the morally right action and behaves as an honorable warrior. In this he is like Thiodolf in William Morris' romance, *The House of the Wolfings*: at first he is under an evil enchantment, but through an act of his own will, he overcomes the temptation. The evil enchantment, of the Dwarf-made hauberk and the One Ring, respectively, makes both Thiodolf and Boromir behave in ways that run counter to their true nature: both men are brave leaders, selflessly devoted to their warrior companions and their homes, the Great Hall of the Wolfings and the White City of Gondor. Both men reclaim their true nature and ultimately die in accordance with that nature, not alienated from it, as the hauberk and the Ring would have caused them to be.

Within Tolkien's divinely ordered cosmos, Boromir's fall is in a sense a *felix culpa*, or fortunate fall, since his actions are part of the causal chain that brings Frodo to the Crack of Doom with Gollum at his heels. Had the entire Fellowship set out from Parth Galen to Mordor, Merry and Pippin would never have come into contact with the Ents, and Isengard would not have fallen. Boromir's actions also set in motion the circumstances that led Frodo and Sam to Gollum and, ultimately, to Mount Doom. This is not to say that the treachery of Boromir was a good thing, but rather that the event was providential. Taken together, the series of events both leading up to and subsequent to Boromir's fall comprise one example out of many in *The Lord of the Rings* that underscore the notion that even evil deeds and circumstances will be taken up by God and woven into the fabric of His divine will. In the case of Boromir, human weakness faced with overwhelming temptation leads to the warrior's departure from the path that Authority has set before him. His limited vision prevents him from comprehending the possibility for the humble to accomplish great deeds, and his pride prevents him from understanding that no Lord of Gondor can also be Lord of the Ring.

Frodo, too, will make the more difficult but morally right choice. After learning of the history and the danger of the Ring, Frodo freely chooses to follow the path that has been set before him. His choice is doubtless made easier by the support of Gandalf, who promises him, "'I

SEVEN. *Postmodern Monsters and Providential Plans*

will help you bear this burden, as long as it is yours to bear'" (Tolkien, *The Fellowship of the Ring* 61). This is Gandalf's path as one of the stewards of Middle-earth. Frodo, too, is a steward of Middle-earth, but early on he is motivated primarily by love of his home and his desire to protect it. He tells Gandalf, "'I feel that as long as the Shire lies behind, safe and comfortable, I shall find wandering more bearable'" (Tolkien, *The Fellowship of the Ring* 61). Frodo chooses well, but his choice is based on both a sense of moral responsibility as well as love for his home and his people, no matter how provincial they might be. Thus Frodo's sense of stewardship arises from love and selflessness. He knows that he might never return to the Shire, but he would still do his part to preserve it for others. Of course, he will return to his home, but he cannot linger there. Ultimately, it is not for himself that Frodo saves the Shire. Sam, too, is selfless and motivated by love not just for the Shire but for Frodo as well.

Sam begins as an ordinary hobbit, an everyman. Like most hobbits, he is provincial; he has never ventured beyond the confines of the Shire. At first he is motivated only by his desire to protect Frodo, whom he dearly loves. However, as Sam's awareness of the world grows and develops, his motivations become more complex. In "The Stairs of Cirith Ungol," after they have passed through many dangers, and with greater danger yet before them, Sam tells Frodo:

> Beren now, he never thought he was going to get that Silmaril from the Iron Crown in Thangorodrim, and yet he did, and that was a worse place and a blacker danger than ours. But that's a long tale, of course, and goes on past the happiness and into grief and beyond it—and the Silmaril went on and came to Earendil. And why, sir, I never thought of that before! We've got—you've got some of the light of it in that star-glass that the Lady gave you! Why, to think of it, we're in the same tale still! [Tolkien, *The Two Towers* 719–20].

At this point, the reader might ask, what comes "beyond grief?" In Tolkien's worlds, both Primary and Secondary, what lies beyond grief is eternal life, "more than memory," as the dying Aragorn tells Arwen. Sam's account of the story of Beren and Lúthien demonstrates the meaningfulness of stories out of the past. In knowing them, we can better situate ourselves in the flow of time. His account also shows how events from even the very distant past can be connected to the present moment, and therefore those events, as well as knowledge of those events, informs our decisions in the present.

Sam's epiphany helps to demonstrate Northrup Frye's assertion that the stories out of the past show us a way to be in the present. Both Sam and Frodo are able to find inspiration and courage from Beren's story, since Beren and Lúthien were in a similar situation in that they had to travel into the dungeons of hell, Thangorodrim, under the dominion of Morgoth, the Prime Dark Lord. They had to retrieve the Silmaril from the very crown of Morgoth. They, too, had to face the most terrifying and powerful enemy imaginable, and yet they succeeded. And like Frodo and Sam, Beren and Lúthien succeeded largely because of their love for and devotion to one another. As Sam suddenly realizes, he and Frodo are in the same tale as Beren and Lúthien. This new awareness signifies that Sam's journey has been for him an education in the nature of life within a vast providential order. His sensibility enlarged, he now truly understands that his is, after all, a small part in what is a very long narrative indeed, for that story is in fact the "Whole Story."

Sam has come full circle. When he takes his first steps into lands unknown to him, he is apprehensive, for he does not have the wanderlust of Bilbo and Frodo. Perhaps it is grace, or "the Powers," at work when at that moment Pippin spontaneously says, "The road goes on forever." In any event, the phrase prompts Frodo to recall that Bilbo often said that "'there was only one Road; that it was like a great river: its springs were at every doorstep, and every path was its tributary'" (Tolkien, *The Fellowship of the Ring* 72). "The Road" is meant to represent the course of human history. Like a river of time, its flow encompasses the lives of each and every individual.

Evil will arise and fall, just as in an age long past Morgoth, Sauron's predecessor, rebelled, was defeated, and was cast into the void by Ilúvatar. Sauron, too, will be overcome. Nevertheless, evil is inherent in the world, and thus it will not finally be overcome until the end of the world, when Eru Ilúvatar, Tolkien's version of God the Creator, the Supreme Author, incorporates all evil into the Whole Story. Evildoers, the many incarnations of the "Shadow," will always hold a subordinate place in the cosmic order. Thus any particular evil is transient: the great story begun before the Creation of Middle-earth, the story of which the events of *The Lord of the Rings* are only a small part, will continue. In Tolkien's worlds, both

SEVEN. *Postmodern Monsters and Providential Plans*

fictional and real, we must never despair in the face of evil, for, as Samwise Gamgee can see from the heart of Mordor itself, there is "light and high beauty for ever beyond its reach" (Tolkien, *The Return of the King* 932).

Like the storytellers he admired, Tolkien was an accomplished "sub-creator" who imagined not only a world, but an entire cosmos. Into the fabric of this world he wove his love of ancient language and lore, his faith in humanity's potential for goodness and courage, his conviction that the humblest among us are often the most noble, and his steadfast belief that each and every life has meaning and purpose in accordance with God's will. The modernists viewed the past across the chasm of the Great War, and thus for them history is a fractured story. And while Tolkien himself was a participant in the "war to end all wars," he nevertheless maintained a belief in the continuity of God's plan for humanity. For Tolkien the impact of World War I, including and especially his experience as a soldier on the front lines of battle, was profound and lifelong, but not personally destabilizing. After the Great War, modernist writers struggled to achieve a sense of personal, historical, and cultural continuity and meaning. For Tolkien, however, continuity and meaning have their sources in divine will. Thus while the modernist response to the crisis of modernity typically emphasizes a sense of fragmentation, despair, and alienation, Tolkien's literary response to modernity emphasizes hope, selflessness, and fellowship in the quest to rekindle an old light in the world and restore the human community within it.

Bibliography

Bede. *The Ecclesiastical History of the English People*. Ed. Judith McClure and Roger Collins. Oxford: Oxford University Press: 1994. Print.

The Bible. New Revised Standard Version. Introd. Bruce Metzger and Herbert May. New York: Oxford University Press, 1989. Print.

Birzer, Bradley J. *J.R.R. Tolkien's Sanctifying Myth: Understanding Middle-earth*. Wilmington: ISI Books, 2003. Print.

Blake, William. "London." *The Poems of William Blake*. London: B.M. Pickering, 1874. 124. *Internet Archive*. The Library of Congress. Web. 22 Nov. 2013.

Brooks, Van Wyck. "On Creating a Usable Past." *The Dial*. 64.7 (1918): 337–41. *Internet Archive*. The Library of Congress. Web. 30 May 2013.

Carpenter, Humphrey. *J.R.R. Tolkien: A Biography*. Boston: Houghton Mifflin, 2000. Print.

_____, ed. *The Letters of J.R.R. Tolkien*. Boston: Houghton Mifflin, 1981. Print.

Chance, Jane. "*The Lord of the Rings*: Tolkien's Epic." *Understanding The Lord of the Rings: The Best of Tolkien Criticism*. Ed. Rose A. Zimbardo and Neil D. Isaacs. Boston: Houghton Mifflin, 2004. 195–232. Print.

Chaucer, Geoffrey. "The Canterbury Tales." *Chaucer's Poetry*. Ed. E. T. Donaldson. 2nd ed. Glenview, Illinois: Scott, Foresman, 1975. 5–583. Print.

Clausson, Nils. "Perpetuating the Language": Romantic Tradition, the Genre Function, and the Origins of the Trench Lyric." *Journal of Modern Literature*. 30.1 (2006): 104–28. Print.

Curry, Patrick. *Defending Middle-Earth: Tolkien: Myth and Modernity*. Boston: Houghton Mifflin, 2004. Print.

Dickens, Charles. *Bleak House*. 1852. Introduction Barbara Hardy. New York: Everyman, 1991. Print.

Dickerson, Matthew. *Following Gandalf: Epic Battles and Moral Victory in The Lord of the Rings*. Grand Rapids: Brazos, 2003. Print.

Eliot, T.S. "Hamlet and His Problems." *The Sacred Wood: Essays on Poetry and Criticism*. 1920. London: Methuen. 1983. Print.

_____. *The Love Song of J. Alfred Prufrock*." *Poetry*, 1915. Poetry Foundation. JStor. Web. 22 Nov. 2013.

_____. *The Waste Land*. The Dial 73.5 (1922): 473–85. *HathiTrust*. Web. 20 Nov. 2013.

Fawcett, Barry and Elizabeth Jones. "The Twelve Traps in John Gardner's *Grendel*." *American Literature*. 62 (4) (1990): 634–47. Print.

Fitzgerald, F. Scott. *The Great Gatsby*. 1925. Preface Matthew Bruccoli. New York: Scribner, 1992. Print.

Flieger, Verlyn. *Splintered Light: Logos and Language in Tolkien's World*. 1938. Rev. ed. Kent, OH: Kent State University Press, 2002. Print.

Forster, E. M. *Howards End*. 1910. New York: Modern Library, 1999. Print.

Freud, Sigmund. *The Interpretation of Dreams*. 1899. Trans. Joyce Crick. Ox-

Bibliography

ford: Oxford University Press, 1999. Print.

Frost, Robert. "The Figure a Poem Makes." 1939. *The Collected Prose of Robert Frost*. Ed. Mark Richardson. Cambridge, MA: Belknap Press. 2007. 131–33. Print.

———. "Home Burial." *North of Boston*. 1914. 2nd ed. New York: Henry Holt, 1915. 43–49. *HathiTrust*. Internet Archive. Web. 20 Nov. 2013.

———. "The Wood-pile." *North of Boston*. 1914. 2nd ed. New York: Henry Holt, 1915. 133–35. *HathiTrust*. Internet Archive. Web. 20 Nov. 2013.

Frye, Northrup. "The Meeting of Past and Future in William Morris." *Studies in Romanticism*. 21.3 (1982). 303–318. Print.

Fuller, Edmund. "The Lord of the Hobbits: J.R.R. Tolkien." Reprinted in *Understanding The Lord of the Rings: The Best of Tolkien Criticism*. Ed. Rose A. Zimbardo and Neil D. Isaacs. Boston: Houghton Mifflin, 2004. 16–30. Print.

Gardner, John. *Grendel*. New York: Vintage, 1989. Print.

Garth, John. *Tolkien and the Great War: The Threshold of Middle-earth*. Boston: Houghton Mifflin, 2003. Print.

Grant, Patrick. "Tolkien: Archetype and Word." *Understanding The Lord of the Rings: The Best of Tolkien Criticism*. Ed. Rose A. Zimbardo and Neil D. Isaacs. Boston: Houghton Mifflin, 2004. 163–82. Print.

Hipp, Daniel. *The Poetry of Shell Shock: Wartime Trauma and Healing in Wilfred Owen, Ivor Gurney, and Siegfried Sassoon*. Jefferson, NC: McFarland, 2005. Print.

Huttar, Charles A. "Hell and the City: Tolkien and the Traditions of Western Literature." 1974. Rpt. in *A Tolkien Compass*. 1975. 2nd ed. Ed. Jared Lobdell. Chicago: Open Court, 2003. 115–40. Print.

Kocher, Paul H. *Master of Middle-earth: The Fiction of J.R.R. Tolkien*. 1972. New York: Ballantine, 1977. Print.

Lawrence, D. H. *Lady Chatterley's Lover*. 1928. Introd. Kathryn Harrison. New York: Modern Library, 2001. Print.

———. *Studies in Classic American Literature*. 1923. New York: Penguin, 1986. Print.

Lewis, C.S. "The Dethronement of Power." n.d. Rpt. in *Understanding The Lord of the Rings: The Best of Tolkien Criticism*. Ed. Rose A. Zimbardo and Neil D. Isaacs. Boston: Houghton Mifflin, 2004. 11–15. Print.

———. *The Four Loves*. 1960. New York: Harcourt/Brace, 1988. Print.

———. *The Great Divorce: A Dream*. 1946. San Francisco: Harper, 2001. Print.

———. *The Magician's Nephew*. 1955. New York: Harper Collins, 2005. Print.

———. *Out of the Silent Planet*. 1938. New York: Scribner, 2003. Print.

———. *Surprised by Joy: The Shape of My Early Life*. 1955. San Diego: Harcourt, n.d. Print.

MacDonald, George. *The Princess and the Goblin*. 1872. Introd. Ursula LeGuin. New York: Puffin/Penguin, 2011. Print.

Manschreck, Clyde. "Nihilism in the Twentieth Century: A View from Here." *American Society of Church History*. 45.1 (1976): 85–96. Print.

Marx, Karl. *Capital: A Critique of Political Economy*. 1867. Trans. Ben Fowkes. New York: Vintage Books, 1977. Print.

Marx, Karl, and Friedrich Engels. *The Communist Manifesto*. 1848. Introd. Vladimir Pozner. New York: Bantam, 1992. Print.

Melville, Herman. "Bartleby, The Scrivener: A Story of Wall Street." 1853. *Project Gutenberg*. Web. 2 Dec. 2013.

Milbank, John. "Fictioning Things: Gift and Narrative." *Religion and Literature*. 37.3 (2005): 1–35. University of Notre Dame. JSTOR. 12 Aug. 2013.

Morris, William. *The House of the Wolfings*. 1888. Seattle: Inkling Books, 2003. Print.

_____. *News from Nowhere*. 1890. Mineola, NY: Dover, 2004. Print.

_____. *The Well at the World's End*. 1896. *On the Lines of Morris' Romances: Two Books that Inspired J. R. R. Tolkien*. Seattle: Inkling Books, 2003. Print.

_____. *The Wood beyond the World*. 1894. *On the Lines of Morris' Romances: Two Books that Inspired J. R. R. Tolkien*. Seattle: Inkling Books, 2003. Print.

Nietzsche, Friedrich W. *Thus Spake Zarathustra*. 1883-1885. Trans. Thomas Common. New York: Heritage Press, 1967. Print.

Norgate, Paul. "Wilfred Owen and the Soldier Poets." *The Review of English Studies*. 40.160 (1989): 516–530. Print.

Owen, Wilfred. "Dulce et Decorum Est." 1920. *The Collected Poems of Wilfred Owen*. Ed. C. Day Lewis. New York: New Directions, 1963. 55. Print.

_____. "Dulce et Decorum Est." Draft. *First World War Poetry Digital Archive*. University of Oxford. Web. 20 Nov. 2013.

Pearce, Joseph. *Literary Converts*. San Francisco: Ignatius, 1999. Print.

_____. *Tolkien: Man and Myth*. San Francisco: Ignatius, 1998. Print.

Perkins, Agnes and Helen Hill. "The Corruption of Power." *A Tolkien Compass*. 1975. 2nd ed. Ed. Jared Lobdell. Chicago: Open Court, 2003. 55–65. Print.

Purtill, Richard. *J.R.R. Tolkien: Myth, Morality, and Religion*. San Francisco: Ignatius, 1984. Print.

Roberts, David. *Out in the Dark: Poetry of the First World War*. London: Saxon Books, 1998. Print.

Rogers, Deborah C. "Everyclod and Everyhero: The Image of Man in Tolkien." *A Tolkien Compass*. 1975. 2nd ed. Ed. Jared Lobdell. Chicago: Open Court, 2003. 67–73. Print.

Rosebury, Brian. *Tolkien: A Cultural Phenomenon*. New York: Palgrave, 2003. Print.

Schopenhauer, Arthur. *The World as Will and Representation*. 1819. Trans. E F. J. Payne. New York: Dover Publications, 1966. Print.

Shippey, Tom. *J.R.R. Tolkien: Author of the Century*. Boston: Houghton Mifflin, 2000. Print.

_____. *The Road to Middle-earth: How J.R.R. Tolkien Created a New Mythology*. Boston: Houghton Mifflin, 2003. Print.

Smith, Thomas W. "Tolkien's Catholic Imagination: Mediation and Tradition." *Religion and Literature*. 38.2 (2006): 73-100. University of Notre Dame. JSTOR. Web. 18 Dec. 2013.

Stevens, Wallace. "Anecdote of the Jar." 1919. *Harmonium*. New York: Alfred Knopf, 1950: 129. Print.

Sullivan, C.W. "Folklore and Fantastic Literature." *Western Folklore*. 60.4 (2001): 279–96. *Western States Folklore Society*. JSTOR. Web. 2 Aug. 2013.

Tolkien, J.R.R. "Beowulf: The Monsters and the Critics." 1936. *Beowulf: A Verse Translation*. Ed. Daniel Donoghue. NY: Norton, 2002. 103–30. Print.

_____. *The Fellowship of the Ring Being the First Part of the Lord of the Rings*. 1954. Boston: Houghton Mifflin, 2002. Print.

_____. "On Fairy-stories." 1938. *The Tolkien Reader*. NY: Ballantine, 1966. 33–99. Print.

_____. *The Return of the King, Being the Third Part of the Lord of the Rings*. 1955. Boston: Houghton Mifflin, 2002. Print.

_____. *The Silmarillion*. 1977. Ed. Christopher Tolkien. Boston: Houghton Mifflin, 2004. Print.

_____. *The Two Towers, Being the Second Part of the Lord of the Rings*. 1954. Boston: Houghton Mifflin, 2002. Print.

Travers, P.L. "Only Connect." *The Quarterly Journal of the Library of Congress*. 24.4 (1967): 232–48. Library of Congress. JSTOR. Web. 18 Feb. 2013.

Wilson, Edward O. *From so Simple a Be-*

ginning: The Four Great Books of Charles Darwin. New York: Norton, 2006. Print.

Woolf, Virginia. *Mrs. Dalloway*. 1925. San Diego: Harcourt Brace, 1985. Print.

———. *To the Lighthouse*. 1927. San Diego: Harcourt Brace, n.d. Print.

Wordsworth, William. "The World is Too Much with Us." 1807. *The Poetical Works of William Wordsworth*. London: Henry Frowde, 1906. 259. Print.

Yeats, William Butler. "The Second Coming." *A Pocket Book of Modern Verse*. Ed. Oscar Williams. New York: Washington Square Press, 1960. 184. Print.

Index

"Anecdote of the Jar" 11, 168

"Bartleby, the Scrivener" 2, 3, 35–38, 141, 149
Beowulf (Anglo-Saxon poem) 4, 6, 46–53, 61, 66–67, 72, 107, 162
"Beowulf: The Monsters and the Critics" 46, 47, 49, 50, 52, 189
Bible 45
Birzer, Bradley J. 21
Blake, William: "London" 2, 34
Bleak House 2, 34, 35, 45, 102
Brooks, Van Wyck 31–33, 38, 49, 53, 54, 73, 103

The Canterbury Tales (Geoffrey Chaucer) 111–112, 116
Carpenter, Humphrey 3, 9, 64, 78
Catholicism 10, 17, 18, 19, 39, 41, 43, 63, 74, 94, 98, 108
Chance, Jane 5
Christ 18, 49, 50, 52, 70, 77, 78, 98, 99, 107, 109, 127, 157, 174
Christianity 3, 6, 13, 21, 33, 36, 43, 49, 50–53, 63, 69, 75, 77, 78, 84, 93–95, 98, 107, 108, 127, 157, 174
Clausson, Nils 96
Curry, Patrick 11

"The Dethronement of Power" 53, 62, 63
Dickens, Charles: *Bleak House* 2, 34, 35, 45, 102
Dickerson, Matthew 99
"Dulce et Decorum Est" 78, 80, 81, 84, 85, 87–89, 148

The Ecclesiastical History of the English People (Bede) 48, 49, 56, 158
Eliot, T.S. 11, 15, 17, 34, 98, 101, 169; "Hamlet and His Problems" 15; "The Love Song of J. Alfred Prufrock" 35, 135–38, 143, 147, 148, 163–65, 175; *The Waste Land* 102, 103, 11, 112, 114, 140, 163, 169
escapism 64, 66, 70, 71, 79

Fawcett and Jones 162
The Fellowship of the Ring 10, 19, 22, 30, 43, 44, 60, 67, 99, 107, 110, 117, 118, 120, 122, 126, 152, 153, 155, 158, 166, 178, 179, 183, 184
"The Figure a Poem Makes" 16, 102, 106
Fitzgerald, F. Scott: *The Great Gatsby* 11, 109, 115, 116, 122, 123, 127, 133- 145, 147, 148, 163, 172–174
Flieger, Verlyn 160
Forster, E.M.: *Howards End* 2, 3, 39, 55–62, 73, 92, 102, 109, 102, 114–15, 137, 164
The Four Loves 4–5, 176
Frost, Robert 11, 17, 141; "The Figure a Poem Makes" 16, 102, 106; "Home Burial" 15, 16, 91; "The Wood-Pile" 168–70
Frye, Northrup 29, 32, 53, 57, 59, 184
Fuller, Edmund 156

Gardner, John: *Grendel* 48, 56, 61, 136, 159, 162–65
Garth, John 10, 41, 63, 82
the Gospel 10, 45, 54, 70
Grant, Patrick 123
The Great Gatsby 11, 109, 115, 116, 122, 123, 127, 133- 145, 147, 148, 163, 172–174
Grendel 48, 56, 61, 136, 159, 162–65

"Hamlet and His Problems" 15
Hill and Perkins 43
Hipp, Daniel 78, 88
"Home Burial" 15, 16, 91
The House of the Wolfings 47, 51, 79, 120–122, 182

Index

Howards End 2, 3, 39, 55–62, 73, 92, 102, 109, 102, 114–15, 137, 164
Huttar, Charles 109

Kocher, Paul 129, 167

Lady Chatterley's Lover 83, 84, 87–89, 113–15, 123, 140, 142, 143, 147–48
Lawrence, D.H. 11, 98, 163, 169; *Lady Chatterley's Lover* 83, 84, 87–89, 113–15, 123, 140, 142, 143, 147–48; *Studies in Classic American Literature* 37–39
The Letters of J.R.R. Tolkien 3, 6, 9, 17–20, 22, 23, 27, 40–42, 44, 51, 64, 66, 69–74, 79, 82, 83, 85, 86, 92–100, 107, 108, 110, 117–19, 122, 125, 126, 128, 129, 146, 147, 151, 153–57, 160, 166, 176–78
Lewis, C.S. 96, 132; "The Dethronement of Power" 53, 62, 63; *The Four Loves* 4–5, 176; *The Magician's Nephew* 129, 130–31; *Out of the Silent Planet* 93; *Surprised by Joy* 82, 95
"London" 2, 34
The Lord of the Rings 4–7, 10, 17–21, 23, 30, 42, 44, 53, 55, 57, 59, 61–65, 67, 69–73, 75, 79, 86, 87, 92, 95, 99, 107–10, 117, 123, 125, 127, 128, 133, 139, 151, 166, 167, 177, 178, 181, 182, 184
"The Love Song of J. Alfred Prufrock" 35, 135–38, 143, 147, 148, 163–65, 175

MacDonald, George 6, 65, 125
The Magician's Nephew 129, 130–31
Manschreck, Clyde 12–14
Melville, Herman 32, 109; "Bartleby, the Scrivener" 2, 3, 35–38, 141, 149
Milbank, John 44
modernism 3, 5, 6, 11, 12, 14–17, 20–23, 61–62, 70–72, 74, 77, 87, 92–95, 98, 101–2, 104, 106, 108–9, 113–17, 122, 127, 130, 132–40, 142–44, 148, 149, 162, 168, 172, 174, 185
Morris, William 6, 29, 34, 40, 53, 109, 146; *The House of the Wolfings* 47, 51, 79, 120–122, 182; *News from Nowhere* 25, 26–28, 30–33, 38, 40, 45, 59, 69, 115, 119; *The Well at the World's End* 115; *The Wood Beyond the World* 115, 130
Mrs. Dalloway 89, 90, 101, 136, 138, 139, 141, 147, 170–72

News from Nowhere 25, 26–28, 30–33, 38, 40, 45, 59, 69, 115, 119

Nicene Creed 77
Norgate, Paul 81, 83, 85

objective correlative 15, 16, 108, 115
"On Fairy-stories" 68–70
Out of the Silent Planet 93
Owen, Wilfred: "Dulce et Decorum Est" 78, 80, 81, 84, 85, 87–89, 148

Pearce, Joseph 13, 90, 94, 127
Purtill, Richard 44

The Return of the King 23, 30, 65, 68, 72, 100, 133, 156, 185
Roberts, David 81, 82
Rogers, Deborah 75, 108
Rosebury, Brian 15

"The Second Coming" 77, 78, 84, 98, 102, 163, 164
Shippey, Tom 63, 95, 96, 146, 147
The Silmarillion 42, 63, 64, 107, 167
Smith, Thomas W. 39
Stevens, Wallace: "Anecdote of the Jar" 11, 168
Studies in Classic American Literature 37–39
Sullivan, C.W. 74
Surprised by Joy 82, 95

To the Lighthouse 15, 103–6, 112–13, 116, 133, 164
Tolkien, Christopher 20, 22, 41, 45, 46, 64, 70, 79, 85, 92, 94, 97, 151
Tolkien, J.R.R.: "Beowulf: The Monsters and the Critics" 46, 47, 49, 50, 52, 189; *The Fellowship of the Ring* 10, 19, 22, 30, 43, 44, 60, 67, 99, 107, 110, 117, 118, 120, 122, 126, 152, 153, 155, 158, 166, 178, 179, 183, 184; *The Letters of J.R.R. Tolkien* 3, 6, 9, 17–20, 22, 23, 27, 40–42, 44, 51, 64, 66, 69–74, 79, 82, 83, 85, 86, 92–100, 107, 108, 110, 117–19, 122, 125, 126, 128, 129, 146, 147, 151, 153–57, 160, 166, 176–78; *The Lord of the Rings* 4–7, 10, 17–21, 23, 30, 42, 44, 53, 55, 57, 59, 61–65, 67, 69–73, 75, 79, 86, 87, 92, 95, 99, 107–10, 117, 123, 125, 127, 128, 133, 139, 151, 166, 167, 177, 178, 181, 182, 184; "On Fairy-stories" 68–70; *The Return of the King* 23, 30, 65, 68, 72, 100, 133, 156, 185; *The Silmarillion* 42, 63, 64, 107, 167; *The Two Towers* 51, 80, 86,

87, 98, 124, 125, 127, 147, 152, 154, 175, 180, 181, 183
Travers, P.L. 58
The Two Towers 51, 80, 86, 87, 98, 124, 125, 127, 147, 152, 154, 175, 180, 181, 183

Valar 23, 68, 109–10, 117, 128–29, 149–53, 155–57, 166, 177–78
Valinor 23, 117, 119, 128–29, 153, 157, 166, 177

The Waste Land 102, 103, 11, 112, 114, 140, 163, 169
The Well at the World's End 115
The Wood Beyond the World 115, 130

"The Wood-Pile" 168–70
Woolf, Virginia 11, 15, 17, 163, 173; *Mrs. Dalloway* 89, 90, 101, 136, 138, 139, 141, 147, 170–72; *To the Lighthouse* 15, 103–6, 112–13, 116, 133, 164
Wordsworth, William: "The World Is Too Much with Us" 33, 34, 36, 37, 40, 106
"The World Is Too Much with Us" 33, 34, 36, 37, 40, 106
World War I 10, 11, 12, 14, 15, 31–34, 39, 46, 57, 62, 73, 78, 79, 81–83, 87, 92–94, 96, 101–104, 108, 123, 135, 185

Yeats, William Butler: "The Second Coming" 77, 78, 84, 98, 102, 163, 164

www.ingramcontent.com/pod-product-compliance
Ingram Content Group UK Ltd.
Pitfield, Milton Keynes, MK11 3LW, UK
UKHW042011140426
5217IPUK00015B/1105